Roger Casement —
E. M. Forster

THE RISE AND FALL OF THE
VICTORIAN SERVANT

Pamela Horn

THE
RISE AND FALL
OF THE VICTORIAN
SERVANT

GILL AND MACMILLAN
Dublin

ST MARTIN'S PRESS
New York

First published in 1975

Gill and Macmillan Ltd
15/17 Eden Quay
Dublin 1
and internationally through
association with the
Macmillan Publishers Group

7171 0746 9

First published in the United States of America in 1975
For information, write:
St Martin's Press, Inc.,
175 Fifth Ave.,
New York, N.Y. 10010

Library of Congress Catalog Card Number: 75-4247

301.444
H

Printed and bound in Great Britain by
Bristol Typesetting Co. Ltd
Barton Manor, St Philips, Bristol

A KITCHEN PRAYER: THE WORK OF A
GIRL OF NINETEEN, A DOMESTIC SERVANT

Lord of all pots and pans and things, since I've no time to be
A saint by doing lovely things, or watching late with Thee,
Or dreaming in the dawnlight, or storming Heaven's gates,
Make me a saint by getting meals and washing up the plates.

Although I must have Martha's hands, I have a Mary mind;
And when I black the boots and shoes, Thy sandals, Lord, I find.
I think of how they trod the earth, what time I scrub the floor.
Accept this meditation Lord, I haven't time for more.

Warm all the kitchen with Thy love and light it with Thy peace;
Forgive me all my worrying and make all grumbling cease.
Thou who didst love to give men food, in room, or by the sea,
Accept this service that I do, I do it unto Thee.

*Inscribed on a card which was intended to be hung on the wall of
the kitchen; it was given to Mrs E. Brazier of Sangerstead while she
was in service early in the present century.*

If you do not get up early, your business will get the start of you, and
then you may toil hard, and not overtake it all day long. You must
exercise a spirit of subordination, that is, do not set up for mistress
yourself, but be willing to acknowledge the authority, and comply
with the wishes of those under whom you are placed. . . . Frugality
will teach you to make the best use of every thing committed to your
care; suffering nothing to be needlessly consumed through extravagance, or wasted through neglect.

The Young Servant (issued by the Religious Tract Society), 2nd ed.
(1837).

Contents

List of Illustrations

Illustration no. 14 is reproduced by kind permission of Mr T. R. Key. Illustration no. 18 is reproduced by kind permission of the Honourable Mrs G. F. Charlton of Great Harrowden. Illustrations no's 23, 24 and 33 are reproduced by permission of the Master and Fellows of Trinity College, Cambridge.

ACKNOWLEDGMENTS

Grateful acknowledgment is due to the following for their assistance with illustrations: Bedfordshire Record Office, Mr V. C. Buckley, Miss N. Charley, Miss E. Cobham, Mr E. G. Dollymore, Essex Record Office (Spalding Collection), Mary Evans Picture Library, *The Illustrated London News*, Mr E. J. B. Irving, Mr T. R. Key, Mrs G. King, Longleat Estate, Northamptonshire Record Office 'Cartwright (Aynho) Collection', Northamptonshire Record Office, Oxfordshire County Libraries, Mrs Y. Snell, Miss J. Stephen, Mrs M. E. J. Tidmarsh, Trinity College, Cambridge (Munby papers), University of Reading (Museum of English Rural Life), Mr G. Wilkins.

Acknowledgments

I should like to thank all those who have helped in the preparation of this book, either by providing material or in other ways. In particular, my thanks are due to the Master and Fellows of Trinity College, Cambridge, for permission to quote from the Munby Papers and to the staff at the libraries and record offices in which I have worked. These include the Bodleian Library, Oxford, the British Library, the British Library of Political and Economic Science at the London School of Economics, the Public Record Office, London, and the county record offices for Bedfordshire, Berkshire, Buckinghamshire, Cambridgeshire, Cheshire, Essex, Gloucestershire, Hampshire, Leicestershire, Northamptonshire, Oxfordshire and Warwickshire. I am indebted to them for much efficient assistance.

I am equally indebted to the editors of the *Daily Telegraph*, the *Western Morning News* and the *Oxford Times* who inserted appeals for reminiscences, documents and photographs of servant life on my behalf in their newspapers, and to the approximately three hundred people who so kindly answered those appeals. Some of the material they sent has been incorporated in the book and is acknowledged in the notes at the end of the book. But I should like to assure all who wrote to me how much I appreciate their co-operation.

Finally, I owe a debt of gratitude to my family for help in the preparation of this work, and in particular to my husband, who has assisted in countless different ways. Without his help neither this nor any of my books could have been written. He has encouraged me throughout, and his advice and guidance on the organisation and content of the book have been invaluable.

PAMELA HORN, *January 1975*

I

The Origins of Domestic Service

The disciple is not above his master, nor the servant above his lord.

Matt. 10 :24.

FOR AS long as there have been rich and poor in society there have been domestic servants to minister to the wants of the well-to-do. As Aristotle observed, 'From the hour of their birth some are marked out for subjection, others for rule.' It was the task of the underlings to provide personal service for their master or mistress and to carry out the hard and unpleasant chores of the household. In the Ancient World, indeed, the word 'servant' was often synonymous with that of 'slave', since few free men or women were willing to perform the menial labour which domestic service entailed. In Rome this meant the discharge of 'the duties of domestic attendance, the service of the toilet, bath, table and kitchen, besides the entertainment of the master and his guests by dancing, singing and other arts'. But in more recent times, at least in Britain, the hewers of wood and drawers of water have been without this ultimate social stigma of slavery.

It is to medieval England that we must turn for an examination of the origins of domestic service as it is understood today. The evidence is scattered and difficult to assess, for even in the Middle Ages the term servant often carried with it a wider meaning than is the case nowadays. In its broadest sense, it might cover the youths of gentle birth who undertook servile duties for a limited period as pages or waiters in manor-house or castle in order to improve their education and because 'nobility and convention . . . decreed that young men of good social standing should receive part of their training by attendance on nobles of recognised power and reputation'. As late as the sixteenth century Henry, Earl of

Worcester, was said to be attended 'not by footmen but by gentle-men and gentlemen's sons', while the waiters who served Henry, Earl of Derby, were all of gentle birth, being either the heirs or younger sons of 'independent gentlemen of first rank in the country'. Most of these would pass into political or courtly life within a few years, although a few might remain to make their careers as stewards or 'comptrollers' within their patron's house-hold. Not until the seventeenth century, more particularly follow-ing the disruptions of the Civil War, did changes in domestic habits and ceremonial bring to an end the practice of sending young gentlemen into noble service for instruction and training. But by the eighteenth century the 'domestic menage of the great house had been completely altered . . . even the upper servants were in the majority of cases the sons of labourers, artisans or small farmers rather than recruits from the ranks of reduced gentlemen'.[1]

Of course these earlier 'servants' of gentle birth were not menials in the true sense of the word. Their status as gentlemen was always assured and their duties were limited. In the case of a gentleman usher, for example, these consisted of governing 'all above stairs, or in the presence of his lord', arranging for, and supervising, the waiting at meals, ensuring that 'the greate chamber bee fynne and neatlie kepte', and having 'at com-maundemente, all the gentlemen and yeoman wayters and see into their behaviors and fashion, that they be civill, comelie and well, and if any defecte bee, in any of them, they are to instruct them in curteous manner, which is both good for them, and bettereth the lord's service'.

The position of such men was certainly very different from that of the domestics employed to scour the pans, clean the rooms and launder the clothes. For a realistic picture of the early English domestic servant one must go to the writings of Bartholomaeus Anglicus, a Friar Minor who wrote in the first half of the thirteenth century. His work enjoyed considerable popularity and was translated from Latin into English towards the close of the next century by an energetic Cornish priest, John Trevisa. According to him, 'the servaunt-woman' was 'ordeyned for to lerne the wyve's rule, and is put to office and werke of traveylle, toylynge and slubberynge'. She is to be fed upon 'grosse [coarse] meate' and 'kepte lowe under the yoeke of thraldome and of servage', if necessary by beating; she is to be allowed little time for rest either by night or by day. Yet despite this depressing description of the fate which seemed to await servants, many clearly escaped its worst excesses for, as Dorothy Stuart has pointed out, from early times 'two sharply-contrasted' types of domestic emerged from the mass, 'to be encountered again in life and in literature as the centuries unfold : the "pampered menial" and the down-trodden drudge'.[2]

For most servants in medieval England the best chance of assuring for themselves comfort and security (the two main objects in life) was to obtain a position in the household of a noble family. Here food was plentiful, there were many fellow-workers to share the daily chores, and even if they had to sleep communally on rushes in the great hall of the manor-house, at least the atmosphere was less smoky and fetid than in the small huts in which the mass of the population still dwelt. One such household was that of Eleanor de Montfort, the mid-thirteenth-century Countess of Leicester, who kept over sixty servants—most of them men. Among the relatively few women employed was the laundress, who was an indispensable member of any household of size or standing. Her position was also one of the hardest, since, as contemporary preachers pointed out, it was she who had to 'turn and beat and wash and hang' the clothes in order to get them clean and dry. At the lowest level were the countless grooms and boy attendants, including lads who minded the horses and hounds or served as helpers and scullions for upper servants. Their wages were low, and they were often recruited from among the local people around a particular manor. When the household moved on, such casual workers would be paid off and dismissed.

During the Middle Ages the retainers of a great lord could run into hundreds. Thus when the Earl of Warwick went up to parliament in the middle of the fifteenth century, he was accompanied by six hundred liveried servants. But many of these would have been, in reality, armed retainers rather than domestic servants proper.

Outside the ranks of the nobility and gentry few households in the country districts would require the help of servants. In most villages only the priest would have need of a full-time housekeeper, although a few of the more prosperous farmers may have engaged maids to help in the household as well as in the dairy and the fields, where their main energies would be concentrated. In the towns, where domestic comfort was rather greater, the families of more substantial merchants and clothiers would likewise employ domestic assistance, but in the majority of households in both town and country the wife and daughters would carry out the daily chores for themselves.

By the sixteenth century this position was slowly changing. The rising standard of life among the middle orders in society was creating a growing demand for domestics, and despite the large establishments of the greater nobles, an increasing proportion of servants were now employed in families of moderate means—a trend which was to persist and intensify up to the early twentieth century. Women, who were cheaper to employ and easier to discipline than men, were always more numerous in these smaller households, although most servant-keeping families in Tudor England would endeavour to employ 'the services of at least one man to run errands and attend on the master of the house'.

Despite the general improvement in accommodation during the sixteenth century, the quarters of the majority of servants remained primitive. Although pillows, bolsters and mattresses of chaff were appearing on the beds of the more fortunate, most were expected to sleep on sacks of straw, spread out in hall or attic. As the Elizabethan cleric William Harrison gloomily noted, 'If they had any sheet above them it was well, for seldom had they any under their bodies to keep them from the pricking straws that ran oft through the canvas of the pallet and razed their hardened hides.' Not until the following century did separate sleeping accommodation for servants become common, while as late as the eighteenth century it was still customary to 'sleep the men in the cellars, the women in the attics, often in a long single dormitory'. In the smallest houses, where only one or two servants were kept, things could be a good deal worse; these unfortunates might have to fit into any hole or corner in kitchen or cellar that they could find.

Under the Tudors the position of the servant in the social order was clearly defined. At the same time the growing power of the monarchy was reflected in such acts as that of 1504 prohibiting the employment of male retainers other than household servants.[8] The enforcement of this legislation led to the disbanding of the private armies which had so swelled the households of the nobility in the previous century and had promoted internal conflict. For the ordinary servant, Tudor legislation (the Statute of Artificers, 1563) laid down that hirings were to be for a year, unless an explicit statement to the contrary were made, and neither party could break the contract on his own initiative. Should the servant be responsible for a breach, he might be imprisoned in the House of Correction, although for his master the penalty for a similar offence was a fine only. It was also established that a servant must place the whole of his time at the disposal of his master, and all lawful commands were to be obeyed. Although in the course of the two following centuries the practice of annual hirings fell into abeyance in favour of monthly or half-yearly agreements, the provisions relating to obedience to a master's orders were retained and, indeed, strengthened by the courts in the nineteenth century. The chastisement of inefficient or lazy maids was likewise accepted practice, especially up to the end of the seventeenth century, while slovenly or negligent behaviour could be punished by fines as well as beatings. In one sixteenth-century Somerset household, where the master was high sheriff and thus had a special dignity to maintain, fines ranged from a penny for swearing or slatternly dress and twopence for absence from family prayers to sixpence for unpunctuality in serving dinner. These were deducted every quarter from wages, along with the cost of breakages. The list invites comparison with a similar one posted in a Surrey household nearly two centuries later. The range of fines is much the same, except for an overriding five shillings imposed on anyone defacing the list; but absence from family prayers no longer brought a penalty, nor did swearing (except at meals), and the sixpenny fine was limited to offences such as letting the dogs lick the plates.

During the seventeenth century the middling orders of society, who had been advancing under the Tudors, now began, in the words of one writer, to 'leap into prominence' and to carry their demands for domestic staff with them. At this stage a moderate household would consist of 'a cook maid, a chamber maid or housemaid, possibly a waiting woman, a man servant and an odd boy', but some establishments were far smaller than that. In 1619, for example, the bakers of London indicated that a typical bakery of that time consisted of a man, his wife and children, four paid employees (or journeymen), two apprentices and two maidservants. Each of the maids was paid 10d. a week, plus her keep.[4]

In rural areas most of the servants employed in smaller households were still engaged on the land as servants in husbandry rather than domestic servants. So although it has been estimated that in Stuart England 'a quarter or a third of all families in the country contained servants', it was as farm workers or dairymaids that they were primarily engaged.[5] In some cases a single drudge, perhaps a child obtained from the Poor Law authorities, would provide the only purely domestic help in a household—often under conditions of the grossest exploitation. Frequently this employment of young paupers would take the form of an 'apprenticeship to Housewifery', undertaken for a purely nominal premium, so that the girl concerned might later 'become a good servant . . . able to get her own living'.[6] She would receive no wages but was fed and clothed by her master.

At the other end of the servant-keeping scale in seventeenth-century England were the large households of the nobility, many of which were characterised by that predominance of male workers which they had displayed in earlier years and which was in marked contrast to their position two centuries later. At Woburn Abbey, the seat of the Earl (later Duke) of Bedford, in the 1660s and 1670s 'no women were to be found in the kitchen. There the men reigned supreme, with the clerk of the kitchen at the head of the staff.' After him, the chief personage was the cook who had to assist him 'a heterogeneous collection of scullions and turnspits'. Some of the youngest of these helpers received no wages at all, but were merely fed and clothed, while others were paid as little as 10s. a year. The Earl of Bedford also regularly employed about eleven or twelve footmen (whose wages ranged from £2 to £6 per annum) and a large number of young boys who acted as pages but were partly employed in the stables as well. They, too, received little or no cash payment but were clothed and fed, and probably lived in hopes of obtaining promotion one day. By contrast, the permanent female staff was limited to seven or eight workers only.[7]

A similar picture of the predominance of males over females in the largest establishments emerges from a catalogue of the household of the Countess of Dorset at Knole in the 1620s. Ranging from the chaplain at one end of the scale to footmen and pages at the other, she kept a male staff of ninety-three; but the women, including two housekeepers and various laundry-maids, numbered only twenty-one.

However, as wages began to rise more rapidly, especially during the eighteenth century, and as more and more male servants displayed an unwelcome spirit of independence and insubordination, this situation started to change, at least at the lower end of the servant hierarchy, among scullions, pages and the like. The upper ranks still tended to be the preserve of the men, although even here the position altered, so that housekeepers came increasingly to take over the duties of the former clerks of the kitchen. Overall earnings varied widely, according to the status of the servant and of his employer, and the £1,000 a year earned by the steward of an eighteenth-century Duke of Devonshire might be contrasted with the £4 to £6 a year earned by scullery-maids and stable-boys in humbler establishments—income levels which were, incidentally, still applicable to many young workers well into the next century, despite the general upward movement of wage rates during the eighteenth century and beyond.

This tendency for wages to rise was reinforced in the last decade of the century by the inflationary pressures of the French wars. But a major factor was the 'accelerated growth of the middle classes that accompanied the commercial and industrial expansion' of the eighteenth century. As always, increased prosperity brought in its train a greater demand for servants. Lesser men followed the example of their better-off neighbours as far as they were able, so that a correspondent in *The Craftsman* could complain in the middle of the century that 'There is scarce a mechanick in town who does not keep a servant in livery.' Although exaggerated at the time, this statement would have had more than a germ of truth in it a hundred years later.

With the growth in demand for servants came the higher wages which so exercised the minds of employers, even in country districts. At the beginning of the century, maids in rural areas could be recruited for as little as £2 10s. to £3 a year, but by 1784 such a man of middling income as Parson Woodforde, rector of Weston Longeville, Norfolk, had to pay a new cook five guineas a year, 'tea included'. Similarly, James Wissman, an oyster-merchant of Paglesham, Essex, appointed maids-of-all-work at £4 a year in the 1780s and 1790s. Wissman usually

B

settled the wages bill of his maids once a year only, but in the interim, advances were made to them for the purchase of bonnet ribbons, clogs, combs and other small items; the maids also drew money when visiting the local fairs at Paglesham, Rochford and Burnham.

In larger establishments servants were even more expensive. At Englefield House in Berkshire, where there was a resident staff of six in 1800, the cook-housekeeper was paid £23 per annum, plus 'two guineas for tea', while the maids received £8 per annum. London, too, was a high wage area. One critic reported early in the 1770s that his landlord had had to pay 'to a fat Welch girl, who was just come out of the country, scarce understood a word of English, was capable of nothing but washing, scouring and sweeping the rooms and had no inclination to learn any more, six guineas a year, besides a guinea a year for her tea'.[8] For better-class maids a wage of £8 a year and an allowance for tea were quite common.

Men could secure much higher figures, and in London a well-trained personal servant 'might command anything from fifteen to twenty guineas a year'. At Englefield House the butler was paid £20 per annum and the coachman £18 18s. It was not surprising that in these circumstances the number of male servants began to diminish, at least as compared to the lavish establishments of earlier centuries. Nevertheless La Rochefoucauld, who visited England in 1784, observed that there were still 'certain English noblemen who have thirty or forty men-servants', while another critic, Silliman, writing of well-to-do families just over twenty years later, claimed : 'One great point of emulation is to excel all rivals in the number of footmen. Some of the coaches had two, three and even four footmen, standing up, and holding on behind the carriage, not to mention occasionally a supernumerary one on the coachman's box.'[9] Similarly, the *Morning Post* reported in June 1777 : 'Lord Derby's coachman, and footmen, with their red feathers, and flame-coloured stockings, looked like so many figurantes taken from behind the scenes of the Opera House.' Certain of the more fashion-conscious even employed gorgeously decked negro servants for the same purposes of ostentatious display.

It was in these circumstances, and with a growing tendency to regard the employment of liveried men-servants as a not altogether desirable luxury, that in 1777 Lord North introduced a tax of one guinea per head on male domestics in order to help meet the cost of the American War of Independence. He estimated that there would be 100,000 men covered by the tax, and that the revenue would benefit to the tune of £105,000 per annum. But like similar measures adopted subsequently, the duty was so widely evaded and its collection so inefficiently organised that its yield fell far short of expectations. Eight years later the younger Pitt introduced a more severe impost, not only increasing the duty on the men in accordance with a sliding scale, but also introducing a new tax on female servants. This latter caused a great outcry, although the proposed level of duty was only 2s. 6d. per annum for one woman servant, 5s. per annum for two, and a maximum of 10s. per head per annum for the employment of three servants or more. As a result of the protests (critics called the levy 'unmanly'), Pitt agreed that families should be allowed one tax-free female servant to every two children; the loss thus caused to the exchequer was to be met by bachelors over the age of twenty-one paying double the rate for *their* maids. Nevertheless, despite the concession, the female servant tax was never popular, and in 1792 it was repealed.

But the attitude adopted towards the men remained harsh. In 1785 the employer of one or two male servants paid a tax of £1 5s. per head per annum; for a household of three or four servants the duty was £1 10s., and so on, on a sliding scale, until the employer of eleven male servants or more had to pay £3 a year for each of them. Bachelors were required to find an additional of £1 5s. per head per annum over and above these basic duties for any men they employed. The taxes were raised again in 1798 and 1808, while in 1786 a new duty on hair-powder hit those who desired their footmen and coachmen to wear powder. By 1808 the servant duty had, indeed, become so severe that the employer of one male servant was now paying £2 4s. per annum; of two servants, £2 16s. for each of them; of three, £3 7s. per annum, and so on until for eleven servants or more the formidable sum of £7 1s. per head had to be found. Bachelors had, as before, to pay an extra duty, but this had been raised from £1 5s. per servant to £1 14s.

Although in the course of the nineteenth century the duties on male servants were substantially eased, it was not until 1937 that the Finance Act at last abolished the tax; the duty on hair-powder had, meanwhile, disappeared in 1869. But, given existing wage levels, the extra burden imposed by the taxes would clearly encourage employers to substitute cheaper female labour for that of the men. This tendency was reinforced during the nineteenth century by the growing range of jobs available to men outside the ranks of domestic service. Consequently, while some estimates suggest that in the first years of that century women servants exceeded the men by less than eight to one, by 1881 the census report could claim that the males then employed were outnumbered in the proportion of twenty-two to one.[10]

But if rising wages and higher taxes were two causes of complaint among the servant-keeping classes of George III's England, a further reason for dissatisfaction arose from the growing avarice of the servants themselves in demanding 'vails' or tips. Even in the 1500s it had been common to tip footmen who brought gifts, or servants who carried out particular personal services, while the records of the Earl of Bedford in the later seventeenth century reveal a long list of presents bestowed on those who brought goods or messages to Woburn, and show 'how much money, in a great household was expended in that way'. But by the eighteenth century the demands had become so excessive that they were 'a barrier to social intercourse. . . . To dine with the nobility, with their considerable retinue, could be a ruinous business, costing at least a couple of pounds.' According to Jonas Hanway, the servants in some houses adopted a fixed schedule of rates, 'so much to be paid by the guest for having taken breakfast, so much for having drunk tea, so much for having eaten dinner'. Throughout Europe the domestics of Britain became notorious for their exactions, causing Baron de Pöllnitz to remark in 1738 : 'If a Duke gives me a dinner four Times a Week, his Footmen would pocket as much of my Money, as would serve my Expences at the Tavern for a Week.'[11] Callers to see the master of the house were expected to contribute, too, and those who failed to do so might be told that the master was not at home. Even visitors who played cards paid dearly for the privilege of having a pack supplied by one of the servants.

Dean Swift satirised this growing greed and independence of domestics in his *Directions to Servants*, which was published in 1745. The work purported to instruct butlers, cooks, footmen, housemaids, nurses, etc. on their duties and included such items as:

> When you have done a fault be always pert and insolent, and behave yourself as if you were the injured person.
>
> The cook, the butler, the groom, and every other servant should act as if his master's whole estate ought to be applied to that particular servant's business.
>
> If you find yourself to grow into favour with your master or lady, take some opportunity to give them warning, and when they ask the reason, and seem loath to part with you, answer that a poor servant is not to be blamed if he strives to better himself. Upon which, if your master hath any generosity, he will add five or ten shillings a quarter rather than let you go.

Any maid who waited upon a young lady of fortune was likewise advised : 'Let it be known what lady you live with; how great a favourite you are; and that she always takes your advice; the fine fellows will soon discover you and contrive to slip a letter into your sleeve or your bosom; pull it out in a fury and throw it on the ground—unless you discover at least two guineas with it.'

So troublesome did servant relations become in some households that employers began to express public disquiet. Typical of the adverse comments was that in the *London Chronicle* of 1767 : 'Can a master expect fidelity, love or gratitude, from a servant who is always grumbling when the house is not filled with vail-giving company; and lives with him with such uncertainty, that his staying or going from quarter to quarter depends mainly on the number and disposition of the visitants?' By the early 1760s there are accounts of meetings being held first in Scotland and later in England in order to discourage the custom of vails, and of supporters of reform pledging their word of honour 'that in visiting one another they would give no money to servants, nor allow their own servants to take money from their guests'. Although, as will be seen, the reform movement did not entirely eliminate the practice, it did see an end to some of the worst excesses.

A further change to emerge by the early nineteenth century related to dress. Until that time women servants wore no distinguishing livery, although footmen and coachmen were, as we have noted, richly adorned in gold and silver braid, with tricorn hats, 'bags, toupées and ruffles'. Maids, on the other hand, often

wore clothes handed down to them by their mistresses or purchased second-hand, and there were complaints that when female
servants attended their mistresses in the streets, 'if the mistress be
not known, it is no easy matter to distinguish her from the maid'.
Daniel Defoe was one of many who wrote of the social problems
to which this could lead :

> I remember I was put very much to the Blush, being at a
> Friend's House, and by him required to salute the Ladies, and
> I kiss'd the chamber Jade into the bargain, for she was as well
> dressed as the best. Things of this Nature would be easily
> avoided, if Servant Maids were to wear Liveries, as our Foot-
> men do; or obliged to go in a Dress suitable to their Station.
> Our Charity Children are distinguished by their Dresses, why
> then may not our Women Servants?[12]

Although his plea met with no immediate response, by the beginning of the nineteenth century attitudes were altering. It became
more and more common for maids to wear plain and simple
clothes for indoor duties, even though a measure of freedom in
outside attire was still permitted. Leigh Hunt, writing in the
1820s, described the maidservant's dress at that time in the
following terms :

> Her ordinary dress is black stockings, a stuff gown, a cap, and
> a neck-handkerchief pinned corner-wise behind. If you want
> a pin, she just feels about her, and has always one to give you.
> On Sundays and holidays, and perhaps of afternoons, she
> changes her black stockings for white, puts on a gown of better
> texture and fine pattern, sets her cap and her curls jauntily,
> and lays aside the neck-handkerchief for a high body, which,
> by the way, is not half so pretty.[13]

Gradually this sort of clothing merged into a uniform of print
dresses, white caps and aprons for mornings, and black dresses
for afternoons. This became the characteristic female servant
attire until well into the twentieth century.

Nevertheless, variations in dress and in attitudes towards tipping were not the most important changes which the nineteenth
century brought about. Far more significant than either was the
increase in the number of servants employed in a century which
saw the true burgeoning of the middle classes. Alongside this there

developed the view that the employment of domestic staff was in itself a sign of respectability and an indicator of social status. And as small shopkeepers, tradesmen and clerks moved in growing numbers into the servant-keeping classes, so the distinctions between employer and maid were more firmly drawn. Whereas in the mid-seventeenth century Samuel Pepys and his wife often treated their maids as friends and companions (and sometimes, in the case of Samuel, as something rather more intimate), their nineteenth-century counterparts adopted a more rigid approach. Nowhere was this clearer than among employers whose own station in life was uncomfortably close to that of the maid they kept, and for whom the preservation of petty distinctions of rank was all-important. While a Lord Chesterfield, writing from the security of his own unassailable social standing, could view menial servants as his 'equals in Nature . . . inferiors only by the difference of our position', the preoccupation of countless Victorian employers was to get servants to recognise that their inferior status (or 'humble station in life') was the 'clear will of God as laid down in both Testaments'.

In the nineteenth century, then, the numbers of those able to afford resident domestic staff rose sharply, and it was in these years that domestic service reached its peak. By 1901 it was not only the major employer of women in the country, but, with a total labour force of nearly one and a half million persons, it formed the largest occupational grouping of any kind—bigger than mining, engineering or agriculture. In this *female* servants were numerically predominant. And it was the Victorian era, with all its strengths and its foibles, that was the real heyday of the domestic servant.

SERVANT HEYDAY

2

The Servant-Keeping Classes and Their Problems

No relations in society are so numerous and universal as those of
Masters and Servants—as those of Household Duties and the per-
formers of them
SAMUEL and SARAH ADAMS, *The Complete Servant* (1825).

Without the constant co-operation of well-trained servants,
domestic machinery is completely thrown out of gear, and the
best bred of hostesses placed at a disadvantage.
The Servant's Practical Guide (1880).

FOR ANY nineteenth-century family with social pretensions at
least one domestic servant was essential, even if at its lowest level
this merely meant the recruitment of a thirteen-year-old 'skivvy'
from the local workhouse at a wage of a shilling a week. Certainly
when Seebohm Rowntree conducted his survey of York in 1899,
he took 'the keeping or not keeping of domestic servants' as the
dividing line between 'the working classes and those of a higher
social scale'. Most of his contemporaries would have agreed with
him—including those like the family of Josiah Crawley, the pro-
verbially impoverished perpetual curate in Anthony Trollope's
Last Chronicle of Barset, who struggled to keep a maid on an
income of £130 per annum, although the carpets were in rags
and the furniture shabby and broken.

Outside the pages of fiction there were many similar examples.
Thus when another perpetual curate, Patrick Brontë, moved with
his wife and six children to Haworth in Yorkshire in 1820, he
took with him two maids, although his stipend was only about
£200 a year. And over seventy years later, an assistant master at
an elementary school in North London, who was earning less than
£200 per annum when he married in 1895, nevertheless con-

trived to employ a resident servant up to the First World War. In order to do so, he and his wife had to give extra music lessons.

Beyond the basic minimum of one, the number of domestics employed was regarded as a rough guide to status *within* the ranks of the socially superior. Those more fortunately placed talked in hushed tones of 'poor Mrs So-and-so' who only had a maid to wait upon her, while there are accounts of hostesses deciding precedence at their dinner table in accordance with the number of servants kept by their guests.[1] As in earlier centuries, well-to-do families employed as large a staff as they could afford, since by so doing they could impress the world with the grandeur of their style of living and could indicate that they were persons of consequence. Lady Cynthia Asquith expressed the typical view in an account of her childhood in late Victorian England : 'There was never . . . any virtue other than economy in keeping only one instead of several servants.'[2]

Those who fell within the servant-keeping classes varied widely in both social position and income. An investigation of the census returns for the mid-Victorian period confirms just how modest the occupations of some of these people could be. In rural market towns like Wantage (then in Berkshire), Thame in Oxfordshire and Fakenham in Norfolk, where approximately one household in six kept a resident maid, around two-fifths of the employers were small tradesmen—drapers, grocers, plumbers, coal merchants, corn dealers and the like. In the main they relied upon the services of the most common form of English domestic, the maid-of-all-work, and it is significant that in the 1871 census not far short of two-thirds of the nation's 1·2 million female servants fell into the 'general' category.

The work required in these poorer households was frequently hard and drudging. Even Mrs Beeton, in her *Book of Household Management*, considered the general servant

> deserving of commiseration : her life is a solitary one, and in some places, her work is never done. She is also subject to rougher treatment than either the house or kitchen-maid, especially in her earlier career : she starts in life, probably a girl of thirteen, with some small tradesman's wife as her mistress, just a step above her in the social order; and although

the class contains among them many excellent kind-hearted women, it also contains some very rough specimens of the feminine gender, and to some of these it occasionally falls to give our maid-of-all-work her first lessons in her multifarious occupations.[3]

Often when the employer had a shop he also expected the maid to serve behind the counter or assist in other ways, while the farmhouse servant, like her Tudor and Stuart predecessors, was normally required to help with the dairying as well as with the household chores. But perhaps most exploited of all nineteenth-century maids-of-all-work were those employed in cheap lodging-houses, particularly in London. The novelist George Moore described in moving terms his encounter with one such girl (named Emma) while he was living at a Strand lodging-house at the end of the nineteenth century, and his testimony can speak for the rest. Every morning Emma rose at five o'clock,

scouring, washing, cooking, dressing the children; seventeen hours at least out of the twenty-four at the beck and call of landlady and lodgers; seventeen hours at least out of the twenty-four drudging in and out of the kitchen, running up-stairs with coals and breakfasts and cans of hot water, or down on your knees before a grate, pulling out the cinders with those hands—can I call them hands? The lodgers sometimes threw you a kind word, but never one that recognised you as one of our kin; only the pity that might be extended to a dog. . . . To know nothing but a dark kitchen, grates, eggs and bacon, dirty children; to work seventeen hours a day and to get cheated out of your wages. . . . [The landlady] owed you forty pounds. . . . I calculated it from what you told me; and yet you did not like to leave her because you did not know how she would get on without you. Sublime stupidity ! . . . I remember you once spoke of a half-holiday; I questioned you, and I found your idea of a half-holiday was to take the children out for a walk and buy them some sweets. . . . [You] were taken by this fat landlady . . . and you will be thrown away, shut out of doors when health fails you, or when, overcome by base usage, you take to drink. There is no hope for you.[4]

Higher up the servant-keeping scale came the professional

classes, doctors, clergymen, bank managers, and the more substantial businessmen, who would probably aim to employ about
three servants, since this was regarded as the minimum necessary
if the household were to be 'complete in all its functions'. In the
late Victorian period these would normally comprise cook, housemaid and parlourmaid, or if there were young children in the
family, a nursemaid. Among employers within this group was a
Hertford bank manager who from 1897 to 1911 earned £600 a
year, 'plus a free seven-bedroomed house with three quarters of
an acre for a garden'. He kept a resident cook, a housemaid and
a nursemaid, plus a daily knife-boy, who was paid 1s. a day to
perform such miscellaneous tasks as cleaning the family's boots
and shoes, carrying in the coal, chopping the wood, and cleaning
the knives.[5]

Much more favourably placed were employers like the rector
of Odell in Bedfordshire who during the 1890s kept seven resident
servants for a family comprising himself, his wife and ten children.
The servants included a governess, a nurse and nursery-maid, a
cook, a parlourmaid, and a 'tweeny', who combined the duties of
a housemaid with those of a kitchenmaid. Although the staff
seemed large, there was a great deal of work to be done. Since
there was no water upstairs and no bathroom, cans of hot water
had to be carried upstairs daily to fill the hip-baths in every room.
There were three breakfasts to prepare—for the nursery and the
school-room at eight o'clock and for the dining-room, where the
parents ate, at nine o'clock. The rector's youngest daughter recalled: 'There must have been at least fifteen oil lamps to fill and
trim daily. A gardener and coachman were also employed, and
their daily work consisted in pumping water to the house twice a
day, and at least fifteen pairs of boots to clean daily. . . . On
Monday mornings women from the village came up to the
laundry at the Rectory to do the household washing. This caused
great excitement, as it was the one link the maids had with the
outside world.'[6]

Yet even comfortably placed households such as this contrasted
sharply with those of the aristocracy at the top of the servant-
keeping hierarchy, with their retinues of retainers and establishments which often constituted 'a settlement as large as a small
village'. In the 1890s the Duke of Westminster, one of the richest
men in England, employed over three hundred servants (includ-

ing ground staff) at the family seat at Eaton in Cheshire, while at Welbeck Abbey about ten years later the Duke of Portland had a staff of around 320—including fourteen housemaids and thirty-eight male and female servants in the kitchens and allied departments. The reminiscences of Frederick John Gorst, who worked there as a young footman, reveal that 'The estate of Welbeck Abbey was more like a principality than anything else; there were scores of people working beside me whom I did not know. . . . Within the borders of Welbeck Abbey, His Grace the Duke of Portland, wielded an almost feudal indisputable power.'[7]

On a more modest scale, another landed family, the Harcourts of Nuneham Courtenay, Oxfordshire, employed a domestic staff of almost twenty, supplemented by occasional temporary helpers, and their account books give an idea of the cost of maintaining a substantial number of servants. During the period 1883-90 inclusive, the wages, board wages (i.e. cash in lieu of food) and liveries of the male and female domestics ranged between £789 15s. and £1,025 6s. 6¼d. per annum; in five of the eight years the annual total was above £950. These figures exclude both food eaten by the servants when not on board wages, and a large part of their travelling expenses. In most years the separate 'travelling account' showed an expenditure of between £3 and £5 on this score, but in 1883, when the family spent a great deal of time at Hastings and London, expenditure on servants' travelling amounted to over £32.[8] Similarly, at Englefield House in Berkshire, where the Benyons employed around twenty-three resident domestics, the wages bill alone—exclusive of board wages, board and liveries—varied between £530 and £620 per annum, during the period 1886 to 1891 inclusive.

Domestic life in the large establishments was carefully structured, and each department was under the control of the head servant belonging to it. At Welbeck, Gorst lists sixteen different departments, including the gardens, gymnasium, racing stables and golf course. General supervision, as regards the men, was undertaken by the house steward or butler, and of the women by the housekeeper. 'These personages were regarded by the under-servants, shut away in their own quarters and never permitted to be seen in the front part of the house after the family and their guests had left their bedrooms, almost as kings and queens. Only the head servants, body servants, and those in attendance on the sitting rooms, or dining-room, would be likely even to know their employers by sight.'⁹

In certain households the practice of keeping servants out of sight was carried to eccentric excess. The household regulations of the aged third Lord Crewe stipulated that 'No housemaids were ever to be seen at Crewe Hall except in chapel, "when a great number would muster, only to disappear mysteriously directly the service was ended".' Failure to observe this rule could lead to instant dismissal. A similar policy was adopted by the tenth Duke of Bedford, who died in 1893. 'To cross his path, unless he wished to see you, was little short of a crime, and any of the women servants who met him after twelve o'clock in the day, when their duties might be supposed to be done', could immediately lose their place. Indeed, according to Lady Cynthia Asquith, in really well-ordered households no housemaid was ever seen with broom and duster in hand. Except for the bedrooms all the housework had to be done before any of the family or their guests came downstairs, a refinement which meant very early rising for the maids. But, as she rather complacently concluded, both employers and employees 'knew their places, and kept to them as planets to their orbits'.¹⁰

When the landed families moved to London, in mid-May, for the 'season', or to Scotland for the grouse-shooting on the 'Glorious Twelfth' of August, they would take a number of their servants with them. Additional staff might also be hired locally, although a few servants were almost invariably kept permanently in the town house on a care and maintenance basis, receiving board wages. To servants the opportunity to travel with the family to a new residence was a welcome break in the usual routine. In an autobiographical fragment, one young servant, Hannah Cullwick, recalls her delight when, in the spring of 1855, as a young kitchenmaid at Lord Stradbroke's residence, Henham Hall, Suffolk, she was told to accompany the family to London for two months. Four servants were taken—the butler, a footman, a housemaid and Hannah. 'It was a nice little house in South St., Park Lane & there i had to wait on the butler & the town housekeeper & clean their sitting room—do the front steps & all the lowest places underground, but i liked the work.' On her evenings off she was free to go for walks in the park or to visit friends.

At Longleat, where an indoor domestic staff of forty-three was kept at the beginning of the twentieth century, about seventeen servants were ordered to accompany the Marquis of Bath and his family each spring when they moved to London. The situation in other large establishments was much the same: the London season, with its balls, receptions and dinner parties, was a busy time for those working 'below stairs', and experienced staff were essential.

On visits to the continent, a well-to-do family would also take some of their servants with them. In the 1840s when the Earl of Ormond and his family visited Germany and Italy they were accompanied by two maids, a footman and a French cook, while in 1900 the Mulhollands of Beccles in Suffolk were attended by twelve of their permanent staff when they rented a villa in Cannes for three months. For some of the younger servants this was their first trip abroad; as one of the junior Mulholland maids recalled, her face was a 'shining light' as she made a brief tour of Paris on the journey south.

Yet these large households, impressive though they were, absorbed only a small minority of the total domestic work-force. And by the end of the nineteenth century rising wages and falling farm rentals were obliging some landed families to cut back on their establishments.[11] The majority of maids therefore worked in one- or two-servant homes. Even in London, which in 1891 contained between one-fifth and one-sixth of the nation's female domestics and where large establishments were by no means uncommon, Charles Booth, in the course of his survey of working conditions in the metropolis, discovered that over half of the female staff were employed in one- or two-servant households; less than one-quarter lived in households of four servants or more.[12] Twenty years later a national estimate suggested that four out of every five employers kept a resident staff of one or two members only.[13]

At the same time, it is a tribute to the growing prosperity of mid-Victorian England that despite the expenditure involved, the number of families able to afford domestic help increased sharply. During the period 1851-71, while the total of separate families increased by 36 per cent, the figure for female servants rose by over 56 per cent. The 1871 census report revealed, indeed, that during the previous ten years the greatest ever rise in female servants had occurred, observing rather critically: 'Wives and

c

daughters at home do now less domestic work than their pre-decessors : hence the excessive demand for female servants and the consequent rise of wages.' At this date a peak of 12·8 per cent of the female population of England and Wales was engaged in domestic service or allied occupations, such as those of washer-woman and charwoman.[14]

But in the ensuing forty or so years up to the outbreak of the First World War the position of employers proved rather less favourable. Although there was certainly no retrogression in the position of the middle classes, the rate of progress slackened off. Whereas total incomes above £150 per annum (i.e. the exemp-tion level for income tax for much of the period, as well as the recommended minimum needed to employ a servant) had grown at about 45 per cent in the 1860s and 33·2 per cent during the 1870s, by the 1890s the advance had been cut to 26 per cent, and in the period 1901-11 it was only 24 per cent.[15] Furthermore, while retail prices were falling in the late nineteenth century, certain other of the more characteristic items of middle-class expenditure—housing, education and servants—were rising in cost. The wages of female servants increased by perhaps a third during the period 1871-1901, while the average age of servants also rose—another tendency making for greater expense.

Indeed, a growing reluctance to enter service, especially on the part of younger girls, became apparent towards the end of the century. They resented the drudgery, the regimentation, the un-becoming clothes and the coarse, work-reddened hands and arms which were their lot as domestics, preferring instead to seek em-ployment in shops, offices and factories. And, as employers found to their cost, even those youngsters who did become maids were often ready to move on if they did not like their situation. Accord-ing to one dissatisfied contemporary, the servant no longer *lived* in her mistress's home, but 'merely [hired] herself out for a short time'. When she grew tired of the place, she left, 'embarking on a new venture in the best spirits in the world'.[16]

By the 1890s, writers on household affairs were beginning to lament that it was 'no longer regarded as honourable' to enter domestic service, and were calling it 'the unpopular industry'. The trend was encouraged by improvements in educational pro-visions following the passage of the 1870 Education Act. In fact, as the 1901 census showed, comparing 1881 with 1901, there had actually been a *decrease* of over 7 per cent in the number of female domestic servants aged 15-20 years, notwithstanding an increase of 28·1 per cent in the total number of females in this age-group. Whereas in 1881 over one-third of all domestic servants had been in the 15-20 age-group, by 1911 the proportion had fallen to 28 per cent; by contrast, women aged between 25 and 45 had increased their share from 24 per cent to about 32 per cent of the total over the same period.

Yet for female domestic servants of all ages, numbers did not indicate a decline, but rather a dramatic slowing down in the rate of expansion. In 1881 the resident female domestic work-force had been put at 1,230,406; by 1901 it had risen to 1,330,783. (The 1891 figures are not comparable, as in this census alone women and girls working in their own families as servants, house-keepers, etc. were included in the aggregate servant figure.) By 1911 the number had advanced only a little to 1,359,359, or excluding those employed in hotels, lodging- and eating-houses, it stood at 1,271,990. The 1911 census also demonstrated how much more thinly servants were spread among households just before the First World War as compared to earlier years. In 1881 there had been 218 female domestics to every 1,000 families in England and Wales, but by 1911, the proportion had fallen to 170 per 1,000 families. Hence the complaints of 'shortages' of servants which proliferate at the turn of the century and the 'pitiful' stories of ladies left temporarily without staff, such as those recounted by Lady Bunting in an article in the *Contemporary Review* of 1910: 'No-one to cook the dinner, answer the door, attend to the children and carry out the many other requirements of an ordinary household. In many cases the mistress is absolutely incapable of taking on the duties which the servant has done and she finds herself more of a "dependant" than the servant.'

For men-servants, on the other hand, the situation was rather different. As we saw in Chapter 1, their employment peak had been passed well before the end of the nineteenth century. In 1851 there were reported to be 74,323 indoor male servants; by 1901 the figure had fallen to 64,146, and in 1911 to 54,260, or excluding those working in hotels, lodging- and eating-houses, to 42,034. And whereas in the earlier Victorian years a male servant had been considered essential for those aspiring to gentility—so that in the city of London of the 1840s and 1850s 'it would have been considered a dreadful thing for a lady of birth to go out walking without a man-servant behind her'—by 1900 all but the grandest families were engaging the cheaper alternative of a parlourmaid to replace butler or footman or even page. It was a trend warmly welcomed by Charles Dickens among others. In an article on 'Old and New Servants' which appeared on 20 July 1867, he contrasted the speedy and quiet service of a maid with what he claimed were the idle and sottish manners attributable to many male servants and concluded that all too often the men were kept 'for the ostentation of the thing'. Families were prepared to 'undergo endless domestic tortures for the vicarious display of crested buttons and bits of lace'.

The 'luxury' aspect of the male servant was also emphasised by the continued levying of the servant tax, which in 1853 was set at £1 1s. per annum for men over the age of eighteen and 10s. 6d. per annum for boy servants. Under the Revenue Act of 1869, the tax was again altered to 15s. per annum for both categories—a change which one Member of Parliament deplored as inflicting 'great hardship on the farmer or small trader, who kept a boy, by making him pay 15s. duty instead of 10s. 6d.' But his protest was unavailing and the tax remained at 15s. per annum until it was abolished in 1937.

The changing position of servants *vis-à-vis* their employers, which the above facts indicate, was also brought out by amendments to the suggested size of domestic establishments which appeared in the various manuals on home management published through the period, including the numerous revised editions of Mrs Beeton's *Book of Household Management*. This work first appeared in serial form during 1859 in Samuel Beeton's *English Women's Domestic Magazine* but was published in book form in 1861. The following extracts are taken from the 1861 and 1906 editions of the work.

Income	Servants
1861	
About £1,000 a year	A cook, upper housemaid, nurse-maid, under-housemaid, a male servant.
About £750 a year	A cook, housemaid, nursemaid, and footboy.

Income	Servants
About £500 a year	A cook, housemaid, and nursemaid.
About £300 a year	A maid-of-all-work and nursemaid.
About £200 or £150 a year	A maid-of-all-work (and girl occasionally).
1906	
About £1,000 a year	Cook, housemaid, and perhaps a man-servant.
From £750 to £500 a year	Cook, housemaid.
About £300 a year	General servant.
About £200 a year	Young girl for rough work.

By the early twentieth century the suggested minimum annual income needed to keep a resident general servant (i.e. maid-of-all-work) had thus risen from £150 to £300.

Alongside these general changes, there were also regional variations in the size and incidence of domestic employment to be taken into account. In the mining and manufacturing areas, where the groups likely to employ servants formed a smaller proportion of the total population and where alternative occupations for girls and women existed, the number engaged in domestic service was at its lowest. It was larger in the agricultural districts and greatest of all in towns like Brighton, Bath and Cheltenham, which were the 'habitual resorts of the wealthier classes'.[17] Whereas in London in 1881 the proportion of indoor domestic servants (male and female together) was put at 1 to every 15 persons, in Brighton it was 1 to every 11, and in Bath 1 to every 9. In the agricultural counties of Norfolk, Suffolk and Essex the average was 1 to every 21, but in Lancashire it stood at a mere 1 to 30, and in Durham at 1 to 31. Ten years later it was calculated that about 1 in 5 of *all* females living in Bath aged ten or over was in service; in York, Reading and London the proportion was put at about 1 in 7, but in Halifax, Bury, Bolton, Rochdale, Blackburn and Burnley it was a mere 1 in 20 of the same female age grouping.[18]

In the cotton and woollen towns especially, few *local* girls chose to go into service, with its long hours and restricted leisure, when they could earn higher wages and, thanks to the Factory Acts, have more free time by entering the mills. Their attitude was summarised by 'A Working Girl' in a letter to the *Leeds Daily News* of 6 November 1889, and subsequent correspondence in the newspaper confirmed that her view was fairly typical among the local mill workers : 'A great many girls prefer to go into a clothing factory . . . because they are not tied so much as servant girls, and, not only that, a great many general servants do not get sufficient food. . . . Girls that work in factories earn their money and know how to spend it to the best advantage.'

Well-to-do householders in the industrial areas either had to recruit their staff from away—or do without. In the small Lancashire cotton town of Colne, for example, the 1871 census showed that only one in every twenty-three households had a resident servant at all (compared to one in every six in such similarly small towns as Thame in Oxfordshire and Fakenham in Norfolk, both situated in rural areas). A mere quarter of the Colne maids had been born in Lancashire. Most had migrated from agricultural districts in Yorkshire, Cumberland, Westmorland and Wales. The same situation prevailed in larger industrial towns, including Preston, where the greater number of domestics were said to be immigrants 'from purely agricultural villages'. By contrast, Blackpool, with its reputation for holidays and amusements, had far less difficulty in recruiting staff. It was even able to attract girls to service from industrial centres like Liverpool, Preston and Clitheroe as well as from the rural areas in its own hinterland and from nearby counties.

London, too, with its insatiable demand for servants depended on large-scale immigration, while, in any case, many better-off householders here were prejudiced against employing girls born in the capital, as they were thought to be dishonest and insubordinate. Areas such as Kensington, St George's, Hanover Square, Hampstead and Lewisham, which had the highest percentage of servants, were also the districts where the lowest proportion of adult females had been born in London : 'The domestic servants were usually recruited from the countryside, and there were a sufficient number of servants in the wealthy districts to affect the statistics.' Throughout the mid- and late Victorian period female domestic servants constituted nearly a quarter of the female population of the West District of London.[19]

But it was the employer of servants in the North of England who had the real difficulty in satisfying his needs, and whose problems became ever more acute as the rate of growth of the domestic work-force slumped in the later nineteenth century. One would-be employer from North Shields complained in 1910 that there was 'an overflow of Shop Girls, Typists and Female Assistants of every description', but a 'perpetual cry for good domestic servants'. The 1911 census bears out his contention. In Lancashire there were only 97 female indoor domestic servants to every 1,000 families, in the West Riding of Yorkshire 100 per 1,000 families, and in Durham 102—as compared to the national average of 170 per 1,000 families, and figures of 307 per 1,000 in Bath, 415 in Bournemouth, and 630 in the small Surrey town of Weybridge.

Some householders sought to overcome their staff problems by recruiting so-called 'lady helps' from among gentlewomen who had fallen upon hard times and who could be turned into 'upper servants'. But although the idea was canvassed from the 1870s, it did not work out.[20] 'Like the governess the lady help was neither in one world nor the other. In a house with several servants she was inevitably a source of friction.'[21] Indeed, in their desire to preserve their status and self-respect, the lady helps often ate their meals in odd corners rather than with the other domestics. The difficulties to which that sort of situation gave rise, as well as the limited number of 'ladies' prepared to undertake the work, soon eliminated this solution to the shortage of maids, though in conditions of growing shortage in the early twentieth century, the idea was to be revived (see Chapter 9).

Discussing the question in July 1892, *The Spectator* referred to a report that lady servants operating under an organisation called the Household Auxiliary Association proposed to eat apart from the other servants and to do no 'scrubbing, blacking of boots or carrying of heavy weights upstairs'. In the journal's view, in 'an ordinary family where the servants number between four and nine', such discrimination would be highly undesirable and would 'reduce a household to anarchy. If ladies are to go into ordinary household service, to be anything else, that is but governesses, housekeepers, or companions, they must be willing to place themselves on a level with the rest of the servants in the house.'

Other employers used more part-time workers, daily cleaning women, etc., and sent out their washing to a laundry, while a small minority adopted the modern solution of labour-saving appliances. But most still adhered to the view that it would be a 'betrayal of civilisation if a gentlewoman boiled an egg for herself', and there was a reluctance to install labour-saving devices 'when the whole function of servants was to do the drudgery'. Lord Willoughby de Broke, writing in the 1920s, recalled with pride that at the family seat at Compton Verney in Warwickshire during his youth, a ton of coal was burnt in the kitchen every day. 'I have had the privilege of seeing the sirloin hanging by a chain, slowly turning round and round and being basted by the stout kitchen wench, whose face was quite as red and nearly as hot as the huge open fire in front of her. We did not bake the good joint in some patent, poverty-stricken, war-begotten, labour-saving monstrosity . . . as we do now.'[22] In any case, the most important labour-saving device of all, a sensibly designed house, was still lacking.

In the hard-pressed North of England a few more adventurous souls were prepared to consider the employment of foreigners to ease their domestic problems. The *Leeds Daily News* of 8 December 1899 pointed out that Scandinavian girls had been 'imported to South Shields, Sunderland and other Tyne ports to act as domestic servants on account of the scarcity of English girls. Their employers state that they are attentive and industrious, and without any of the foibles of English domestics. In Norway and Sweden there is plenty of female labour available, and as steamers are constantly running between those countries and our northern ports, girls for service in English homes are readily obtained.' In its issue of 15 November 1899 the same newspaper also published an enthusiastic account of male 'cooks and general servants' from Germany and Switzerland, who were prepared to perform domestic duties in return for an opportunity to learn the English language. One German valet-de-chambre had agreed to undertake the duties of a housemaid for this reason, and according to his employer, he proved so efficient as to do the housework 'twice as well as the normal housemaid and in about half the time. The brasses shine like gold throughout the house . . . and the dust disappears like magic. He is a noiseless creature and most deeply respectful in manner.'

Yet, despite these eulogies, foreign servants remained a tiny, exotic minority in the total domestic work-force, and employers had to be content with such of the home-grown variety as they could recruit. Even among men-servants 'European foreigners' numbered less than one in thirteen of the total work-force at the turn of the century, and among the womenfolk they were too few to be accorded special mention in the general census reports.[23]

It is now time to examine how servants *were* recruited and to consider what pre-service training, if any, the youngest of them was likely to have received before they obtained their first situation.

3

Getting a Place

Engaging domestics is one of those duties in which the judgement
of the mistress must be keenly exercised.

MRS I. BEETON, *Book of Household Management* (1861).

SINCE THE vast majority of working-class girls in Victorian England went into service at an early age, the attention of a mother
and her daughter began to turn to the question of getting a place
as soon as the girl had reached about twelve or thirteen. In the
middle of the nineteenth century, indeed, the search might begin
still sooner. Hannah Cullwick was only eight years old when, in
1841, she left the charity school at Shifnal in Shropshire to take
a situation in the household of a friend of her mother's.[1]

One difficulty was that not all smaller employers liked to
engage servants from their own immediate locality. The diary of
the Rev. W. C. Risley of Deddington, Oxfordshire, reveals that
he rejected a candidate for the post of footman purely on the
grounds that he had 'friends living in the Place', to whom he
might, presumably, have betrayed secrets of the Risley household.
Similarly, a former servant from the Ewelme area of the same
county recalled that it was usual for youngsters in her parish to
be sent at least twenty miles away from home—'probably to discourage followers or to stop the girls running home'.[2]

But even if the *first* position were obtained locally, sooner or
later most youngsters from the country districts would have to
move away to the towns, since it was here (especially in London)
that the bulk of the vacancies for servants lay. In fact the 1891
census report critically observed that the openings for early
domestic employment were stripping 'the rural districts of their
young girls, and [causing] . . . the lads exceptionally to outnum-
ber the girls in country places between the ages of 10 and 20'.
Such a situation led to stresses within village society and was one

minor factor in the extensive migration of young men from rural areas which occurred in the last years of the century.

Before reaching an age when permanent employment could be contemplated, many girls would have been gaining a little experience in household chores by helping their mother or taking an occasional day or weekend job in the home of a neighbour. This is made clear by entries in school log-books, like that at Cublington in Buckinghamshire, where the mistress noted on 28 June 1877 that 'Agnes Beckett [had] made 12 attendances in 9 weeks—am told she is nursemaid to Mrs White in this village.' On 16 July came the further entry : 'Agnes Beckett left, gone out nursing for good.' Backed by the practical training thus gained, such girls would start their full-time careers as nursemaids, and it is surprising to note that in the 1871 census nearly one-fifth of all 'nurses' employed in full-time domestic service were under fifteen years of age. There were even 710 girls under the age of *ten* so occupied—a signal act of faith on the part of some parents, it would seem.

Other girls carried out simple cleaning jobs in their spare time while still at school. Thus Mrs Wrigley of Cefn Mawr in Wales, who was born in 1858, began earning her living when she was about seven or eight : 'I went out cleaning the floors and back-yards on a Saturday for a penny a time, and a piece of bread and butter. I also carried dinners and suppers to the iron forge for twopence a week.' At the age of nine she embarked on a more serious stage in her career—one followed by many girls—by obtaining a post as day servant at the vicarage. 'There was another servant, but I did not stay long, for we were rationed with our food and everything was locked up. My mother was glad for me to go out for food alone.'

Most youngsters would stay for about a year in these 'petty' places, saving as hard as they could so that they might buy their uniforms in readiness for the move into full-time residential employment. For only a few lucky girls were given clothes by their employer or by some local well-wisher, such as the clergyman's wife.[3] And fewer still had mothers like that of Mrs Emily Caldwell of Marlborough, Wiltshire, who had sufficient cash—and foresight—to take out a small insurance for each of her daughters in readiness for the day they went into service and had to buy a uniform.

While in their petty places, the girls learned something of the way a household was run, for the standards demanded by even a modest middle-class family were likely to be very different from those they had encountered in their own poverty-stricken, overcrowded homes. Many did not even know the names of the items of furniture or kitchen utensils they were expected to clean, and household manuals prepared especially for the young servant often contained instructive pictures of the most common of these items.

But it was workhouse or orphanage children who were particularly likely to experience this difficulty, since although they were taught to scrub floors and to polish rough wooden furniture, they had no idea how to carry out more delicate tasks like dusting china ornaments, or even cleaning carpets. As a contemporary sympathetically noted, when such girls went out to work they were 'frequently called stupid because they [were] unacquainted with the names and uses of kitchen articles, whereas it is simply ignorance from not having seen or used them'. Certainly one former servant who was brought up in an Irish orphanage in the 1890s remembers her bewilderment when in her first place she was 'taken to the kitchen—introduced to the huge kitchen range (never having seen one before) given a flue brush, and told to clean the range and the flues; blacklead the whole; set the fire and leave all ready for morning'.[4]

Towards the end of the nineteenth century some writers on domestic affairs, seeing the emergence of servant 'shortages' and the growing reluctance of girls to enter service, began to canvass the view that elementary schools should play a greater part in preparing children for a domestic career. As early as 1859 the Rev. R. Gurney, Clerical Secretary of the Church of England Education Society, had suggested that in girls' schools the 'industrial element' ought to be 'more largely introduced, so that we might look to them with more hope for a better and higher principled class of household servants than they now furnish'.[5] Similarly, 'A Late Lady Overseer from Leamington' wrote to the *Royal Leamington Chronicle* of 28 May 1872, calling for instruction to be given in 'washing and ironing and cleaning grates and making fires. . . . It is lamentable to see that the present system of education (especially in schools under Government inspection) is ruining the daughters of our agricultural poor for domestic service, and so leading many into the broad road which leads to destruction.'

Most elementary schools ignored these hints and confined their domestic instruction to needlework. But in a few instances the strictures were taken to heart, and training of a more specialised type was provided. The Royal Commission on the Employment of Children, Young Persons and Women in Agriculture, 1867-69, drew attention to several of them. Thus at Well in Lincolnshire it was reported that, in addition to the customary needlework every afternoon, one girl was always employed in the service of the schoolmistress, and others were engaged in cleaning the schoolroom, the grates, the outhouses, and carrying out any additional work required on the premises. 'The oldest girls take it by turns one quarter of the year, and one day in every week, to prepare a dinner for eight or ten of their school-fellows. . . . The girls are responsible for all the arrangements, the dishing-up, the service, washing up &c.' To what extent this experiment and others like it were inspired by a genuine desire to train the girls and to what extent by the wish to recruit unpaid labour for cleaning the school and school-house it is not easy to decide.

Special domestic servant training schools were also organised, usually financed either by individual philanthropists or by charitable organisations. In London, according to Charles Dickens's *Dictionary* for 1879, there were no less than twenty charities concerned with this particular question, ranging from the Clapham Servants' Training Institute, which catered for girls of 'good character' only to the Refuge for the Destitute, which sought to train 'female criminals for service'.

Occasionally public funds might be used for the same purpose. The Dallington Domestic Economy School, founded in the last years of the nineteenth century by Northamptonshire County Council, gave girls 'a thorough training in all branches of a housewife's or domestic servant's' duties. The school was residential and accommodated up to thirty pupils. They were selected at the age of fourteen, stayed for eight months, without holidays, and were boarded free. A surviving timetable for 1897 classified the main subjects of the curriculum as housework, laundry and cookery, plus dressmaking and mending. The day was divided into three sessions, running from 6.30 a.m. to 9.30 a.m.; 9.30 a.m. to 12.30 p.m.; and 2.30 p.m. to 4.30 p.m. on every day except Sundays.[6]

In England and Wales as a whole local education authorities were running ten domestic servant schools and eighteen domestic economy schools by 1914. Four of the former and twelve of the latter were in the London area.

At the London domestic service schools, girls were taken between the ages of thirteen and fifteen and were trained for two years. 'Parents had to pay fees of thirty shillings a year (a considerable outlay for a working-class family in those days) unless the girl was lucky enough to get a scholarship, awarded after an examination and interview.'[7] Unlike the training provided at Dallington, a third of the curriculum was devoted to general education, such as reading, history, arithmetic, singing, etc., with the remaining two-thirds spent in acquiring the practical household skills. 'At the end of the first year the pupil decided in which branch to specialise and went on to qualify as kitchenmaid, scullery-maid, housemaid, under-parlourmaid or laundry-maid and to get a job in a private house.' In all, the domestic service schools catered for about 350 pupils.[8]

Domestic service training was likewise given in special boarding schools established under the Poor Law Certified Schools Act of 1862. The candidates here were normally orphans or the off-spring of destitute families. But sometimes, as with Sandbach Industrial School, the Poor Law authorities would join with local philanthropists to provide a training centre for non-pauper children. At Sandbach a number of the pupils were appointed 'each week to do the washing connected with the church and the master and mistress's house, and also on three days a week the same girls cook[ed] by means of a gas stove meat dinners for all the sick of a parish'. The bills for these dinners were sent each quarter to the Poor Law Guardians for payment.

On a smaller scale, Anne Sturges Bourne of Eling in Hampshire financed a servants' training school in her own village, and her venture was typical of many undertaken by well-meaning ladies, who allowed the trainees to work for part of the time in their own households. Miss Sturges Bourne declared that her object was 'to substitute good service training for the chance first places [girls] now get'. In 1853 she described, perhaps rather enviously, a visit to another similar institution : 'Ds. of Sutherland has a school of 40 girls boarded & lodged—who besides their own house work learn in her laundry, & she gets them places—very well for a fine lady. But I wd. not have 40 girls if I could—& I think the only reason mine have done well wh. always surprises me, is that they are few & like a family & can be studied individually.'

Nevertheless, none of these activities should blind one to the fact that for the majority of girls, the only instruction received before they sought their first place was that gained at home, in addition to what might be picked up through part-time employment.

For both young servants and old 'getting a place' was a matter of vital importance, and several possible courses of action were open to this end. Firstly, there was reliance upon information passed on by members of the family or friends who were already in service; or perhaps applicants just 'heard' of a vacancy through local gossip. In the case of youngsters living on a large estate, like that of the Duke of Westminster at Eaton in Cheshire or the Duke of Devonshire at Chatsworth in Derbyshire, there was always the hope of being taken on at the 'big house' as a fourth housemaid or a scullery-maid or, for the boys, as a page. These posts were valued because of the security they offered, the usually good living conditions and the opportunity they provided to enjoy some of the reflected glory of the employer's social position. But not all landowners followed a practice of local recruitment. They preferred instead, like many smaller men, to obtain their staff from away. An investigation of mid-Victorian census returns reveals, for example, that Lord Camoys, an Oxfordshire estate owner, had only one Oxfordshire-born servant among his resident indoor staff of twenty-three; similarly the Harcourts of Nuneham Courtenay had only two Oxfordshire-born servants out of their staff of twenty-one—and neither of these had been born in the immediate vicinity of Nuneham.

A second possibility for those seeking employment was to secure the help and advice of local gentry or clergy in the rural areas, and of tradespeople in the towns. In villages it was quite usual for the squire's or clergyman's wife and daughters to interest themselves in the careers of the children of 'their' parishioners and to seek situations for them in the households of their friends if they had no vacancy in their own establishment. One such family was the Henleys, who were major landowners at Waterperry in Oxfordshire. On 11 April 1851 Grace Henley wrote to an acquaintance, Ellen Fane, about the possibility of one of her family's page-boys (aged seventeen) being employed by Lady Dashwood of West Wycombe, Buckinghamshire. 'He expects 9-pounds the first year, and hopes Lady Dashwood will raise him to ten pounds the next year if he suits. . . . I am sure we owe you many many thanks for helping on so many of our parishioners. It is such a good thing for them to get them out into nice places and I hope they will all do well.' In a subsequent letter to Lady Dashwood on the same subject, Ellen herself declared : 'Waterperry seems to supply different houses with servants, for Mrs John has got a housemaid from there—I think at last it will be in the geographical dictionaries as a place famous for its servants.' Lady Dashwood must have agreed, for not only did she hire the young page but also a kitchenmaid recommended from the same source.

Anne Sturges Bourne, too, approached friends on behalf of her protegées—and was in turn approached by them. Indeed, in 1853 she confided to her closest friend, Marianne Dyer : 'Getting places & people to fit is one of the chief employments of life.'

The use of tradespeople as unofficial registry offices was equally widespread, especially in towns, and it was a practice recommended by Mrs Beeton : '[Tradespeople] generally know those in their neighbourhood, who are wanting situations, and will communicate with them, when a personal interview with some of them will enable the mistress to form some idea of the characters of the applicants, and to suit herself accordingly.' This role of shopkeepers was also valued by the servants, and Hannah Cullwick describes how on more than one occasion she made use of their services. Thus in July 1868, when her existing employers were due to leave London for the Isle of Wight, she was 'lucky enough' to hear of a vacancy just a fortnight before she was due to lose her place. 'The Greengrocers wife told me of it, & so in my dinner hour one day i went after it.'[9]

Where personal contacts failed, advertising in a newspaper or even attendance at one of the annual hiring or 'Mop' fairs might be resorted to. Although in fairly widespread use in the eighteenth century, by the middle of the nineteenth the Mop was coming into disrepute, partly because of the slave-market atmosphere it engendered, as men and women stood around waiting to be hired, and partly because of the drunkenness that too often accompanied its festivities. Dairy-maids and maids-of-all-work looking for

1 Staff employed at Easton Lodge, Essex, by the Countess of Warwick, c.1900.
Standing (left to right): *men:* footman, valet, butler, footman; *women:* housemaids and laundry-maids. Seated: head housemaid, cook, housekeeper, parlourmaid, head laundry-maid. Front row: kitchenmaid, scullery-maid, kitchenmaid.

*2 Lady Isabella Battie-Wrightson and her staff, Culsworth Hall, Yorkshire,
1911.* In front of table (left to right): Lady Isabella, lady's maid, steward,
housekeeper, assistant housekeeper. Behind table: gamekeeper, housemaid,
chauffeur, footman, gamekeeper, head gardener, housemaid, under-butler,
kitchenmaid, under-butler, housemaid, footman, housemaid, gardener, kitchenmaid, odd-job man, butler, page-boy, housemaid, two gardeners. The photograph
was taken at a tea-party given for the officers and men of the King's Own
Yorkshire Light Infantry.

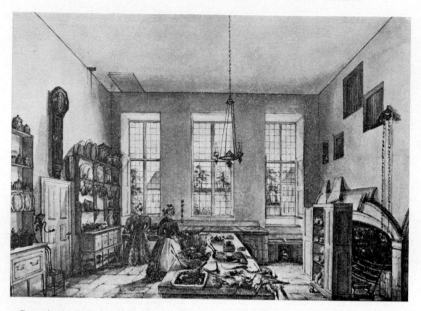

3 *Drawing of kitchen at Aynho House, Northamptonshire, 1847.* On the centre table game is waiting to be dressed and in front of the fire is a drying cupboard for crockery. Overhead hangs a 'chandelier' of three oil lamps.

4 *Drawing of laundry at Aynho House, Northamptonshire, 1847.* On the left is a large box-mangle. Linen baskets hang on the wall and an airing frame is suspended from the ceiling. This would be lowered when in use.

places on farms were the servants most likely to use the Mop, but in the early Victorian period a few cooks and housemaids also attended. They would usually wear special ribbons and carried a distinctive mark to indicate their particular skill; cooks, for instance, wore a red ribbon and carried a basting spoon, while housemaids wore a blue ribbon and held a broom.

As regards newspaper advertisements, although this particular solution to the problem of 'engaging domestics' was omitted from the first (1861) edition of Mrs Beeton's *Book of Household Management*, it had certainly been used from the eighteenth century with some success, and by the end of the 1860s, in a fresh edition of her book, Mrs Beeton declared it 'one of the commonest modes of procuring servants'. In some cases, where the youngest servants were involved, advertisements were inserted on their behalf by upper- or middle-class friends, like the wife of the vicar of Sydenham, Oxfordshire, who advertised on behalf of a protegée in *Jackson's Oxford Journal* of 13 July 1872 : 'A lady wishes to find a place under a Cook for a young girl of 16. She has lived with her for two years, and is very honest, quick and good tempered.'

The majority of advertisers confined themselves to a bare statement of the details of the situation being sought or offered, but occasionally social, racial or religious restrictions would be introduced. Such phrases as 'No Irish need apply', 'No crinolines allowed' or 'Must be of the Church of England' throw an interesting sidelight on conditions in early and mid-Victorian England.[10] And as the domestic work-force grew and households became more complex, so the range of positions advertised became wider. On 3 January 1832 *The Times* had 'nineteen servants asked for or requesting positions in seven different categories'. In the issue of 10 January 1870—and by no means untypically—there were 'a hundred and seventy-seven offers and requests [in] thirty-three separate species'. In the provincial press a similarly wide choice of situations was indicated, although here there were more vacancies suitable for the young servant seeking his or her first place. Most advertisers seem to have stressed the need for youngsters to be 'strong' or 'hard-working', and where boy servants were required there was usually the additional proviso that the successful candidate must be willing to make himself 'generally useful'.[11]

In the selection of butlers and footmen, appearance entered

D

into the matter. A butler seeking a situation in or near Oxford in February 1872 carefully pointed out that he was 'five feet ten inches' tall, while in an advertisement in *The Times* in 1850 one footman immodestly described himself as 'tall, handsome, with broad shoulders and extensive calves'. He went on to state that he preferred Belgravia, or the north side of the park. Another footman offering his services specified 'six months a year in town and if an inconvenient neighbourhood, five guineas extra salary'.

But none save the most self-confident would dare to make their requirements as explicit as this—and certainly not if they were married. Employers preferred their servants to be single, and even a diligent married man might have difficulty in securing a place. Thus the Rev. W. C. Risley of Deddington, who was seeking a 'footman out of livery', noted on 7 June 1865 : 'Mr Wyatt's servant (Swaby) from Broughton came over to offer his services. He was a married man—and on that account was objectionable —respectable and character good—Mr W. parted with him for that Reason only.'

It was not until these various alternatives had failed that most Victorians turned to a servants' registry office. Although a number of respectable registry offices did exist, many—especially in the larger towns—had for long earned a doubtful reputation as the resort of prostitutes or the lowest grade of servant only. Indeed, there was a well-known saying : 'When down and out start an agency for servants,' while in the eighteenth century registry offices had been seen as a means of practising 'the good old Trade of Pimping'.

Towards the end of the Victorian era a number of charitable organisations sprang up to try to restore the good name of the registry office. One such was the Associated Guild of Registries, which was formed to press for the compulsory registration of such institutions under government supervision. As its honorary secretary, Leonora Yorke Smith, pointed out in a pamphlet issued in 1901, the blameworthy offices operated on two levels. On the one hand they took entrance fees from the girls without any intention of finding employment for them, and on the other, they carried on an

outwardly . . . respectable trade . . . as a cover for the vilest of transactions. . . . Scores of desirable sounding situations which have no real existence are advertised by these Registry Offices daily. Country girls come up to the towns in response to these baits, only to find that the particular opening in question 'is just filled up'. Another is sure shortly to occur, the victim is informed; meanwhile she can have comfortable quarters in the Servants' Home attached to the Registry. And then the tragedy works itself out. Completely in the hands of the proprietors of the establishment her fate, if she is ascertained to be friendless, is likely to be that if rescued at all it is too late.[12]

It was because of this situation that a special act of 1907 empowered the London County Council to keep a register of the agencies within its area, and to issue licences, to be renewed annually. But elsewhere public control remained incomplete, the option of exercising regulative powers being left to the local authority concerned, under the permissive Public Health Amendment Act of 1907. Many authorities took no action at all, and according to the Ministry of Reconstruction's *Report . . . on the Domestic Service Problem*, issued in 1919, it was possible 'for an agency which [had] been deprived of its licence in the London area to continue its business in an area where there happens to be no control'. Such a situation was clearly unsatisfactory.

Yet the properly run registry office performed a useful function, and despite the existence of the unsavoury organisations, there were always many others which were completely reliable—like the famous agencies in Marylebone run by Massey's and by Mrs Hunt in the 1890s and early 1900s. Each catered for both male and female servants. At Mrs Hunt's agency newly arrived servant girls slept in the attic while they waited to be placed. Fashionable ladies were given their own private cubicles on the premises and might interview as many as twenty or thirty girls before deciding on the successful candidate. 'On the stairs was a "roll of honour" with the names of grand clients inscribed in gold letters, together with the details of the long periods they had kept butlers, cooks and other upper servants.'[13] The various short-lived domestic workers' trade unions as well as charitable organisations, like the Girls' Friendly Society and the Metropolitan Association for Befriending Young Servants, also set up their own registries, even though the main interest of these latter was with the moral welfare of the young. The Girls' Friendly Society, a Church of

England organisation established in 1874, had within a decade formed branches in most parts of the country with registries attached. In London alone there were twenty-two lady registrars, and in 1885 the Society claimed to have received through them 1,889 applications from mistresses and 408 from servants (in addition to others which were 'not accurately returned'), and had found places for 683 girls.

At the beginning of 1867 Hannah Cullwick made use of one of the respectable agencies at the Soho Bazaar, London. Upon arrival she sat in the office with several other servants waiting her turn for her name to be put down.

> They have prayers there together at a certain time in the morning, and the man over it all wears a white tie, and speaks to us each about religion & gives us tracts before going up stairs to sit in the room where the ladies come to look at us, & so the Soho Bazaar is reckon'd a good place to wait for a place at, & i went there for the first time. I paid ½ a crown—the price for the lower servants—it's 5/– for cooks or upper ones & i was shown the way up stairs, and where to wait. ₂ . . the ladies begun to come in & i felt very nervous till one lady spoke to me & she ask'd me to follow her, & that was to another room where the ladies sat and hir'd you or ask'd you questions.[14]

If there were no appointment forthcoming on the first visit, then return calls must be made for as long as was necessary. One girl who used the services of an Essex registry office early in the present century remembered the sheer monotony of the whole business : 'We had to . . ₂ stay there all day. . . ₂ It was weary and tiring spending days there.'

But no matter how a situation was obtained, for those eventually short-listed for closer consideration, the interview itself could be an ordeal. Hannah Cullwick remembered nervously walking up and down in front of a large house in Norfolk Square where she was to be interviewed for the position of cook, 'feeling half afraid to venture'. Some employers treated the applicants kindly and considerately, while occasionally it was the aggressive servant who turned the tables on the mistress and 'interviewed' her. Jane Carlyle, wife of the famous Victorian writer Thomas Carlyle, wrote of a determined female 'with a face to split a pitcher', who came for an interview at the Carlyle house in Chelsea. 'After

surveying me—rather contemptuously I must own—she proceeded to ask me a string of questions, which I answered to see
how it would end. "Did I keep no more servants than *one*?"
"Had I much company?" "Was I in the habit of often changing
my servants?" ' But this was a challenge Jane was well able to
meet. 'I answered as often as they seemed to require changing,
and on the whole I *shouldn't suit her*, I was afraid.'

In the bigger households the interview had a special formality
and ritual. In major establishments the house steward might
engage and dismiss both the male and female servants, but if
there were no house steward, then the housekeeper would engage
the women, and the butler the men, while the master and mistress
would normally recruit their personal attendants, such as the
valet, lady's maid and nurse.

Certain families, such as the Benyons of Englefield House in
Berkshire, kept a detailed servants' book. This meticulously recorded the date on which each servant entered the household and
the date he or she left, as well as information on wages and a brief
summary of the former experience of the applicants, including the
names of previous employers. There were also lists of questions
prepared to be put to the applicants for the more senior posts.
When engaging a butler, for example, Mr Benyon apparently
raised the following points :

Where did you live last, and for how long?

Why did you leave, and when?

What was the establishment, and what were you?

This is a regular Family—prayers every morning—punctual
—the Plate is under your charge, and you will help clean it—
You will lay the Breakfast things, & answer the Drawing Room
Bell before 12 o'clock.

I keep the key of my own Cellar, & give you out Wine as it
is wanted, of wch. you keep an account.

I order everything, and pay for everything—you order nothing except by my direction.

Can you brew? You give out the Ale yourself in a fixed
allowance. Can you read and write? Are you married? A
Protestant—Healthy—no Apothecaries' Bills—no perquisites
—how old are you? You will valet me.[15]

Among those who underwent this scrutiny was James Blake, who was appointed on 21 June 1869 and remained with the family until May 1886. Biographical notes indicate that at the time of his appointment he was 'aged 37—unmarried—lived 7 yrs. with Col. Biddulph—learnt particulars of the Place from Pitt, the going Butler. Wages £65 a yr. 1st year then £70.'

The under-butler was subjected to a similar examination but was also informed that he must 'clean the Plate . . . the Lamps, Knives, and Tables in Dining Room'. He was required to wear his hair powdered, with powder provided by himself, but was supplied with '1 suit of Livery—2 Undress Suits—1 Hat—a Great Coat when required—and a jacket & trousers for working in when wanted and 4/– a day Bd. wages'.

Nor did women members of staff escape regulation. Applicants for the post of cook-housekeeper were asked about their professional skills—whether they could prepare soups, entrées, pastry, confectionery, etc., as well as truss poultry, game and venison. They had also to prepare 'Broth & Gruel for the Poor and Sick'. The housekeeper was responsible for the household linen '& see that it is mended every Monday. Look after the Rooms when there is Company. Keep order & quiet in the Family, and not let the Maids go out without your leave, & to take care that they are dressed quietly. Keep a regular Account of everything.'

Likewise, records of late nineteenth-century applicants for what appears to have been the position of lady's maid with the Harcourts of Nuneham Courtenay show that questions were asked not only about past experience but also about the occupation of the candidate's father (if still living), while details of personal appearance were noted. The wearing of hair in a fringe seems to have been especially frowned upon.[16]

Once the interview had been successfully accomplished, the final hurdle to be overcome was the securing of a satisfactory 'character' by the prospective mistress from the previous employer. This was one of the most vexed aspects of domestic service. As Mrs Beeton observed,

In giving a character, it is scarcely necessary to say that the mistress should be guided by a sense of strict justice. It is not fair for one lady to recommend to another, a servant she would not keep herself. . . . It is hardly necessary to remark, on the other hand, that no angry feelings on the part of a mistress towards her late servant, should ever be allowed, in the slightest degree, to influence her, so far as to induce her to disparage her maid's character.

Unfortunately not all employers followed these strictures, and as early as 1792 an act had been passed to prevent 'the counterfeiting of the characters' of servants. Under its provisions anyone giving a false character for a servant in writing, knowing it to be false and the servant unfit for a situation through drunkenness, dishonesty or other similar defect, could be fined £20 with 10s. costs. A similar penalty was imposed on a servant who presented a counterfeited character, and failure to pay could mean that the offender might be imprisoned for up to three months with hard labour. There are a few examples of Victorian servants being caught out by these provisions, but in most instances the act proved a dead letter and disputes over the 'character question' persisted.

Sometimes employers gave a good character reference to a servant they were dismissing purely because they knew that without this he or she would be unable to obtain a fresh situation. In August 1879 a heated correspondence was conducted in the columns of *The Times* over what one writer called 'the way in which too many ladies give unwarrantable characters to servants whom they wish to get clear of'. He described how his wife had engaged a parlourmaid with an excellent character reference from her previous employer :

The third day she was with us on being found fault with in the very mildest manner, she flew into a most violent passion and used such language to my wife that she had to come to me; on my telling the girl she must go, she . . . refused to leave the house. I had to call a policeman and eject her.

When the servant's former employer, a vicar's wife, was approached on the matter she admitted that the girl had given trouble : 'I consider —— has mistaken her vocation and is only fit to be a barmaid.' Other correspondents had similar tales of woe, and one writing under the name of 'Pollaky' suggested that every servant should be issued with a special service-book which she would obtain from the local police and where 'several blank leaves . . . all numbered in print' would provide space for each employer to enter not only the period the servant had remained in the family 'but also the cause for leaving and other general remarks as to conduct, &c.' Although the writer claimed it was 'a well-known custom abroad', it was a solution which smacked too much of state regulation and Prussian efficiency for the taste of most mid-Victorian readers of *The Times*.[17]

Nevertheless in 1902, 1903 and 1904 attempts were made by private Members of Parliament to introduce a False Characters Bill 'for the better prevention of giving False Characters to servants, and of offences connected therewith'. On no occasion did the measure progress beyond its first reading.[18]

But the character question was even more serious for the servant, since there was no *legal* requirement for an employer to give a character reference at all. Any mistress of a vindictive turn of mind could, by withholding this document, in effect deprive a servant of his or her livelihood. As Frederick Seward, a butler at Flockton manor, Wakefield, pointed out in a letter to *The Times* of 21 August 1879, 'At the whim of the master, the servant starves or he lives.' Furthermore, if an employer stated that a servant, who was in fact blameless, was lazy or dishonest, this was only actionable if the servant could *prove* that the employer had acted with express malice. Such a point was extremely difficult to establish, and a servant's only consolation was the knowledge that if his master maliciously *defaced* a testimonial which was the servant's own property, then legal action could be taken. But few servants would have the financial resources needed to pursue the matter in the courts anyway.

The early years of the twentieth century saw several abortive attempts by private Members of Parliament to bring in a bill 'to make it compulsory upon employers to supply a Reference Note to a person leaving their employment and deserving one', but like the False Characters Bill already mentioned it never progressed beyond the first reading.[19]

Only when all formalities, including the obtaining of a satisfactory character reference, had been completed could the servant consider himself or herself properly hired. For the youngest girls, especially those with some distance to travel and who were going into residential service for the first time, the separation from home and family was keenly felt. One former maid, who left her Birmingham home for service in Chislehurst on 24 October 1888, recalled that she started to cry as soon as her father had seen her on to the train at New Street Station. She was fourteen years old at the time. And Flora Thompson, who witnessed several such departures from her own North Oxfordshire hamlet of Juniper Hill at the end of the nineteenth century, has described the occasion in moving terms :

> The tin trunk [containing the girl's clothing and other posses-sions] would be sent on to the railway-station by the carrier and the mother would walk the three miles to the station with her daughter. They would leave [Juniper Hill], perhaps before it was quite light on a winter morning, the girl in her best, would-be fashionable clothes and the mother carrying the baby of the family, rolled in its shawl. Neighbours would come to their garden gates to see them off and call after them 'Pleasant journey! Hope you'll have a good place!' or 'Mind you be a good gal, now, an' does just as you be told!' or, more com-fortingly, 'You'll be back for y'r holidays before you knows where you are and then there won't be no holdin' you, you'll have got that London proud!'

Flora recalled one particular parting, where the couple walked off in the early morning, with the mother enveloped in her large plaid shawl and the girl dressed in a bright blue poplin frock which had been bought second-hand—'a frock made in the ex-treme fashion of three years before, but by that time ridiculously obsolete'. They started off cheerfully, even proudly, but, when some hours later, Flora saw the mother returning alone, she was limping, for the sole of one of her old boots had parted company with the upper. 'When asked if Aggie had gone off all right, she nodded, but could not answer; her heart was too full.' What the girl herself felt, bound for an unfamiliar new life among strangers, can only be imagined. 'Probably those who saw her round, stolid little face and found her slow in learning her new duties for the next few days would have been surprised and even a little touched if they could have read her thoughts.'[20]

Yet it was all part of the growing-up process, and despite their private misery, these young girls realised that they must learn to live with the unfamiliar difficulties. They knew that they must not fail, for their parents could not afford to keep them in idle-ness at home. And it was, in any case, an experience which they shared with large numbers of their fellows, for by the early 1880s no less than one in three of *all* girls between the ages of fifteen and twenty was employed as a domestic servant. The vast majority of them were country-born and bred.

4

The Daily Round: Female Servants

[Indoor domestic service] is practically monopolised by the female sex. . . . Of females above 5 years of age, one in nine was an indoor servant.

General Report of the 1881 Census of
Population of England and Wales.

THE carefully maintained social distinctions which existed amongst the servant-keeping classes were matched by even firmer divisions among those they employed 'below stairs'. Each member of staff was expected to know his or her place in the general scheme of things, and woe betide anyone who stepped out of line. One girl remembered how her first job as a 'tweeny' was 'hell. But I did not suffer at the hands of my employers, but at the hands of my fellow servants. There was far more class distinction and bullying and misery below stairs than can be told in a letter.'[1]

At the summit in the largest establishments, on the female side, came the housekeeper, although in more modest homes, where no housekeeper was kept, pride of place would be held by the cook. The lady's maid, who normally came just below the housekeeper on the scale, was in a special position because of her close personal relationship with her mistress, to whom she had sole responsibility. For this reason she was often regarded with suspicion and envy by her fellow-servants. Next came the nurse, the housemaids, kitchenmaids, scullery-maids and laundry staff. Each position was carefully graded, and promotion was valued accordingly. One former servant, for example, remembers that when she was upgraded 'from scullery-maid to kitchenmaid . . . the lady's maid could say good morning to [her] before the scullery-maid'.

At the very bottom of the servant ranks came the most numerous class of all—the maid-of-all-work or 'general servant'—who was found only in the smallest households. She was expected to carry out 'in her own person all the work which in larger establishments' was accomplished by a whole range of domestics. Naturally the duties varied with the circumstances of each individual household for, as Mrs Beeton declared, 'the mistress's commands are the measure of the maid-of-all-work's duties'. But an idea of what this could mean may be gained from the diaries of Hannah Cullwick. In 1860 Hannah was employed as a maid-of-all-work by Mr Jackson, an upholsterer of Kilburn, for whom she had worked for about five years. Her diary entry for 14 July in that year reads

> Open'd the shutters and lighted the kitchen fire—shook my sooty things in the dusthole & emptied the soot there, swept & dusted the rooms & the hall, laid the cloth & got breakfast up— clean'd 2 pairs of boots—made the beds & emptied the slops, clear'd & wash'd the breakfast things up—clean'd the plate— clean'd the knives & got dinner up—clear'd away, clean'd the kitchen up—unpack'd a hamper—took two chickens to Mrs Brewer's and brought the message back—made a tart & pick'd & gutted two ducks & roasted them—clean'd the steps & flags on my knees, blackleaded the scraper in the front of the house —clean'd the street flags too on my knees—had tea—clear'd away—wash'd up in the scullery—clean'd the pantry on my knees & scour'd the tables—scrubb'd the flags round the house and clean'd the window sills—got tea at 9 for the master & Mrs Warwick in my dirt but Ann [a fellow-servant] carried it up—clean'd the privy & passage & scullery floor on my knees— wash'd the door [?] & clean'd the sink down—put the supper ready for Ann to take up, for i was too dirty & tired to go up stairs.

The mind reels at the sheer range of the duties she was expected to perform from the time she rose at about 6.30 a.m. until she went to bed at around 11 p.m. Yet countless other diary entries confirm that the day was a typical one during her career as a maid-of-all-work. Thus on 1 January 1871, when she was employed by a widow named Mrs Henderson and her daughters at Gloucester Crescent in Paddington, a diary entry showed that she had to dig

> coals and [carry] em up ... and anything that wants strength

& height i am sent for or called up to do it. All the cabs thats
wanted i get, if the young ladies want fetching or taking any-
where, ive to walk with them and carry their cloaks or parcels.
I clean all the copper skuttles and . . . clean the tins and help
to clean the silver and do the washing up if Im wanted and
carry things up as far as the door for dinner—and clean four
grates and do the fires and irons, sweep and clean three rooms
and my attic—the hall and front steps and the flags, 2 area
railings and all that is in the two areas and all that is in the
street.

Nor was this all. In addition to doing the household scrubbing,
she prepared the meals for herself and her fellow-servants (a
housemaid and a 'boy').

On one occasion when the Hendersons went away for a fortnight's holiday, Hannah was given the task of spring-cleaning the
house on her own. This included re-laying carpets and washing
down paintwork, as well as dusting and polishing all the rooms
from the attic down to the scullery : 'i work'd with a good heart,
getting up at six a.m. . . . and was often at work till twelve o'clock
by gaslight. . . . i work'd so hard, & saw nothing but dust & *dirt*,
till i really felt sick over it, & was obliged to go out one afternoon
to forget it.' Nevertheless the task was completed in time for her
employers' return, with the sole exception that she had been unable to clean behind the pictures in the dining-room because they
were so large and heavy : 'i got it over pretty well, & all as straight
& nice as i could by the time they came home, & the first thing
Missis ask'd me was if i had taken the pictures down in the dining
room—i said, "No Maam, but i did as much to them as i could",
& she seem'd determined to be dissatisfied & so made that a reason
to be angry, instead of thanking me as i thought she would. My
hands *smarted* from so much holding of brooms & brushes, but
they was too *hard* to blister.'[2]

Hannah was a woman of considerable physical strength and
one who was extremely hardworking and conscientious, and who
took great pride in her work. Yet her experience was not unique.
The reminiscences of other maids-of-all-work confirm both the
drudgery and the wide-ranging character of the tasks to be performed by the general servant. This was recognised by the books
on household management. Mrs Beeton advised a systematic

programme to carry out any special cleaning that might be required alongside the normal daily chores. Thus on Monday the drawing-room might be thoroughly cleaned; on Tuesday, two of the bedrooms; on Wednesday, two more; on Thursday, any remaining bedrooms and the stairs; on Friday, the dining-room, hall, and kitchen utensils; and on Saturday, the cleaning of the kitchen and the plate, as well as a general 'arranging of everything in nice order'.

Furthermore, for those youngsters who were employed on a farm, like Mrs Florence Davies of Whichford, Warwickshire, work in the dairy would add to the other burdens of servitude. Each day she had to skim the milk, clean and scald the milk pans, the separator, the strainer, and the milk buckets, as well as scrub the dairy itself. And on one afternoon every week there was 'churning and making the butter a 2-hour work & about 30 to 40 lb. to pot up, weigh, mark, ready for market'. Another former farmhouse servant, who was born in Norfolk, remembered that when she started work at the age of eleven in about 1901 she was too small to reach the churn and so had to stand on a stool in order to help with the butter making. 'When that was done I had to wash up all the pans. . . . It was then getting well into the afternoon, and it was time for their tea and mine. I got their tea ready in the dining-room and mine in the kitchen. When I had finished tea and washed up, there were the faggots of sticks to get for the fire in the morning. Then I had to go all round the fields to collect the eggs, then see they were all clean and rolled in paper to take to the market.'[3]

Although Mrs Beeton optimistically concluded that 'a bustling and active girl' engaged in a general servant's place would always find time in the afternoon or evening to do a little needlework for herself, provided she lived with 'consistent and reasonable people', the evidence available makes this difficult to believe. Only where the household was a very small one, consisting of perhaps one elderly lady, like Miss Matty's home in *Cranford*, would there seem to be much opportunity for leisure.[4] More realistic, therefore, was Mrs Beeton's additional comment that 'A general servant's duties are so multifarious, that unless she be quick and active, she will not be able to accomplish this. To discharge these various duties properly is a difficult task, and sometimes a thankless office.' Those were surely sentiments with which

Hannah Cullwick, Florence Davies and many others would have agreed.

But the varied activities expected of the general servant in the small household were in marked contrast to the situation in the largest establishments, where every member of the staff had his or her own special duties, and where each senior servant headed a department—so that the cook or chef controlled the kitchens, the housekeeper the housemaids and stillroom maids, the head laundry-maid the laundry, and so on. And the fact that around three-fifths of the female servants in mid-Victorian England were maids-of-all-work should not blind one to the duties of the remaining, perhaps more fortunate, two-fifths.

As regards the most senior female staff member, the housekeeper, there were, according to the 1871 census, 140,836 of these reported in England and Wales; they formed around one-ninth of the total domestic work-force and were the next most numerous category to the general servant. But there was considerable latitude at that time as to what situations could be covered by the vague term 'housekeeper'. Not all housekeepers were in 'gentlemen's service', as a random examination of the census returns soon reveals. Thus at Fakenham in Norfolk each of the six housekeepers reported in 1871 was engaged in a working-class or tradesman's family—the employers comprising two railway porters, a tailor, a chemist, a hairdresser, and a superintendent registrar. In all cases except the last the housekeeper was the only domestic employed. Again, at Belper in Derbyshire, of ten housekeepers recorded in 1871 only one was employed in a well-to-do household—that of the Strutt family—where fifteen other servants were also kept. She alone of the ten would have been occupied with the sort of duties which most books of household management attributed to the housekeeper. The rest were fulfilling the role of substitute wife or mother, and their duties would largely parallel those of the general servant.

Yet for the women who were engaged in the bigger establishments—and an income of at least £1,500 to £2,000 a year was considered necessary to afford a housekeeper (in the currently accepted sense of the term)—the position was one of considerable responsibility. Except in the few cases where a house steward was also engaged, the housekeeper was second-in-command in the household, after her employers. Mrs Beeton pointed out that

[She] must consider herself as the immediate representative of her mistress, and bring, to the management of the household, all those qualities of honesty, industry, and vigilance, in the same degree as if she were at the head of *her own* family. Constantly on the watch to detect any wrong-doing on the part of any of the domestics, she will overlook all that goes on in the house, and will see that every department is thoroughly attended to, and that the servants are comfortable, at the same time that their various duties are properly performed.[5]

She had to deal with her subordinates firmly but fairly, and carry out her own duties with method and order. The large bunch of household keys she carried was a symbol of her authority, and more than one subordinate learned to tremble on hearing the jangle of those keys as she walked along the corridor. Hannah Cullwick, for example, remembered with deep unhappiness the unfriendly treatment she received from the housekeeper at Lord Stradbroke's residence near Ipswich, when she took up an appointment as a kitchenmaid in 1855:

i'd made her a curtsy & when she made no answer i thought i was sure she was unkind & my heart begun to fail me. . . . i made haste & put my cotton frock & cap & apron on to be in the kitchen by 6. Mrs Smith the housekeeper was most unkind to me in ordering, & i was ready to say i'd go back in the morning, & i told Bill the groom i would but he said "never mind *her*—she's drunk & doesn't know what she's about—you stop & you'll get on all right"— . . . Mrs Smith gave up coming in the kitchen after 2 or 3 months.[6]

But not all subordinates escaped the eagle eye of their superior as easily as that.

The housekeeper was normally responsible for engaging and dismissing all of the female staff except for the lady's maid and the nurse. She was expected to be a 'steady middle-aged woman . . . moral, exemplary [in conduct] and assiduous to the harmony, comfort and economy of the family'—an ideal to which Lord Stradbroke's housekeeper seemingly did not conform. Both she and the cook were always referred to as 'Mrs' by the other servants whether they were married or not. It was simply a mark of respect.

5 *Restored Victorian kitchen at Longleat House, home of the Marquis of Bath.* Much energy must have been expended by the maids in keeping clean the gleaming copper cooking pans which are ranged along the walls.

6 *Restored cook's pantry at Longleat House.*

7 Coachman at Blenheim Palace, Oxfordshire, c.1900.

8 Porter at Blenheim Palace,
Oxfordshire, 1912.

9 First footman to the Marquis of
Willingdon, 1937.

In addition to directing other female staff members, the house-keeper's duties included supervision of the household linen and the china closet, and superintendence of the stillroom department, where cordials and preserves were made and stored. She also made the decisions on the arrangement of the bedrooms, includ-ing, in consultation with her mistress, allocation of the rooms to be occupied by visitors and their servants. A knowledge of first-aid was also desirable, so that she could 'distil healing waters' and concoct simple medicaments like liquorice lozenges or scurvy-grass wine for invalids.

At Longleat the Marchioness of Bath remembered the house-keeper performing 'feats of alchemy, distilling rose water from dark damask roses, producing pot-pourri from an old family recipe, preserving fruits, making jam, candying peel, bottling morello cherries in brandy, drying lavender to keep the linen cupboard sweet, and forever harrying the stillroom maids'. The short spiral staircase which wound its way from the housekeeper's room to the stillroom seemed 'to be haunted by the jingling sound of the clustered keys which the housekeeper wore at her waist; and the smell of the old stillroom itself—that delicious combina-tion of hot bread, biscuits, coffee and herbs'.

Control of the household stores and authority to order fresh stocks were further important responsibilities, but ones which might give an opportunity to the dishonest housekeeper to cheat her employer. For she alone kept the books and recorded the items purchased, her mistress normally examining the accounts only once a week and sometimes less frequently than that. But the more cautious and cost-conscious employers were aware of the dangers and adopted a policy of stricter regulation. At Englefield House in Berkshire it was a condition of service that Mr Benyon himself issued his housekeeper with her stores in fixed quantities and at set intervals. He alone ordered fresh supplies. Similarly at Bulstrode Park, Buckinghamshire, surviving correspondence be-tween Sir John Ramsden and his housekeeper, Mrs Dee, during the early 1890s indicates that even when her master was away from home, she had little freedom of action. In a letter dated 16 February 1893 she not only had to ask Sir John to order some roller blinds but also such minor items as 'soda and hearthstones. We are nearly out of both.' On another occasion she wrote to order more oil, soap and candles: 'We have just now two oil

E

stoves on in the dairy burning, and the cream freezes so the butter cannot be made without precaution.'

The housekeeper's daily round began with her appearance in her own special room (often called the 'Pug's Parlour' by irreverent juniors) at 7.30 a.m., when she overlooked the arrangement of the stillroom to see that the china had been given out for breakfast, together with the table-linen. She would direct the activities of the stillroom maid, who was in effect her personal servant. At eight o'clock she poured out the tea and presided over breakfast for the senior servants (the butler, lady's maid, valet, and sometimes the cook) in the housekeeper's room, after which she would once again check the stillroom arrangements for the family breakfast. 'She then gives out the stores for the day, and assists the stillroom maid to wash up the china in use, and puts the preserves away that have been on the breakfast-table; she makes the rounds of the bedrooms, and sees that soap, candles, writing-paper, and inkstands have been attended to, and that the drawers and wardrobes have been properly dusted and papered. . . . At one o'clock she leads the way into the servants'-hall and takes her place at the head of the dinner-table, and carves one of the joints; she then leads the way to the housekeeper's room, and takes the head of the table, and helps the sweets or cheese.' The other senior servants would also eat in the housekeeper's room. In the afternoon she would arrange the dessert for dinner, and would make both the tea for the drawing-room five o'clock tea, and the tea and coffee sent in after dinner.

Many housekeepers would reserve to themselves the more intricate items of cookery only, such as the making of confectionery, preserves, wines and pickles, but in more modest households the offices of housekeeper and cook would be combined.

'She makes the preserves and bottles the fruit; she is referred to respecting all domestic arrangements; she keeps the housekeeping accounts, and the greater part of the needlework required in the house is done by her, with or without assistance, according to the amount of work to be got through.' So runs an account of the housekeeper's duties in *The Servant's Practical Guide* of 1880. Most of the other books on domestic management followed a similar line.

The housekeeper often assisted her mistress in dispensing charity among the neighbouring poor. She would also organise entertainments for the children of estate workers and ensure that they showed due respect towards their benefactors. Some house-keepers stayed in one household for many years, becoming almost members of the family—like Susan Clarke, who was appointed to Englefield House, Berkshire, in 1854 and remained with the Benyons over twenty years. Mrs Munns, a successor, stayed for over nine years. The position of such employees as Mrs Fairfax in Charlotte Brontë's novel *Jane Eyre* emphasises the close links which could exist between the housekeeper and the family she served.

Lady's maids, who stood on the next rung of the household ladder, were always a small minority of the domestic work-force and were found only in the homes of the wealthy. An income of at least £2,000 a year was suggested as necessary to afford such a luxury, although sometimes, in humbler households, a house-maid would carry out certain of the duties of the lady's maid. She was generally disliked by lower servants because of the airs and graces she often assumed, and because her proximity to her mistress made her suspected of tale-bearing. Then, too, she was dis-tinguished from the rest by always being known as 'Miss ——'; but, as the anonymous author of a pamphlet on the duties of the lady's maid warned, the privileges thus enjoyed were only tem-porary : 'I trust you will bear constantly in mind that your eleva-tion into comfort and luxury—your better clothes, your seat in the dressing-room and on your master's carriage, are only circum-stances in your service, and not given you to last. Your heart should still be where your station is—among the poor.'[7]

To be properly qualified for her situation the lady's maid would usually have received an education superior to that of her fellow-domestics, 'particularly in needlework and the ornamental branches of female acquirements'. Some would undergo special training in dressmaking and millinery before taking up their chosen career, and for this reason the maids were often drawn from a more prosperous background than most of the other female staff. The Harcourt family records indicate that three of the applicants for the position of lady's maid at Nuneham Courtenay in the late nineteenth century comprised the daughters of a cashier in a Liverpool timber merchant's office, of a city clerk, and of a gamekeeper on a Scottish estate. But the most sought-after lady's maids, at least among the fashion-conscious, were French or Swiss, the former being preferred an account of their greater vivacity and superior skill in dressmaking.

The successful lady's maid was neat in person, able to speak pleasantly, to read and write well, 'handy and tolerably quick with [her] needle, and . . . trusted to tell the truth and not to gossip'. Her conduct must be 'uniformly influenced by correct principles, and strict regard to religion and moral obligations'.[8] Absolute honesty was essential, since the maid would handle her mistress's jewels and clothing. The temptation secretly to wear 'dresses and caps' from her employer's wardrobe while she was away from home must be firmly resisted. Vanity was a particular danger, and maids were warned to be 'more careful about the condition of [their] underclothes than about the make of [their] gowns and caps. Girls who mimic their ladies' mode of dress, and flaunt about in their cast-off finery, are seldom found to have nice, dry, smooth hair, and good underclothes.' But most important of all, the lady's maid must be willing to perform for another woman 'those intimate services which nine women out of ten are modest enough to wish to do for themselves'. She must be prepared to dress, undress and re-dress her mistress as often as the engagements of the day required and yet remain good-tempered, quiet and efficient.

Other duties included laundering the most delicate articles of clothing in her mistress's wardrobe and preparing beauty preparations and lotions. Many of the books on household management contained recipes for lotions to remove freckles, cure pimples or make the hair grow thick and glossy. Skill in hairdressing was another essential qualification, and Mrs Beeton advised all would-be entrants to initiate themselves 'in the mysteries of hairdressing' before taking up their duties.

Although the work of the lady's maid was not physically arduous, she was very much at the beck and call of her employer. If her mistress attended a dinner party or ball, she was required to stay up until late at night in order to await her return. A good deal of her time would inevitably be spent alone, sewing, ironing, making millinery or engaged in other similar tasks, and most writers on domestic matters felt it was important that she should keep her mind fully occupied at these times rather than allowing it to dwell on trivialities and gossip. Some advised the keeping of a Bible or a book of poetry open in front of her 'to help to save her mind from wandering into unprofitable channels'; she could then while away the time by learning a psalm or a few verses of a poem like Goldsmith's *Deserted Village*. At the same time she must guard against envying her mistress's privileges :

> As long as the rich pay for what they desire to have they have every right to please themselves. . . . The chief purposes of the many comforts and conveniences that rich people have about them is to set their time and thoughts free for their serious occupations. . . . A rich lady has a great many servants not because there is any pleasure in ordering a number of people about but because she wants to save her own time and thoughts by hiring other people to do, without any care of hers, what she likes to have done. . . . Her mind is free for her children, her friends, her books and all the serious things she has to think of.[9]

But although her position had many advantages, there was always the fear that as the lady's maid grew older she would lose her place and might have difficulty in obtaining another. More than for other members of staff, mistresses preferred their personal attendants to be young, and 'the older a lady's maid grew the smaller were the wages offered her. Among middle-aged ladies' maids the unemployment problem was serious. A lucky few became housekeepers, but this was not a form of promotion popular in the servants' hall. If the lady's maid did not marry, her future was bleak. And in the matrimonial market she had two handicaps : she had, almost certainly, ideas above her station and she did not know how to cook.'[10] Yet all the signs are that the ambitious servant was prepared to face these hazards in order to become a lady's maid.

The cook, the third of the senior servants, was—unlike the housekeeper and lady's maid—found in a whole range of households. Not surprisingly, skills varied widely, and there was a world of difference between the dishes produced by a 'plain' cook working in a two- or three-servant household and those of the 'professed' cook in a large establishment. In the very wealthiest households a male chef would be employed, but those who desired to obtain the benefits of more elaborate cooking without the cost of maintaining a male cook might employ a man for a short time to teach their own staff. The diaries of Caroline Clive, wife of the rector of Solihull, show that in December 1841 this solution was adopted for a month, although not without snags. Caroline thought they were all 'in a fair way to be sick' as they were 'obliged to eat a goody every day that he may teach and [the cook] may learn'.

In bigger establishments the cook would be assisted by both kitchenmaids and scullery-maids, and it was their duty to come down first in the morning to light the fire and to sweep and clean the kitchen in readiness for the cook to begin her work. In some cases the senior kitchenmaid would also be expected to prepare and cook the meals for the servants' hall, while the cook herself concentrated on preparations for those 'above stairs'.

In the hot, badly ventilated atmosphere of the kitchen both the cook and her assistants had to work extremely hard, and it was small wonder if, in surroundings which encouraged the intake of liquor, some cooks earned a reputation for drunkenness. Yet if they were skilled in their profession, mistresses were prepared to overlook this. For, as *The Servant's Practical Guide* observed, 'Some ladies stand very much in awe of their cooks, knowing that those who consider themselves to be thoroughly experienced will not brook fault-finding, or interference with their manner of cooking, and give notice to leave on the smallest pretext. Thus when ladies obtain a really good cook, they deal with her delicately, and are inclined to let her have her own way with regard to serving the dinner.' Most cooks also expected to have per-quisites—dripping, rabbit skins, old tea-leaves and the like—which they could sell at a profit. But this proved a fruitful source of dispute with cost-conscious employers, who sometimes thought they took too much. One anonymous critic considered that the term 'perquisite' was so 'comprehensive, so elastic, and accom-modating, that it is made to embrace and signify almost every-thing in the various departments of the house—anything, in fact, convertible or transferable, from "*torn up*" damask cloths and *broken* silver, to rags, old brass, and metal of every description'. She told cautionary tales of cooks who had secretly ordered large quantities of butter which they had then converted into 'dripping' and had sold to dealers.[11]

It would seem that some of the suspicions of employers were justified. Margaret Thomas, who began her career as a kitchen-maid in a large household in London, remembered that the same quantity of provisions for the servants' hall came from the grocer's each week, and 'these were never all used up in the time, so occasionally I was sent to post a parcel to the cook's home just as it came from the shop. As well she had commission from the tradesmen every month when the books were paid, and woe betide them if they didn't turn up with it, there were complaints about their goods until they did.'[12]

During the morning the cook would prepare the soup for the following day, 'as soup is seldom made the day it is required to be eaten', and would then turn her attention to the pastry, jellies, creams and entrées which were required for the evening dinner. She would also prepare the dishes required for luncheon above stairs. These would usually be served after she had eaten her own dinner at midday. According to *The Servant's Practical Guide*, the afternoon was 'very much at the cook's disposal, except on the occasion of a dinner party, or when guests are staying in the house, when there is naturally more work to be done'. On these occasions the kitchen staff lived in a state of tension, with the cook working at top pressure.

Normally it was in the early evening that the serious business of the day began. Between five o'clock and nine o'clock was 'always a very busy time with the cook; dishing up a large dinner is an arduous duty, the greatest order and regularity being maintained in the kitchen the while, perfect silence is enjoined save when an order is given concerning the work in hand. . . . When the dinner has been duly served the cook's duties for the day are over, and the remainder of the kitchen work is performed by the kitchen-maids.'[13] That was no light task either, for a full-length dinner for eighteen persons might produce as many as five hundred separate items to be washed up afterwards.

The most numerous class of cook was the 'plain' cook, working in a small household where no kitchenmaid or scullery-maid was kept and where the general work of the house was carried out by a housemaid. She would, of course, lead an existence entirely different from that of her 'professed' counterpart described above. Unlike the cook in a large establishment, she would have duties to perform unconnected with the kitchen itself. She would be expected to sweep and dust the dining-room, clean the grate, light the fire, and sweep and clean the front hall and front door-step, in addition to carrying out the work of the kitchen. Like the maid-of-all-work, she would rise at 6 a.m. in the summer and 6.30 a.m. in winter in order to light the kitchen fire and get through her work upstairs before putting the kitchen in order and cooking the breakfast. Plain cooks were only expected to produce simple dishes—with dinners generally consisting of fish, a joint and vegetables, and a pudding or tart, and luncheons of either a joint, vegetables and plain pudding, or cold meat, salad and potatoes. According to *The Servant's Practical Guide*, kitchen-maids who had trained in a large establishment were reluctant to take on the situation of cook in a small family, since this would involve a loss of caste, and so most plain cooks in small families were self-taught, and for this reason often had 'as much to un-learn as to learn'.

After the evening dinner had been served at 6.30 or 7 p.m., the plain cook would carry out the scullery-maid's work of clean-ing dishes and scrubbing kitchen tables. These tasks had to be completed before she went to bed, for 'if the cook were to put off washing the dishes, plates and cooking utensils until the following morning, it would not only be untidy and unmethodical, but it would be throwing a burden of too much work upon the follow-ing morning'. It was also her duty to see that the doors and windows of the basement were fastened securely, that the kitchen fire had burnt low, and that the gas in the kitchen and passages was turned off before she retired for the night.

Girls who went as kitchenmaids or 'between maids' ('tweenies'), working partly as housemaids and partly as kitchenmaids in smaller households, were, of course, the real drudges of this cate-gory of servant. They had to prepare the food for the cook, carry out all the pounding and chopping and the staff cooking, as well as the washing-up and scrubbing, unless they had the help of a scullery-maid. The kitchen ranges had to be blackleaded, and in large households, like Longleat, there were hundreds of copper cooking utensils to polish and keep clean. Longleat had, in addi-tion, a huge elm working-table and three large cooking-ranges, which burned mostly charcoal and also heated the water. One range was used for roasting, casseroles and stews, another for baking, and the third for boiling kettles and general cooking.[14] Two kitchenmaids, a vegetable maid, a scullery-maid and a daily woman were responsible for keeping all this in good order and for assisting the chef. But in smaller households it was very different. A former servant from Little Canfield, Essex, recalled that when she took up her first place as kitchenmaid she had

> to get up at 5.30 a.m. blacklead a six foot cooking range, light the fire, scrub the kitchen tables and floor, then call the Cook and upper servants at 7 o'clock (with tea). It was a large house with a basement kitchen and scullery. I was given a thick taper to light my way down the back stairs, and told not to put on my shoes, so as not to disturb anyone. I shall never forget the horror of that first morning, the crunch under my stockinged feet when I opened the kitchen door to find the floor and all round the fireplace thick with huge black beetles. When I told Cook about it she laughed and boxed my ears when I said I was frightened. . . . One day I found some strange looking tins with curved sides, which Cook said were beetle traps, I set these for several nights with a bait of brown sugar, and destroyed hundreds of them by plunging the tins into a pail of hot water. . . . My job other than cleaning was to prepare and cook the vegetables and learn to make sauces, sometimes three or four different ones with a seven course dinner, but as cook was so often drunk, I had to do a lot more.[15]

During her employment in this place she was frequently beaten and ill-treated by the cook.

Yet if the cook and her assistants were responsible for the culinary comforts (or otherwise) of the home, the housemaids were the people who ensured that it remained clean and orderly. Given the cluttered state of the rooms, with their numerous hangings, heavy furniture, countless ornaments of glass, china and silver, and carved, gilt-framed mirrors and pictures, the task was not an easy one. Sometimes in smaller establishments, the housemaid would also perform certain of the duties of a parlourmaid, such as laying the table for meals, waiting at table, answering the door and announcing visitors.

In well-to-do homes, where several housemaids were employed, the head maid would be responsible for supervising the work of her subordinates, and perhaps dusting the ornaments and cleaning the furniture in the principal apartments. The juniors would each have their own special duties. Margaret Thomas remembered that in one large household where she worked in Yorkshire, the fourth housemaid worked entirely for her fellow-servants, the third was employed in the schoolroom, and the second performed general duties. She 'had to be downstairs at 4 a.m. every morning to get the sitting-room done before breakfast. The second housemaid had a medal room to keep clean where the medals were set out in steel cases, and had to be polished with emery paper every day. I think, because she had to get up so early, she was off duty at noon until evening. The head housemaid did light jobs. They all did sewing.'

In small households, where the majority of younger maids worked, there were no opportunities for this kind of division of labour; and it is significant that the 1871 census shows that while housemaids were the third most numerous category of servants recorded, nearly one in three of them was under the age of twenty. For them the day would begin at about 6 or 6.30 a.m. Before breakfast the housemaid was expected to sweep and dust the drawing-room, the dining-room, the front hall and the other sitting-rooms, as well as to tidy the grates and light the fires. To clean the carpet she would spread some damp tea-leaves over it and would then sweep them up with a small hard brush, working on her knees. Lamp glasses and candlesticks had to be polished, and if a cage bird were kept—and this was a very common feature in Victorian homes—its cage, too, would have to be cleaned.

Then, if there were no lady's maid or valet kept, the housemaid would carry up cans of hot water to the bedrooms so that the family could wash. After her own breakfast she would make the servants' beds, sweep, dust and arrange the rooms and clean the front staircase and front hall. Before making the best beds she would remove any velvet chairs or other furniture likely to be damaged by dust and would don a special apron to protect the bedclothes from her working-apron and dress. One young housemaid remembers, indeed, that even in the 1920s her employer, a doctor's wife, 'always inspected my fingernails to make sure they were clean' before she was allowed to make the beds. Mattresses had to be turned, pillows smoothed and, of course, no dust was to be left under the bed. Grates would be cleaned, fires lit, and slops emptied. All basins, water-jugs and chamber-pots must be carefully washed and, when necessary, scalded. Windows had to be wiped clean; a maid who neglected to do this on one occasion recalled that her mistress noticed the omission and 'put a large cross with her finger' on the offending window to indicate disapproval. Once a week each bedroom had to be cleaned thoroughly, with mattresses brushed, curtains shaken, paintwork washed down, looking-glasses polished, brass curtain-rods burnished and floors well rubbed. The conscientious housemaid, especially in the towns, also kept a sharp look out for insects and, in particular, for bed bugs, which had to be guarded against with 'incessant care'. There was a constant danger that bugs would be brought into the house with 'tradesmen's parcels, by visitors coming out of an omnibus or hackney-coach, and even in the clean linen from the wash. . . . The housemaid should not complain of the trouble of taking down the whole bed, each time there is found that there is a bug in it.'[16] Jane Carlyle's household in Chelsea was one of many Victorian homes periodically turned upside down by the discovery of the dreaded 'bug'.

If fires were kept in the bedrooms during the day, it was the housemaid's duty to attend to them—as it was usually also her duty to keep filled the coal-scuttles throughout the house, unless a footman or hall-boy were kept for the purpose.

In the evening she prepared the bedrooms, turned down the beds, filled the jugs with water, closed the curtains and took up a can of hot water for each person to wash. After the family had gone down to dinner she again made a round of the bedrooms and put them in order. Her last duty was to take up a can of hot water to each bedroom and dressing-room at night, and also a warming-pan or hot water bottle if her employers required it. During the day the housemaid had to make sure that each bedroom was supplied with soap, candles, clean towels, writing-paper and anything else required. And at all times she was expected to answer promptly the ringing of her employer's bell.

Some mistresses tested the honesty and the industry of their housemaids by leaving coins on the floor or under the edge of the carpet; the maid was expected to hand them quietly over when they were discovered. One Norfolk girl who found several such pennies eventually told her father, and he informed the mistress that his daughter 'was to pocket any pennies . . . found among the dirt'. The girl ruefully added: 'I never found another one.' But most maids were too afraid of losing their place to follow this example.

The question of breakages was another thorny problem. In some houses it was the rule that a servant was forgiven if she admitted immediately that she had broken an article, but in other cases fines were imposed—in order to discourage carelessness—even when the practice was, strictly speaking, illegal.[17] But concealment of a breakage was felt to be the worst sin : 'It is not only mean and dishonourable to an earthly master, but it is a sin against God,' declared the anonymous pamphlet *Common Sense for Housemaids*, published in 1850.

Most servant-keeping families with children would endeavour to employ a nursemaid, and in the mid-Victorian years this was the preserve of younger girls, with over half of all nursemaids under the age of twenty. The majority of these were little more than child-minders employed in the households of tradesmen or clerks. They were responsible for dressing and undressing the children, playing with them and taking them out for walks. Needless to say, a few of the more ruthless were also accused of administering Godfrey's Cordial or other narcotics in order to keep their charges quiet. But, as the anonymous author of *The Servants' Guide*, published in 1830, declared, this was a practice which 'should be guarded against. Opium, in every form, weakens the infant and brings on the most distressing diseases.'

It was only in bigger establishments that the head nurse or nanny was held in awe and had almost complete authority in bringing up the children. In such cases the youngsters usually saw their parents for little more than an hour or so each day, when they were sent down for inspection in the drawing-room during the late afternoon.

The head nurse in these larger households would run her own department quite separate from the rest of the family. There were constant demarcation disputes between the nanny and the rest of the staff, particularly in regard to the cleaning and fetching and carrying which were the responsibility of the nursery housemaid or one of the footmen. Sooner or later the nurse antagonised the cook, too, by her demands for special food for the children, or her rejection of certain dishes. Both nannies and children would have separate meals in the nursery away from the rest of the household.

Some women used their authority to make the lives of both their charges and their subordinates thoroughly miserable. F.

Anstey, for example, remembered that during his childhood the family were

> under the despotic rule of a nurse whose name was Fanny Channer—a dark, sallow, hard-featured woman of about thirty. We were fond of her and, after her peculiar fashion, she was fond of us—but she led us a hard life. Before she came to us she had been a nurse at an orphan asylum, and she never outgrew an impression that stern discipline was what we required. At breakfast, our porridge, for which I conceived an incurable dislike, was served with nothing to make it more palatable, and I was compelled to swallow it, protest and bellow as I might. She also issued an edict that any crusts we had left overnight were to be eaten before we touched our bread and butter, and we obeyed until our father accidentally discovered this prohibition and put an end to it. We had plenty of wooden bricks but Fanny, for no particular reason, made a rule that only six long bricks and twelve short ones were to be permitted.[18]

Lord Curzon recalled that his nanny, Miss Paraman, behaved with even greater cruelty and vindictiveness towards her helpless charges.

> She persecuted and beat us in the most cruel way and established over us a system of terrorism so complete that not one of us ever mustered up the courage to walk upstairs and tell our father or mother. She spanked us with the sole of her slipper on the bare back, beat us with her brushes, tied us for long hours to chairs in uncomfortable positions with our hands holding a pole or blackboard behind our backs, shut us up in darkness.[19]

Needless to say, only a small minority of nannies displayed this kind of brutal authoritarianism, and the single-minded devotion which Sir Winston Churchill accorded his nurse, Mrs Everest, amply demonstrates the other side of the coin. For twenty years, until her death in 1895, she was 'destined to be the principal confidante of his joys, his troubles, and his hopes', and his early correspondence from school contains many anxious inquiries as to her health and well-being. Mrs Everest was not only the friend and companion of Churchill's youth, schooldays and early manhood, but she remained a warmly cherished memory throughout his life. For many years after her death he paid an annual sum to the local florist for the upkeep of her grave. Another nanny, who stayed with her employer's family for over fifty years, was remembered by her charges with equal devotion. One of them wrote, more than twenty years after her death : 'My brother and I worshipped her—she used to lend us money, defend us in family rows and never bossed the other staff.'[20]

Nevertheless, most head nurses considered it their prime duty to inculcate discipline into their charges and to ensure that the nursery was run with clockwork efficiency. Sarah Sedgwick, who went as nursery-maid in a large household near Doncaster before the First World War, recalled the strictness of the daily routine :

> To look after [two children] there was the head nurse, the under-nurse, the nursery-maid, and a maid to wait on the nursery, and in the winter a footman who came up every two hours to make up the fires. . . . I had to get up at five-thirty. The nurseries were a day nursery, a night nursery, a lavatory, the room I shared with the under-nurse, and a kitchenette. I had to light the nursery fires at six o'clock, and I had my fire guard to clean. . . . At 7.30 I had to call the head nurse with a cup of tea, and at eight o'clock the children had their breakfast. . . . Everything had to happen to the minute. At ten sharp we were out with the prams, and pushed them until half-past twelve. Luncheon was one o'clock. Then from two until half-past three another walk with the prams. This was followed by tea at four o'clock. Then there was dressing up the children before they went downstairs, and they were taken into the drawing-room to the minute, and brought up again to the minute. Then there were their baths to get ready, all the water to be carried. Then bed. I was supposed to be in bed myself at 9.30, but that was something which could not always happen to the minute, for with the washing, ironing, and running in of ribbons I couldn't get done in time. . . . In the evening the head nurse changed into something simple, but evening dress when there were visiting ladies' maids and valets, and went to her supper in the housekeeper's room. But the under-nurse and myself never mixed with the rest of the staff, we had our supper in the day nursery.[21]

Although in many respects the life of the nurse was isolated and lonely, there were compensations when she met colleagues while out walking with her charges. This was especially the case in London, where the nannies congregated in Hyde Park. Many would walk miles to reach it, ignoring nearer, greener but less fashionable recreation grounds. 'Here the gossip seethed and flowed, though transmitted often through the Nanny medium of nods and chuckles, pursed lips, raised eyebrows, shaken heads, fiercely criticising their employers, boasting about them, complaining, reminiscing . . . and all the while watching and discussing their charges, reprimanding misdemeanours. . . .' Most head nurses were extremely snobbish and would not allow 'their' children to associate with the offspring of families whom they considered inferior.

The final category of female servant to be discussed—the laundry-maid—was, like the nanny, a product of the richest families only, albeit without any of the nurse's awe-inspiring position. In 1871, when there were over 1·2 million domestic servants, only about 4,500 of them were classed as laundry-maids. The laundry itself consisted of a washing-house, an ironing-room and drying-room, and sometimes a drying-closet heated by furnaces. It was usually separated from the house, and here the laundry-maid would begin each week by carefully entering in her washing-book the articles committed to her care. White linen had to be separated from muslin, coloured cottons and linens from woollens, while the coarser kitchen or greasy clothes would form a fifth pile. These greasy cloths would be put to soak in a tub filled with unslaked lime and water. Washing and rinsing would usually take up three days in each week, and in large households the quantity of items to be laundered was enormous. A former laundry-maid employed by Lady Mary Fitzwilliam at Abbey Moulton, for example, remembers that she and two colleagues had to wash a thousand table napkins a week among other things. One ton of primrose soap and half a ton of soda were delivered each year for the washing. Thursdays and Fridays were normally devoted to mangling, starching and ironing. 'To be able to iron properly', Mrs Beeton pointed out, 'requires much practice and experience. Strict cleanliness with all the ironing utensils must be observed, as if this is not the case, not the most expert ironer will be able to make her things look clear and free from smears, &c.'[22]

In some households other members of staff were also called in to help the laundry-maids. At the beginning of the nineteenth century Mrs Wollaston, the wife of a merchant and banker living in Clapham, and with a staff of six female servants, wrote that the successful candidate for a vacancy as housemaid would

> have to get up with the laundry-maid to wash at 1 a.m. every Monday morning and will till 5 or 6 a.m. according whether it is summer or winter, and whether there are grates to clean. Then comes in to do her housework which employs her till 10.30 a.m. or 11 a.m. when she returns to the washing till 9 p.m. She had nothing more to do with the linen or the getting it up, but twice a year helps the laundry-maid wash beds and other furniture. She washes her own things every four weeks in summer and every three weeks in winter, and it must be got up and quite finished in the day.[23]

But as the nineteenth century drew to its close, fewer and fewer families maintained their own laundry, especially in the towns, where drying ground was scarce. They preferred the cheaper alternative of sending their washing out, while perhaps relying on a weekly washerwoman to launder the more delicate items of clothing at home. Such women would come for two shillings a day and a meal of bread and cheese. Nevertheless, some families continued the old traditions, and even in 1890 the Harcourts of Nuneham Courtenay had a laundry in full swing, with laundry wages costing about £107 5s. per annum.

5

The Daily Round: Male Servants

Every English man-servant is apt to consider himself a specialist and the remark of the butler in *Punch*—'In other houses the maids mostly carries up their coals theirselves'—fairly represents the attitude of men towards certain duties which might reasonably have been expected of them. This want of elasticity on the part of the Englishman has led to his gradual disappearance from all except the most wealthy households. Fashion no longer insists on the presence of a man in fine livery at the front door, and his services as a hall-mark of respectability are in consequence at a discount.

CHARLES BOOTH and JESSE ARGYLE,
'Domestic Household Service' in *Life and Labour in London*, ed. Charles Booth, 2nd Series (1903).

THROUGHOUT the nineteenth century domestic service was pre-eminently the preserve of women workers. Even in 1851, when there were over 74,000 men-servants reported in England and Wales, they were outnumbered more than ten to one by the three-quarters of a million female domestics. Thirty years later the gap had widened still more, so that the 1881 census estimated that the men were now in a minority of twenty-two to one. Indeed, notwithstanding various changes in the classification of indoor male servants which make comparisons of the various census reports rather difficult, it does appear that from the beginning of the 1850s their numbers were on the decline—despite short-term upward fluctuations within that general trend.[1]

By contrast the number of *outdoor* male servants—coachmen, grooms, gardeners, etc.—continued to grow to the end of the nineteenth century. Consequently, while there were about 22,000 'private coachmen and grooms' in 1851, by 1871 the total had exceeded 37,000 and in 1901 had topped 75,000. Only after the

F

turn of the century, when the chauffeur was beginning to make his mark, did some decline occur, but even then the combined total for private coachmen, grooms and motor-car drivers still showed an increase. Domestic gardeners, too, advanced from 74,603 in 1881 to 87,000 in 1901 and 118,739 in 1911. The very large rise between 1901 and 1911 was, however, attributed not only to the 'growing interest in gardens' but 'to omissions, on account of faulty returns, from the number classified under the heading in 1901'. Nevertheless, it is evident that more and more householders in Victorian England felt it necessary to have a carriage of their own and to employ a gardener, at least on a part-time basis. As early as 1861 a contemporary had observed: 'In our own day an equipage of some sort is considered so necessary an appendage to a medical practitioner, that a physician without a carriage (or a fly that can pass muster for one) is looked upon with suspicion. He is marked down *mauvais sujet* in the same list with clergymen without duty, barristers without chambers, and gentlemen whose Irish tenantry obstinately refuse to keep them supplied with money.'[2] Other professional men experienced similar pressures to conform.

Yet it was not the employment of coachman or gardener but of the male indoor servant that was for long regarded as the prerequisite of gentility. And it was the allegedly arrogant behaviour of this group which aroused the ire of contemporaries like Charles Booth and Lady Violet Greville. The latter, in an article on 'Men-servants in England', which appeared in the *National Review* in February 1892, particularly condemned the sort of flunkey who had

a wholesome contempt for poor people, small families, and genteel poverty; and talks of *us* and *we* in connection with his master. . . . He may be seen lounging superciliously on the door-steps of a summer afternoon, his coat thrown back, his thumbs in his waistcoat armhole, regarding the passing carriages and their well-dressed occupants with approval, or glaring contemptuously at the small boy with a parcel, and the poor music mistress who arrives on foot and timidly asks whether the young ladies are at home.[3]

Nevertheless, if such faults existed among male domestics in the bigger establishments, it must be remembered that a large number of the men were employed in a single-handed capacity, alongside a small staff of women servants, and that around one-third of *all* resident male indoor servants in mid-Victorian England were under the age of twenty. Many of these had a whole range of menial duties to perform and were merely the masculine counterparts of the maid-of-all-work. One such was a Suffolk lad, Robert Savage, who went at the age of twelve to work as a kitchen-boy at a large farm in his home village. His day commenced when he rose at 6.30 a.m. in order to hand over the milking pails to the cowman; they were kept indoors for cleanliness and the cowman had to come to the kitchen door to fetch them. His next task was to make up the copper fire, so that there would be hot water available for the maids to carry upstairs for the family to wash. After the copper came the 'blackstocks'—the open, barred fire-grates which would be lighted to provide heat and for cooking purposes. Then came the cleaning of the boots and shoes of the farmer's family and any guests, and the grinding of coffee for breakfast. His next job was cleaning the knives with a bathbrick and board kept specially for the purpose—a duty which was performed under the strict eye of the cook. There was just time to feed the fowls as well, before breakfast at nine o'clock.

After breakfast Robert carried out further duties, including the collection of vegetables needed for dinner, chopping the kindling wood and filling the old brass-bound coal-scuttles. As kitchen-boy he was also expected to peel the potatoes for the cook.

In the afternoon there were the fowls to feed again, the cows to fetch from the fields, the eggs to collect, and any other odd jobs which might be required either in the kitchen or outside. He was expected to pluck the chickens eaten in the household and to draw beer for the gardener, the groom and any other workers who were entitled to a fixed daily quantity. After tea a few other small jobs were carried out before taking the letters to the post office, which was about three-quarters of a mile away. This had to be done before 6.30 p.m. If there were no evening tasks, he could stay in the village to visit his family, but whatever happened he had to be back at the farm before nine o'clock. On some evenings, however, he was required to dig the garden, or if there were visitors he had to stand by to help with their horses when they went home. There were other occasional or seasonal jobs, too, like churning the butter. This was done once a week during the winter and twice a week during the summer. Savage remained a kitchen-boy for two years before moving on to farm work, helping first with the horses and eventually becoming a shepherd.

In the towns, kitchen-boys, or hall-boys as they were sometimes called, did not have the agricultural duties to perform which were expected of lads like Robert Savage, but they would spend more of their time in running errands, answering the door to callers, and perhaps in accompanying their mistress when she went out. In 1872, when Hannah Cullwick went as a maid-of-all-work to the household of a Miss Otway of Eaton Terrace, Euston Square, her first view of her future employer was when she 'saw a lady & a dog & a funny looking lad behind her' walking along the road, the boy acting as escort. At her previous place with the Hendersons in Gloucester Crescent, Hannah had also worked with another young page-boy; but as he was so small she had had to carry in the coal and perform all the heavy jobs of the house.[4]

Some youngsters were employed part-time on these tasks while still going to school—like Mr Fleming of Wallington, Surrey, who remembers working as a houseboy when he was only ten. He recalls:

> My job was to clean knives and forks, chop firewood, carry in coal for the kitchen range and other fires, clean boots and shoes, and sweep the yard daily, whilst on Saturdays a lot more was called for, such as cleaning windows, household brass ware, steel fire irons, etc. There was a separate coal fired boiler in an outhouse which supplied the house itself and a large greenhouse. In the winter I had to ensure that this boiler was working properly by raking it and adding fuel as necessary.

It was with that sort of indeterminate job in mind that boys answered advertisements for a 'Respectable lad . . . to clean boots and knives, and make himself useful', or for a 'Strong respectable Lad, about 18, to look after pony and trap, garden, clean knives and boots and make himself generally useful'. Both of these requests were published in the *Hampshire Chronicle* during 1890, but they are typical of the thousands of such appeals for boy servants which appeared in both the provincial and the national press during the Victorian era.

On the other hand, in more prosperous households an adult

single-handed man-servant would be employed (usually out of livery), and his duties presented a very different picture from those of the young page or kitchen-boy. Although he, too, would normally work alongside a small female staff of perhaps two or three, he was required to combine the duties of butler and foot-man. He was expected to rise early so that he could complete the rough work of the day before breakfast, including getting in coals and wood, cleaning the knives and boots and similar tasks. Very often he would also have to valet the gentlemen of the family, carrying up water for their baths, brushing their clothes and putting out the articles they were to wear for the day. He would lay the breakfast for the family and carry in the food to them, although he was not usually expected to wait at table during this meal.

During the morning he cleared away the breakfast things and washed and replaced them in the pantry cupboard; he trimmed the lamps and cleaned the plate. He also laid the luncheon table and waited at that meal if required. The afternoon was spent in washing the glass and silver used at lunch, attending to the sitting-room fires, answering the drawing-room bell and opening the door to callers. Sometimes he would go out in the carriage with his employer. But if he spent the afternoon at home, he would keep the front hall in order, put coats, hats and umbrellas in their places, prepare and carry in the five o'clock tea and clear it away. In the evening he would lay the dinner table, wait at that meal and clear away afterwards, as well as washing up the glass and silver used. He was expected, if needed, to carry in tea or coffee to the drawing-room after dinner.

Other miscellaneous duties of the single-handed man-servant included preparing the candles for the sitting-rooms, ensuring that the doors and windows of the house were properly secured at night, and drawing the beer needed for the servants' lunch, dinner and supper. Unlike the butler in a larger household, however, he was not expected to brew beer himself or to bottle wine, and his master would normally be responsible for looking after the wine cellar. Finally, he was expected to make himself 'generally useful' in the house—'to move and clean furniture; to clean windows, mirrors, chandeliers, etc.'⁵ The running of errands or taking of messages would probably also fall within his province.

Yet while the single man-servant and the page-boy, with their wide variety of duties, were among the most common of the male servants, it was only in the houses of the rich that the full range of men-servants was to be found. It was here that the house steward, the valet, the butler and the chef practised their skills and supervised the activities of footmen, page-boys and odd-job men. At Longleat, for example, in the early years of the present century the male staff comprised the house steward, the chef, the butler, an under-butler, one groom of the chambers, one valet, three footmen, one steward's room footman, two odd-job men, two pantry-boys and one lamp-boy. And at Eaton, the seat of the Duke of Westminster, the staff comprised a house steward, a chef, two grooms of chambers, one valet, one under-butler, three footmen, one pantry-boy, a kitchen porter, a hall usher, a night-watchman and an odd man. Other stately homes displayed a similar range. At Nuneham Courtenay, for example, the male staff in 1883 included a butler, three footmen and an usher—although by the later 1890s, following the death of Edward Harcourt, a rather more modest regimen was introduced. At that date only a butler, one footman and an usher were employed. Mrs Beeton, writing at the end of the 1850s, considered that the majority of gentlemen's establishments comprised a butler (or servant out of livery), a footman, and a coachman (or a coachman and groom, where the horses exceeded two or three).

The house steward was the most senior member of the domestic staff and was employed only in the wealthiest families. But despite his responsibilities, he enjoyed a very comfortable existence in most households. At Longleat, for example, early in the twentieth century the Marchioness of Bath recalled him as only appearing in the dining-room to 'ensure that all was running smoothly. He was also in sole charge of the household accounts.' By contrast, at Welbeck Abbey, Mr Spedding, the chief steward, was kept fully occupied. Frederick Gorst, one of the footmen, admitted: 'I don't think anyone coveted his job, because he worked harder than all the rest of the department heads put together.' The steward was expected to discipline the staff and check the supplies as well as oversee the accounts. According to the books on household management, he had to be a man of irreproachable character, experienced in household affairs, and able 'by the suavity of his manners, and equable deportment . . . to sustain the reputation of his master and to make his whole household comfortable and happy'.[6] He was expected to supervise the movement of staff from one residence to another, according to the peregrinations of the family he served, and it was he who controlled the packing and safe transit of valuables from one house to another. When a steward was employed, the upper servants would eat in his room rather than with the housekeeper, and if there were visitors, he would escort into dinner the visiting female servant of highest rank—usually the lady's maid.

The butler and under-butler were far more commonly engaged than the steward, the former particularly so. He was a non-liveried servant and wore the gentleman's clothes of the period distinguished by a deliberate solecism such as the wrong tie or the wrong trousers. His duties varied with the status of his employer : 'Where many servants were kept his nominal responsibilities were increased but his practical duties were slight; they could mostly be unloaded on to footmen. If the household employed a butler and one footman, the latter often became the butler's drudge.'[7]

In most families the office of butler was one which commanded respect and even awe. At Longleat he was 'far too grand a figure to roll up his sleeves and work in his own pantry; and in the dining-room he would serve only the wine and the more imposing dishes. Even the house steward would always knock at the pantry door out of respect for the butler.' Butlers were encouraged to adopt an authoritarian attitude towards their subordinates, or, as one handbook put it, 'In all establishments it is [the butler's] duty to rule. In large establishments more particularly, this exercise of judicious power will be greatly required; for under-servants are never even comfortable, much less happy, under lax management.' Lady Violet Greville thought they tyrannised over their employers, too, if they had the chance—particularly if those employers were single elderly ladies. The 'old butler . . . decides what they shall drink, how much they shall drink, and how they shall live, and whom they dare not disturb at odd hours, or in the enjoyment of his meals, by ringing the bell or sending him on a message'.

Nevertheless, in smaller households a butler would usually have to work fairly hard, for it was his task to ensure that the wheels of domestic life turned smoothly. He was also responsible for the household plate and each night would have to make sure that it was carefully locked away. In the mornings he would give out those pieces which were to be cleaned, or in some cases he would clean them himself, along with the silver ornaments from the drawing-room. When the family were away from home he might have to deposit the most valuable items in a place of safety. Thus Keeping, butler to Sir John Ramsden of Bulstrode Park, Buckinghamshire, wrote to his employer on 21 June 1890 informing him that he had taken 'the Plate to the Bank. . . . I left all the chests, 7 in no. as the place they were deposited in seemed perfectly dry.'

If there were no valet kept, the butler might be responsible for caring for his master's wardrobe. He would normally wait at breakfast, luncheon, tea and dinner, together with the footmen, and would overlook the arrangements for each meal. Where only one footman was kept, the butler would assist by laying the breakfast table, waiting at that meal, and then clearing away. He would attend to the lamps, and if the footman had to go out with the carriage early in the afternoon, he would clear away the luncheon and later lay the dinner table.

When dinner was ready he entered the drawing-room and announced that all was prepared. He then stood behind his master's chair while grace was said, ready to remove the dish covers. 'Thereafter he waited at the side table and served the wine, and set and arranged succeeding courses.' The aim was to provide service as quietly and efficiently as possible. At the dessert stage he left to take tea in the housekeeper's room. Before the family returned to the drawing-room he would make sure that the fireplace was in order and that the lamps, candles or gas-burners were operating properly. After this he would go to his pantry to await the bell to attend the company once more; the footman meanwhile was clearing the dinner table and cleaning the plate and glasses.

When the family rang for tea, later in the evening, the butler handed round the cups and saucers and the footman followed behind carrying the urn. The butler's last duty at night was to see that all doors and windows were secured, that the plate was locked up and that the fires were safe.

During the day in households where no footman was kept, or where the footman was out with the carriage, the butler would answer the door to callers and would ensure that the fires were made up in the dining-room, drawing-rooms and various sitting-rooms. During the afternoons if the family were 'at home' he would remain in the front hall ready to announce visitors. In many of the larger country houses, where a letter-bag was used for receiving or despatching letters, the butler would possess a key to this and would be responsible for the distribution and collection of the mail.

But perhaps the butler's most important duty was the traditional one of looking after the wine cellar, decanting the wine for daily use and putting away the decanters after every meal. He had to enter in the cellar book the amount of wine given out and the number of bottles drunk per day. The skilful butler in the large household was also expected to know how to fine or clear wines and to brew beer, and to be competent to advise his master as to the price and quality of the wine to be laid in. Most of the books on household management provided recipes for fining wine: Mrs Beeton suggested that isinglass, gelatine and gum Arabic were all equally suitable for the purpose. They were mixed in with a cask of wine by constant stirring, while the bubbles were skimmed off as they rose to the surface. The mixture was allowed to stand for three or four days before it was ready for use. One cask of clarified wine was sufficient to fine thirteen dozen bottles of port or sherry, according to Mrs Beeton. The experienced butler could likewise detect the adulterations committed by unscrupulous tradesmen; thus 'a piece of chalk the size of a pea could be used to disclose the presence of aqua fortis and oil of vitriol; and an admixture of lime water to port would reveal any alum in it'.

Where the master was a hunting man and no valet was kept, a butler was expected to maintain his employer's hunting gear. One such, John Henry Inch, remembered spending hours during the long winter evenings 'cleaning his master's white leather hunting breeches, working to detailed instructions from Hammond & Co. of Oxford Street, who produced a special powder for the purpose'.

Some employers exerted a close control over their butlers. The Benyons of Englefield House, Berkshire, for example, made it clear that the key of the cellar would be kept by the master, who would give out wine as wanted. He alone ordered items and paid for them, the butler only ordering if directed to do so. No perquisites were allowed. (However, most of the Benyon butlers seem to have been satisfied with the conditions, for they stayed with the family for many years. James Blake, who entered service with them in June 1869, remained until May 1886. His successor, James Chisholm, who came on 7 May 1886 was still at his post when entries in the servants' book ceased early in 1894.) Other families adopted simpler devices, like the tantalus fitted with a locking mechanism which was invented by Sir John Betjeman's grandfather to prevent the servants getting at the drink.

The groom of the chambers was akin in status to the butler but was found only in the largest houses, where there was a multiplicity of public rooms. 'His principal duty was that of receiving and announcing visitors and showing guests to their accommodation. Several times a day he toured his suite of rooms, unobtrusively patting cushions and straightening chairs, adjusting blinds against the sun or placing footstools.' He performed much ceremonial door-opening, when the guests descended from the drawing-room, library and elsewhere to dinner. At meals he was expected to help with the serving. 'It was not the most arduous of callings, but during big house parties the groom of the chambers often persuaded himself that he was earning his money, if only by replenishing the supplies of crested writing-paper which guests removed as fast as he could set it out.'[8]

The footman was the male servant most directly subordinate to the butler, and he was expected to perform a variety of duties, ranging from attending his mistress in the carriage to cleaning knives and boots, carrying coal, cleaning plate, looking after the lamp and candle-holders, waiting at table and answering the bell. In more modest households these latter tasks would be carried out by the cheaper substitute of a page or parlourmaid.

An efficient footman was expected to rise early so as to finish the dirtiest jobs before the family came down. He could then put aside his working dress, tidy himself and appear in a clean jacket to lay the cloth and prepare breakfast for the family. *The Servant's Practical Guide* of 1880 suggested that the footman's day should begin at 6.30 a.m. in the summer and 7 a.m. in the winter. At midday he must be ready, dressed in his livery, to answer the door or take out messages, or carry out any other task required.

In the evening the footman rang the dressing-bell about half an hour before dinner was served, and again at the expiration of that time. Then, wearing his best livery and, in affluent house-holds, with his hair powdered, he would take up his stand to the left behind his master's dining chair, ready to assist in serving. Where a system of dinner *à la russe* was adopted he would help to hand round the dishes. If any of the guests had brought his own footman, the man would stand behind his master's chair, rendering such assistance to others as he could, while attending to his employer's wants throughout the dinner. In the largest households the mistress, too, would have her own footman; and in some cases even the nursery and the house steward would also be supplied with their personal servitor. At Longleat the first footman acted as the lady's footman. When she went out driving he would sit on the box with the coachman—or in later days with the chauffeur—and would open and shut the door for her and wrap the fur rug around her knees. If she had dinner in her room, he would carry up her tray; at the dinner table he stood behind her chair.

Other general duties included looking after the wants of the gentlemen in the smoking room; attending to the lighting of the house as soon as it was dusk; cleaning, arranging and having in readiness the flat silver candlesticks, before the dressing-bell rang in winter, and by ten o'clock in summer; and attending in the front hall when the dinner guests were leaving. If the carriage was ordered out in the evening, the footman would have to go out with it—a duty he did not relish during the cold winter evenings. Given these varied tasks and the long hours involved, a man might walk many miles in the day, up and down stairs and along corridors, in a really large house. Arthur Inch, a footman at Londonderry House, once put on a pedometer during the course of a long day in the busy London season and recorded eighteen miles without leaving the house.

Footmen were allowed two suits of livery a year in most house-holds and were expected to keep them in immaculate order. However, they often had to provide their own hair-powder, if this was worn. Frederick Gorst discovered to his horror that his hair was thinning rapidly thanks to the drying effect of the powder. On one occasion he experimented with hair-oil as a base before he applied the usual soap and powder. All went well for about an hour, then he felt what seemed like droplets of moisture on his forehead and rushed to a glass to see what was happening. 'My "wig" was disintegrating! I rushed to Mr Spedding's office to be excused from duty in order to make a fresh toilet using the tried, old method of violet powder and soap.'[9]

The energy with which the footmen performed their duties varied both with their own character and with that of their employer. But Lady Violet Greville, for one, had few illusions about the average footman : 'He rises as late as possible; he exerts himself as little as he need; he declines to take up the governess's supper or to clean her boots; and he insists on his own breakfast being brought to him in bed whenever his mistress is out of town.'[10] Although her view is exaggerated, the diary of William Tayler, a twenty-nine-year-old footman in the employ of Mrs Prinsep, an East India Company merchant's widow, and her daughter, shows that her fears were not entirely groundless. The diary relates to the year 1837; on 1 January (a Sunday) William describes his situation : 'I am the only manservant kept here as the coachman is only a sort of jobber. Here are three maidservants, very quiet good sort of bodys, and we live very comfortable together.' At the time Mrs Prinsep had some of her grandsons staying with her, and this added to William's duties.

> I got up at half past seven, cleaned the boys' clothes and knives [and] lamps, got the parlour breakfast, lit my pantry fire, cleared breakfast and washed it away, dressed myself, went to church, came back, got parlour lunch, had my own dinner, sit by the fire and red the Penny Magazine and opened the door when my visitors came. At 4 o'clock had my tea, took the lamps and candles up into the drawing room, shut the shutters, took glass, knives, plate and settera into the dining room, layed the cloth for dinner, took the dinner up at six o'clock, waited at dinner, brought the things down again at seven, washed them up, brought down the desert, got ready the tea, took it up at eight o'clock, brought it down at half past, washed up, had my supper at nine, took down the lamps and candles at half past ten and went to bed at eleven. All these things I have to do every day.[11]

Mrs Prinsep was certainly no hard taskmistress and William regularly went out for walks or to visit friends during the day. Thus on 7 January he noted : 'Rose at half past seven; done my work at eleven. Went out and took a walk; back to dinner.' And on 9 January came an entry which would surely have confirmed Lady Violet Greville's worst fears : 'Up at eight. It's realy very little use getting up sooner as the mornings are so dark and I detest working by candlelight and, more than all, I am very fond of my Bed this cold weather. I spent this morning in work and fiddleing about the afternoon.' At between three and four o'clock his Aunt Puzey called on him and stayed to tea. When she left at six he 'took a short walk, got home to supper, went to bed at eleven o'clock'. Similarly on 23 February, his mistress had a small card party in the evening, and one of the gentlemen 'put five shillings into my hand for which I was greatly obliged to them for. I have drunk rather to much wine this evening and that you may tell in my writing, therefore I am of to bed.'

In the largest households a much narrower specialisation would be the order of the day for the footman. Frederick Gorst recalled that at Welbeck Abbey his first evening's employment was to sit, concealed behind a twelve-foot screen, in a corner of the room occupied by the Duke of Portland. 'His Grace disliked ringing a bell for a footman when he wanted something, so the man on duty always sat ready within earshot to answer his "hello", which was his way of summoning us. . . . When we served the Duke and Duchess of Portland at dinner, there were always three men in attendance : two footmen and either the wine butler or the groom of the chambers.' A four-day cycle of duties was in operation at Welbeck. On the first of the four, Gorst was on call all day, serving breakfast, lunch, tea and dinner, with another footman to assist. On day two a colleague was the 'lead' footman and Gorst acted as follow-up. On day three he was only on call in case extra guests arrived and to assist his fellow-footmen as necessary. On day four he was off duty. Then the process began again. The footmen on call were expected to answer the bells, to provide hall duty, and to stand ready to carry out the orders of the Duke : 'His Grace was very punctilious about an immediate response to a bell.'

Yet despite the sometimes frustrating and boring nature of their duties, both butler and footman took pride in their work— in the beautifully cleaned silver, the brightly shining lamps, the tastefully arranged dinner table, and the deft service rendered. Gorst recalled with pleasure the attractive fashion in which, as a young footman at Carden Park, Cheshire, he and Ling, the butler, had prepared the dinner table. It was always laid with a thick baize underlining covered by a white damask cloth. 'Directly in the centre of the table, Mr Ling placed a large bowl of dark red geraniums which had been specially raised in the hothouse. Two silver baskets of fresh fruit and two pairs of five-branch candlesticks, with each candle covered by a fringed silk shade, made a lavish setting. Then the flat silver, and the Crown Derby china with insets of the Squire's crest, the same lush red as the geraniums were arranged.'[12]

Later Gorst became a travelling footman to Lady Howard. He was responsible for accompanying his mistress on her journeys, for purchasing railway tickets, and making first-class reservations for her—with a second-class one for himself. He carried robes and steamer rugs to put over his mistress's knees and feet in the train to keep her warm in the unheated compartment. 'To insure her complete comfort, I carried a hot-water container to place under her feet.' Gorst also looked after the valises and trunks and carried his mistress's jewel case, which was attached to his wrist by a bracelet and chain, like a handcuff. He had a tea hamper prepared in her compartment so that he could serve tea at an appropriate time on the journey. No effort was spared to satisfy her every wish or to provide for her comfort.

Personal appearance was important for any boy aspiring to the position of footman or page in a large household, for only the tall and well-built were considered. Wages often related to height, with the tallest men or boys receiving the highest pay.

The male cook or chef was employed in the most affluent families only, and the hiring of a Frenchman in this position was considered essential for the prestige of status-conscious English aristocrats. French cooks were temperamental beings who expected their masters to take an interest in the elaborate dishes they prepared. Felix, for a short time chef to the Duke of Wellington, left his position purely because the Duke ate the food prepared without giving either praise or blame. Yet even when their masters did show an interest, the French cooks might not be satisfied but exacted extra privileges and were frequently at loggerheads with their English subordinates, to whom they relegated the simpler tasks such as roasting. At Longleat in the late nineteenth century the French chef was Albert Gaillard, who was a friend of the royal chef at Buckingham Palace. When the family were in London he would go to the palace to lend a hand at the big dinner parties, while in return the palace chef came to the Marquis of Bath's residence in Berkeley Square to prepare his own specialities, 'pedestals and statuettes of semolina to decorate the sweets'. Gaillard demanded, and received, a high wage— being paid as much as £130 a year in 1883, well above the level paid to other senior servants at Longleat and more than twice the amount earned by the housekeeper.

At Buckingham Palace at the end of Victoria's reign, M. Menager, the royal chef, had a salary of £400 a year and a living-out allowance of an extra £100. He had a London house and arrived each morning at Buckingham Palace by hansom cab soon after eight o'clock. Although he had eighteen chefs and master-cooks working under him, 'eight with their own tables', he supervised their activities closely and tackled the most difficult dishes himself. Gabriel Tschumi, who went as an apprentice to the royal chef in 1898, recalled that the master-cooks and chefs 'brought their dishes to him at various states of preparation to be passed before they could go on to the next stage', for 'it was M. Menager's task to see that each of the ten courses served daily at luncheon and dinner reached the standard of perfection at which he aimed'.[13]

Lady Violet Greville, however, viewed the employment of a chef with a jaundiced eye:

He is an artist, and as such a Bohemian. He is always out, except when he is concocting some specially delicate 'plat' (the ordinary family dinner being provided by the kitchenmaid); he enjoys a wild liberty denied to the other servants; he stays out late—for is he not assisting his friend Alphonse in the preparation of a banquet at the Duke of S.'s, and is not this part of the necessary experience and deftness required in his stock-in-trade? . . . The man-cook practises his extortions and raises his demands daily. Year by year Italians and Frenchmen invade our shores, and take possession of our kitchens, wielding their 'casserolles' in kingly fashion and ruling obsequious kitchenmaids and scullions with a rod of iron. After a few years they wax fat and retire from the fleshpots of Egypt, with their sausages, their garlic, and their wives, to an old age of comfortable competency in their native land.[14]

The last member of the male indoor staff to be considered is the valet. Like the chef he was something of a status symbol, for all but the richest households adopted the cheaper alternative of allowing the butler or footman to act as valet as well. Only in the case of bachelors might this not apply. Like his female counterpart, the lady's maid, the valet was always numbered among the 'Upper Ten' of the domestic staff; he did not wear livery, nor did he receive an allowance for clothes, but was often given his master's cast-offs.[15] His duties were very similar to those already described for the butler or footman-cum-valet, but the specialised and intimate nature of his work inevitably gave the valet a far closer relationship with his master than applied in these other cases. Even the hostile Lady Violet Greville was forced to admit that the well-trained valet, although 'selfish and untruthful occasionally', was also invaluable :

He never forgets a single portmanteau or bag or hat-box; he reads *Bradshaw* excellently; he takes the tickets, and, tipping the guard efficiently, secures a reserved railway compartment; he brings his master tea, or brandy and soda, at the stations; he engages the only fly at their destination; he has everything unpacked and ready by the time his master leisurely strolls upstairs to dress. . . . He has the soul of a perfect army commissariat. . . . He looks after 'the Guv'nor's' interests in a fatherly way, and advises him to pay an occasional visit to the paternal home, or reminds him to write to his mother and sisters. . . . He has always the same noiseless step and perfect sleekness and politeness of manner, the same absolute good temper and gentleness of tone, with the same subserviency and perfection of voice, the same ardour and energy in his work. Your boots are polished till you can see your face in them; ties are carefully arranged; clothes are ironed; and brushed hats are glossy; the buttonhole is laid out invitingly; hot water is to your hand; your slippers lie in front of the fire; and the obsequious valet stands ready. Who would grudge so many guineas a year for service like this? If he smokes your cigars, your loose cash may lie about freely; he will not touch it. You who are so careless with your studs and sleeve-links possess an attendant who counts and looks after them. If he occasionally helps himself to a glass or two of wine, he pays your bills

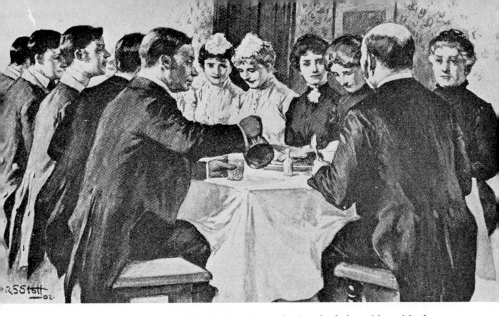

10 The Servants' hall, 1902. The butler sits at the head of the table, with the valet on his immediate left. The other male servants are footmen. Female servants (left to right): two housemaids, lady's maid, cook, housekeeper. In many households it was the custom for the senior servants (the 'Upper Ten') to take their meals in the housekeeper's room.

11 A middle-class Oxford family with their youthful groom, 1900.

12 Indoor and outdoor servants at Deene Rectory, Northamptonshire, 1884.
The rector clearly possessed private means and an unusually large glebe. Most
country clergymen had to make do with a staff of less than half this number.
Standing (left to right): head gardener, two farm workers, under-gardener,
groom and under-coachman, tutor, garden-boy, coachman. Seated: rector's
son, head housemaid, cook, under-housemaid, kitchenmaid, farm worker. The
two boys at the front of the picture are other sons of the rector.

*13 Resident servants employed by a middle-class family at Sydenham Hill,
London, 1900.* Standing (left to right): kitchenmaid, gardener, housemaid.
Seated: cook, parlourmaid.

punctually and in order. . . . The gentleman's gentleman remains an unique specimen of high civilisation acting upon a naturally uneducated nature. There is veneer, but no real value, underneath. Yet, take him all in all, the gentleman's gentleman is agreeable to live with, easy to manage, unobtrusively useful, faithful as far as his lights go, devoted to what he thinks your interest and is amiable and good-tempered, light-hearted and ready-witted. What better can we say of most of our friends?[16]

The model valet, then, was the sort of man who was shrewd enough to spend his day performing trivialities, like ironing his master's bootlaces or making sure that the daily newspapers were pressed before they appeared on the breakfast table, and yet had the art of making them seem important and essential. Nevertheless, not all gentlemen relished the attentions of such servitors. The Duke of Wellington was one of these. 'Perhaps you are not aware', he told Lord Strangford, 'that I shave myself and brush my own clothes; I regret that I cannot clean my own boots; for men-servants bore me and the presence of a crowd of idle fellows annoys me more than I can tell you.' Yet despite his protestations, the Duke did employ a valet who served him faithfully, 'even to the extent of consulting secretly with the Mendicity Office in an effort to eliminate the numerous dishonest contenders for the Duke's charity'. And when in September 1852 the Duke died it was his valet, Kendall, who sent for the apothecary and who remained in close attendance during his master's last hours.

When one turns from the indoor to the outdoor staff, it is the coachman who occupies pride of place, for he was regarded as the most senior of all the liveried servants. At William Lanceley's first situation as a page-boy in the household of the local squire, indeed, it was the coachman who headed the servants' hall rather than a member of the indoor staff.

The good coachman was expected to drive smoothly and not too quickly. Mrs Beeton recommended a pace of seven or eight miles an hour; 'less speed', she considered, was 'injurious to the horses, getting them into lazy and sluggish habits'. The coachman's hands must be delicate and gentle, so that the mere weight of the reins was felt on the bit, and the directions were indicated by a turn of the wrist rather than by a pull. The whip was to be used only rarely, 'more as a precaution' or to encourage than as a punishment.

Where two coachmen were kept and the stable department was large, the head coachman would drive a pair of horses in the barouche or other open carriage, and the second coachman would drive the one-horse brougham. And, according to *The Servant's Practical Guide*, all the night work, 'such as driving the family to a ball, or driving to and from the railway-station', was the duty of the second coachman. Thanks to a law passed in the reign of George I, the drivers of hackney carriages were required to give way to the coaches of gentlemen and could be fined ten shillings for failing to do so.

A coachman was expected to be able to get ready for the road within twenty minutes. But in the ordinary way he would start work at six o'clock in the morning, spend an hour and a half in getting the stable in order and dressing the two horses. 'Washing and cleaning carriage and harness would take between two and three hours and the vehicle would be at the door by eleven o'clock, its windows open and the interior purged of all fustiness.'[17] The master would give orders beforehand as to which direction he wished the horses to face, for it was a sign of a badly managed household if the carriage had to be turned in the street.

In large establishments, where no expense was spared, there might be as many as sixty horses, several under-coachmen and a whole string of grooms and stable-boys to feed and exercise the horses and, if necessary, to act as postilions and outriders. The stable servants usually lived over the stables in a little community of their own, and the cost of their board was often separately recorded in the household accounts, as at Nuneham Courtenay in Oxfordshire. At Longleat, early in the twentieth century, fourteen men and boys were employed in the stables. They included a coachman, a second coachman, a carriage groom, a steel-boy (whose duty was to burnish the bits and metal parts of the harness) and a 'tiger', a small boy in livery who sat upright on the box of the carriage, his arms folded stiffly across his chest, and whose role was primarily ornamental. In the stables there was a fully equipped blacksmith's shop, and once a fortnight the village blacksmith and his lad came over from nearby Horningsham to shoe the horses at Longleat. When the family moved to London for the season they took eleven horses and five stablemen with them. 'In the mews behind the Grosvenor Square house there were stables and a coach house, with rooms above for the coachmen and the grooms.'

It was the responsibility of the head coachman to see that the horses were properly fed and groomed, that the carriages and harness were kept thoroughly cleaned and that the stables and harness-room were in perfect order. It was his duty, too, in some households to order hay, corn, straw, etc., and he would in any case supervise the distribution of feeding stuff to make sure that none was wasted. In smaller households, where only one coachman-groom was kept, various informal duties might also devolve upon him. Thus Jones, coachman to the Rev. W. C. Risley of Deddington, was frequently sent on errands to the nearby town of Banbury, and on occasions he also accompanied Risley's son, Halford, when he went out hunting.

Not all coachmen proved worthy of the trust placed upon them. Tom, coachman to Sir Henry Halford, physician extraordinary to George III and later M.P. for the Southern Division of Leicestershire, was in trouble with the Marylebone police in June 1830, 'having been fined so it seems for assisting some woman to carry off the furniture of Lodgings to the value of 30s.' As Sir Henry ruefully noted, it was his carriage which had been used as the get-away vehicle : 'I have written to inquire about it.' Similarly, in the late 1860s, Emily and Ellen Hall of Ravenswood House, West Wickham, Kent, discovered that their coachman, Cutting, had been driving their dog-cart while they were away from home. He had used it for pleasure trips 'up and down the countryside and [had] tethered Myrtle, the horse, too loosely, while imbibing some refreshment at West Wickham's Star and Garter. Myrtle had trotted off and the cart had upset and damaged a pony carriage owned by Farmer Weaver to the tune of £4. Mr Weaver, being in the cart at the time, had also claimed for damages to himself.' Cutting promised to pay up but did not do so, and the sisters were eventually forced to find the cash themselves.[18] Nor was this their only brush with recalcitrant coachmen. In 1861 one of Cutting's predecessors had secretly been letting the room above the stables to a local ne'er-do-well, who had responded by stealing some of their oats. The coachman had refused to apologise for his action and so had been dismissed.

In humbler establishments, where the driving was carried out by a groom, the latter might also be expected to help around the house and even wait at table. Thus *Jackson's Oxford Journal* for 27 July 1872 contained an appeal for a groom : 'A respectable young Man, accustomed to horse driving, able to wait at table, a member of the Established Church and a good character indispensable.' Sometimes such all-purpose servants lacked sufficient time to wash themselves before they had to wait at dinner, and the odour of stables all too strongly assailed the nostrils of the diners.

The most common of all male servants to be employed in Victorian England was the gardener. His tasks ranged from that of an odd-job man in a small household to the specialised skills of a Joseph Paxton. The head gardener in a large establishment was generally in charge of a great deal of glass—hothouses, greenhouses, conservatories, etc. As well as producing vegetables for the table, expert gardeners were required to grow such luxuries as strawberries, pineapples and melons both in season and out. According to *The Servant's Practical Guide*, it was the head gardener who apportioned out the work among his underlings; he was often something of an autocrat and for this reason was 'usually studied and conciliated by the feminine branches of the family. He objects . . . to his choicest blossoms being cut by his mistress or her daughters, or the finest bunches of grapes being gathered; when his green-houses and hot-houses are to be rifled, he prefers that it should be done by himself rather than by his mistress, and ladies who value their gardeners are inclined to humour this weakness.' At Eaton the Duke of Westminster employed a head gardener and forty under-gardeners, the unmarried men among the latter living in a bothy with a cleaner and a cook of their own. At Welbeck Abbey there were six house gardeners to attend to the subterranean greenhouses and house decorations, as well as thirty to forty general gardeners and forty to fifty roadmen. More modestly, Englefield House, Berkshire, had a garden staff of fifteen in the late 1850s rising to above twenty from the mid-1860s to the mid-1890s; among those employed at the latter date were two women.

After the turn of the century staffs tended to be smaller, but the routine in other respects remained the same. Thus Ted Humphris, who started work as garden-boy at Aynho Park, Northamptonshire, in 1914, was employed alongside a staff consisting of 'Mr Brown, the head gardener, a foreman, whose special responsibility was the greenhouses, a second gardener, known as a journeyman, three men in the kitchen garden'. In addition, two men were occupied full time in the pleasure grounds. Humphris worked from 6 a.m. to 6 p.m. every day except Saturday, when he was permitted to finish early at 4 p.m., and Sunday, which was a day of rest. His wages were 6s. a week. 'One of my tasks during this time was to lead the pony which was used to haul the giant mowers across the spacious lawns in the pleasure grounds. The pony was provided with leather boots to wear over its hooves, to prevent them from damaging the surface of the lawn.' But most of his time was spent in weeding, scrubbing the staging and floors in the greenhouses, running errands and making himself 'generally useful' to the foreman gardener. He had also to prepare the wood and coal and light the fire in the bothy, as well as lay the breakfast table there for the foreman gardener. 'I had very little to do with the head gardener, who in those days was always addressed as "Sir", and in fact one was not permitted to speak to him unless he spoke first.'

Some employers followed the example of Earl Ferrers and entered into a formal contract with their gardener. A surviving agreement between the Earl and William Dean, gardener, dated 14 September 1853, shows that the Earl was to pay Dean 'one Pound a week as Wages, and the use of Three Rooms over the Stables, Coals and Vegetables for the use of himself only'. If Dean wished to leave, or were dismissed, one month's notice or one month's wages had to be given.

A more typical picture of the average gardener's activities was provided by such newspaper advertisements as that inserted on behalf of the rector of Bourton-on-the-Water in Gloucestershire in April 1872 : 'Wanted . . . a middle-aged Man and his Wife— the man as gardener, to manage a kitchen garden and a small green-house, to look after a pony and chaise, and to help in doors; the woman as good plain cook.' Similarly, *Jackson's Oxford Journal* for 11 January 1873 appealed on behalf of a Worcester-shire family for a general gardener : 'There is no under-gardener kept, but sufficient help for the work in the kitchen garden and lawns is always to hand. The salary may fairly be put at 22s. per week. A steady active single man would be preferred, but there will be no objection to a married man; no one, however, need apply without a good character.'

6

Social Life 'Below Stairs'

I'd no one to go to : oh! I cried the first night. . . . I had always
slept in a ward full of other girls, and there I was all alone, and
this was a great big house . . . and they told me to go downstairs,
in a room by the kitchen all alone, with a long black passage. I
might have screamed, but nobody would have heard.

> 'Maids-of-all-Work', anonymous article in
> *Cornhill Magazine* (1874). (The girl quoted in the
> extract had been brought up in a workhouse.)

Troops of men and maid-servants were kept in large town and
country houses in those days. The maids on the lower rungs of the
ladder seldom saw their employers. . . . The upper servants were
their real mistresses, and they treated beginners as a sergeant
treated recruits, drilling them well in their duties by dint of much
scolding; but the girl who was anxious to learn and did not mind
hard work or hard words and could keep a respectful tongue in
her head had nothing to fear from them.

> FLORA THOMPSON, *Lark Rise to Candleford* (1945).

FOR THE majority of servants, employed in small households,
social life below stairs was limited to contact with at most one or
two fellow-workers, and perhaps also the milkman or baker's
roundsman who came with deliveries to the house. Leisure time
was closely controlled by the employer. In larger establishments,
by contrast, a more complex situation existed, since the distinctions of rank which had characterised the working relations of
senior and junior staff (the so-called 'Upper Ten' and 'Lower
Five') were also present at meal times and during off duty periods.
Welbeck Abbey was but one of many stately homes where the
social divisions between the two were 'drawn more strictly' than
among those whom they served. One of the footmen, Frederick
Gorst, recalled :

The Upper Ten took their meals in the steward's dining room and they were waited on by two steward's room footmen. The Upper Ten had white wine, claret, and beer for luncheon and dinner. The china, silver, and glass which was used to serve them, and which was taken care of exclusively by the steward's room footmen, was much finer than the gentry had in some of the smaller houses in England. We, the Lower Five, ate our meals in the Servants' Hall, the old refectory of the Abbey. . . . At Welbeck the upper servants adopted an arrogant attitude towards the under servants. Mr Clancy, the wine butler, was the haughtiest and most pompous of them all.[1]

Nevertheless, in most households the senior staff would join their subordinates in the servants' hall for the main course of the midday dinner each day, before retreating to the housekeeper's or steward's room (the so-called 'Pug's Parlour') to eat their pudding and drink their wine. At Longleat, as in other large households, even this custom had a ritual of its own. The under-servants trooped into the servants' hall first and remained standing in their places until the upper servants had filed in, in order of precedence. Then, when the first course had ended, they left in procession. First marched the steward's room footman carrying, with great pomp, the remains of the joint which had been served, 'followed by the upper servants who then retired to the steward's room for the remainder of their meal; while the housemaids and sewing maids scurried off with platefuls of pudding to eat in their own sitting-rooms'. Usually a joint, chickens or a goose were served at midday, followed by a pudding and cheese; in the evening there was a four-course dinner. 'Callers at the back door stayed long enough to drink a glass or two of Longleat-brewed ale, and leather flagons of this brew with plates of bread and cheese, were always left standing on the servants' hall table for anyone to help himself.'

Needless to say, not all servants, even in the largest establishments, fared as well as this—although food was usually abundant. In some houses maids were given cold beef or mutton or even Irish stew for breakfast, while the midday meal consisted of a hot joint and heavy suet pudding. Furthermore, when the staff's cooking was carried out by an inexperienced kitchenmaid, even good quality food could be rendered unpalatable. In 1892 a butler, writing under the name of John Robinson, complained in an article published in the magazine *Nineteenth Century* that, thanks to the 'tender mercies' of the kitchenmaid, a 'huge badly cooked joint' regularly appeared on the servants' table. 'This appears cold again and again at a succession of suppers and dinners, till some one, nauseated at its continual reappearance, chops it up and assigns the greater part to the swill-tub. This is followed by another joint, which goes the same round and shares the same fate. . . . As matters stand, the servant must either gorge himself with half-cooked meat, or steal what he can from the upstairs table, or starve.'

In the earlier part of the nineteenth century, when tea and sugar were expensive, these items were rarely provided by the mistress, and servants either had to buy them out of a cash allowance made by their employer for that specific purpose, or else (as a number did) make do with the tea-leaves which had been used already above stairs. Even at the end of the century in the more traditional households men-servants were given only beer with their meals. Frederick Gorst remembered his horror when at the age of sixteen he went as an under-footman to Squire Leache at Carden Park, Cheshire, and was offered a horn of beer to drink with his breakfast. He asked the housemaid if he might have tea instead but was quickly told : 'You're not going to get tea for breakfast here! The Squire don't allow it.' John Robinson also strongly disagreed with the custom of providing beer : 'How this pernicious practice is perpetuated passes my comprehension. . . . Hundreds of men get their first start in a drunkard's career from this hateful practice.'

For as long as the senior staff remained at the dinner table, subordinates were not allowed to speak unless spoken to. Usually the steward or the butler would carve the meat, while the housekeeper or cook dished up the vegetables. Each person was served in accordance with his or her position in the household, and the most junior had to wait until last. The highest-ranking servant would then say grace and would give the signal for the meal to begin and also to end. One former man-servant recalled : 'When the butler put his knife and fork down that was the signal for *everyone* to do the same, so God help you if you were a slow eater.'[2]

In all households, both large and small, it was common

practice for the servants to supplement the food supplied for them by leftovers from the meals served upstairs. Supper was very often provided from this source—with the staff in the wealthiest establishments delicately consuming cold chicken, grouse or pheasant. But William Tayler, footman to the Prinsep family, made the best use he could of any leftovers, as his diary entries make clear. Thus on 28 January he noted: 'We get many little nice things that come down from the parlour. . . . I have just had a good blow out of egg hot and am now going to bed.' ('Egg hot' was a hot drink make from beer, eggs, sugar and nutmeg.) Earlier the Prinsep servants had dined at midday on hash and vegetables and had supped on cold mutton and rice pudding.

In the more cost-conscious households, however, store cupboards were kept locked, weekly rations of jam, butter, sugar and tea, if provided, were carefully doled out, and encouragement was given to the servants not to eat too much. In this the various handbooks on household management played their part. Thus *The Young Servant's Own Book*, published in 1883, warned against excessive eating and drinking: 'Eating too much is bad for your health, and drinking too much leads to misery. I do not think it wise for young servant girls to accustom themselves to drink strong tea, with a great deal of sugar; for, after a while, should they have to buy for themselves, they will find it very expensive to do so.' Some mistresses made sure that their servants were strictly rationed not only by locking up the larder, but also by leaving behind just enough for the servants' midday meal if they went out for the day. Mrs Annie Mason, of Guilsborough, Northamptonshire, remembered that when she went into service as a general maid at Stoke Newington, London, at the turn of the century, her mistress left her 'a slice of bread and cheese' for lunch, while she herself went into the city. Another young servant similarly received '2 slices of bread and *mutton* dripping and a cup of drink' for lunch every day while in her first place as a general servant.[3]

Nor was it only the poorer employers who tried to economise on their servants' food. A lady's maid in a 'county' family early in the present century remembered that because of her mistress's extravagance in dress, some of the housekeeping allowance went on clothes rather than food: 'The joint that was bought for the dining-room used to last the servants' hall for the rest of the week.

We usually had it cold with hot vegetables until it finally appeared as a sort of hash which nobody wanted. Tea was bread and butter and a small cake, gooseberry jam one week, and plum the next. We did get occasional treats after dinner parties; anything that wouldn't keep, like ices, we demolished.'[4]

Nevertheless, a strict approach by employers was sometimes justified, as evidence from Bulstrode Park, Buckinghamshire, indicates. Here the servants' hall seems to have been regarded as an open house for casual visitors until Sir John Ramsden was forced to tighten up the regulations. From the mid-1880s a careful record of expenditure and of numbers dining in was kept, and doubtful entries queried. Thus on 1 September 1886 it was noted that there were twenty servants eating in, plus the 'postman extra every day'. On 18 September this latter entry was queried by Sir John's agent, with the cautioning note : 'This was done without any authority. It is to cease henceforth.' When the family entertained and waiters were employed temporarily to assist the regular staff, their meals, too, were recorded in the household accounts. On 9 September, for example, '2 Helpers each had supper on the 9th and breakfast on the 10th.' They were to be classified as 'a half of each day' instead of as one full servant per day, as the original entry showed. Sir John's especial concern appears to have been to cut down consumption of meat, and records of meat purchased or obtained from the family estates were maintained. In May 1887 these showed that with an average of five or six members of the family and two visitors, together with twenty servants and one 'extra', the daily quantity of meat eaten per head had been 1 lb 12½ oz. By July of that year the figure had been cut a little to 1 lb 9 oz, but although Sir John continued to keep a check on the meat supplied during the 1890s, his efforts produced no substantial economies. (As a matter of interest, it has been estimated that the average *weekly* consumption per head of meat in middle-class families during the 1890s was 3·2 lb. So Sir John's servants were faring a great deal better than most of their working- and middle-class compatriots.[5])

The leisure time allocated to servants in the most generous households, even at the end of the century, was normally restricted to a fortnight's holiday each year, plus a half day every Sunday, one day off per month and an evening out weekly.[6] Many fared far worse than this. Thus *Beeton's Domestic Service*

Guide suggested that while in the country 'it [was] customary for servants to have a week allowed them once a year', they should expect no other holidays—although it considered that few people would deny 'a day to an industrious willing servant. In London no yearly holiday is granted; but every six weeks or so a whole day is allowed.'⁷ Nevertheless, many workers would also manage to snatch a little free time to themselves during each day when they could sew or knit or read, even if they were not allowed to leave the house. Of course, this was a penalty in itself when the weather was warm and sunny. In the largest establishments there would often be a comfortable sitting-room provided, perhaps fitted out with a piano. William Lanceley, who served as steward in the household of the Duchess of Connaught, remembered that the Duchess, who was fond of music, installed a piano in the servants' hall. 'It was much appreciated, and in a very short time even the new-comers could play very well. A few took music lessons and these helped the others in their first attempts. There are always good singers to be found in large or small houses, and every one knows that singing with music makes all the difference to a happy evening.'⁸

But most households lacked such refinements, and the maids would have to spend their spare time in the uninviting atmosphere of a basement kitchen. Furniture was usually minimal—a large kitchen table, a few wooden chairs, a dresser, in the drawers of which they might keep their books, needlework or knitting, and perhaps a few basket chairs with cushions for them to relax in. Mrs Panton, in *From Kitchen to Garret*, advised against installing carpets 'in any room where servants live and move and have their being', presumably because although they spent so much time in keeping clean their employer's floor coverings they could not be relied upon to do the same for their own. As a compromise coconut matting or a couple of 'strong Kurd rugs' might be put on the floor of the servants' hall, and, if the servants were responsible and trustworthy, 'an old sofa or a comfortable arm-chair or two' might be installed 'in which they can rest when work is over; but if the servants are young, heedless, or have not lived any time in the establishment, these little additions to their comfort are not necessary'.

In the cramped and spartan conditions, relations between the servants could become strained. There was no way in which they could escape from one another's company. In most households the maids would even have to share their attic bedrooms, although the more senior members of staff had rooms of their own. The frustrations that built up, especially among members of a small staff, are revealed in Hannah Cullwick's diaries. For example, on 1 January 1870 when she had been employed as a general servant in the Henderson household at Gloucester Crescent, London, for about eighteen months, along with Walter, the young single-handed man-servant, and Emily, the housemaid, she wrote : 'i could wish my fellow servants was nicer.' And on 5 January she described why her relations with Walter, at least, were not happier :

> [Walter] & me is not such good friends as we was—he is so rude—swears so i canna bide it. . . . i give up my wrestling bouts for i used to get him down & lay him with his back on the floor, though he's 20 years old & strong—that was only for a game, in the kitchen, but W. was so mad at been master'd by *me* i suppose that he hit me hard, so i said i would never romp with him any more. And Emily, he often kisses her & she's so smart & fine about her work, wears *gloves* to clean grates in, & spends her wages mostly in dressing fine o Sundays, so she despises me wi my old things.

But there were happier times as well. On 7 April Hannah noted that after the midday dinner 'we servants sat a bit, as we do generally if we're not busy—i have ten minutes sleep by the screen & Emily & Walter read at the tales in their weekly papers.'

Hannah's wrestling bouts with Walter were not the first time she had joked in this way with one of her fellow-servants. In 1868, when she was employed briefly as a cook at the Saunders household in Norfolk Square, she had teased the footman, Gower, by saying that she was sure she could 'carry him easy, & before the housemaid & Ann i lifted him & carried him round the kitchen table'. By so doing she aroused his enmity and eventually he revealed to Mr Saunders that she was corresponding with Arthur Munby, the barrister whom she secretly married five years later. Although Hannah was able to persuade her employer that she had committed no wrong, she was still forced to leave.[9]

Male servants often had more liberty than female, partly

because they were frequently sent out on messages and could loiter on the way there and back, and partly because it was common in many households for them to go out for an hour or so in the morning when they had finished their work. Lady Violet Greville considered that they spent too much time in public houses or in one of the many servants' clubs which were established in London. 'Clubs are an immense institution and a great resort of servants. They are of all sorts, from those as exclusive as the Marlborough or Arthur's to others bristling with as many secret rules and regulations as the Freemasons' brotherhood are popularly supposed to enjoy.'[10]

Lady Violet Greville's account was written in the early 1890s, but as early as the 1830s the leisurely lifestyle of a servant such as William Tayler corresponded closely to her description. For example, on 4 February 1837 he wrote : 'I took a walk this morning, drew a picture this afternoon of my going home and alarming my friends. Have been out this evening and had my screens raffeled for. Got just about as much for them as they cost me therefore I had all my labour for nothing. Fire screen makeing will not do.' Similarly on 9 February he 'took a long walk. . . . Began drawing a paire of pictures for an old lady who has been bothering me for some a long time. Played at whist this evening; won a penny. Went to bed at eleven with a very bad head ache.' Sometimes Tayler stayed out so long that his fellow-servants 'grumbled very much because I left them to answer all the doors and bells'. But this certainly did not deter him from following his accustomed social round—or from paying secret visits to his wife and family, who were lodged comfortably nearby.

Occasionally the monotony of life 'below stairs' was relieved by visitors. Some employers made it a rule that their servants were not to have visitors of their own, but in most cases callers continued to come to the household either clandestinely, when the master or mistress was out, or openly, if they were duly authorised. William Tayler, for one, entertained many friends at the expense of the Prinseps—as on 11 January 1837, when the family were in bed with influenza and he acted as host to a relative, John Tayler, a shoemaker from Turnham Green. John arrived in the morning and stayed to lunch, dinner and tea. After his departure two more people came to the house. Two days earlier William had entertained his 'Aunt Puzey' to tea.

Sometimes the entertainment developed into a real party. In December 1837, when the Prinsep servants organised their 'muffin feasts', friends were invited to share in the fun, while on 27 December William went out to a party given 'by some servants. There was card playing, fiddleing and danceing and some singing, plenty to eat and drink.'

Hannah Cullwick and her fellow-domestics at the Hendersons also organised surreptitious celebrations from time to time. On 4 January 1872, for example, a birthday party was held in honour of Emily, the housemaid, and Hannah wrote :

> we bought some crumpets, & every thing extra as we wanted. Ellen [Hannah's sister] came in & Walter to tea & Mr & Mrs Shiach after—the parlourmaid from next door after she'd clear'd the dinner, & then we had oranges & nuts and port wine—all drinking her health, and the [music] box was at play every now and then, but we had to be quiet so as we wasn't heard up stairs. . . . i got the supper at 9—E. paid for a lobster salad & that with our usual bread & cheese was enough & i paid for the extra beer—we all enjoy'd ourselves & sung what songs we knowd. . . . We was order'd to prayers afore ten, so our company had to sit very quiet till we came down again— then i got the parlour supper—clear'd ours and got up to bed by 11.[11]

Occasionally the servants would be invited to watch (though not to take part in) the fun at parties held by their employers, especially at Christmas time. Thus in 1863, when Hannah was working as a maid-of-all-work for Mr Foster, a Kilburn beer merchant, she and the hired waiters were invited upstairs after the Christmas Eve dinner to see 'the acting in the other room' and to listen to the singing. After supper was over 'the Master had the hot mince pie up wi a ring & sixpence in it. They had good fun over it, cause Mr Grant got the ring & a young lady the sixpence. We had no fun down stairs, all was very busy till 4 o'clock & then to bed.' But at least the kitchen was decorated with greenery, and when Mrs Foster came down on Boxing Day to pay Hannah her wages, she noticed the mistletoe hanging up. But Hannah was able to assure her that 'ther'd bin no one kiss'd yet'. She also received small Christmas boxes not only from the Foster family but from regular visitors to the house and from tradespeople with whom the Fosters dealt. In all, she collected £2 in 1863, including 14s. 2d. from four of the household's regular guests.[12]

Other servants had rather less happy memories of their Christmas gifts. Mrs N. Parkin, who entered service at the age of fourteen for a wage of 5s. per week, remembered her excitement when on Christmas Day her mistress rang for her to fetch her present 'from the huge festive tree which stood in the lounge. I shall never forget my feelings as I rushed back to the kitchen and, with trembling fingers, undid the glittering string and gay paper wrapping containing my gift . . . two working aprons!'[13] And as late as 1925, a young kitchenmaid, Jean Rennie, recalled her bitter disappointment when the 'dress length' she had received from her mistress turned out to be 'of that god-awful pink cotton—a length sufficient to make a morning dress—for work. . . . I never made it up and I never wore it.'[14]

As might be expected, Christmas arrangements in the largest houses were more lavish. The Marchioness of Bath has described how at Longleat every Christmas there was a grand servants' ball given in the dining-room, to which the local tradesmen who served the house were also invited. The custom was for the Marquis of Bath to open the ball with the housekeeper, while the Marchioness danced with the house steward. The Lancers was always the second dance. 'When I first came to Longleat, as the wife of the son of the house, I was partnered in the first dance by the butler, and in the Lancers by the head groom, a charming bandy-legged little gnome who steered me through the figures of the dance with skill and command.'

On Christmas morning itself all of the under-maids came to see Lady Bath, and each received the traditional gift of a dress. That night, however severe the weather, the maids went out to dance in the courtyard. They would bob around in their thin dresses on the rough paving stones 'while the gentry watched them from the windows above'. Carol singers came from Horningsham and accompanied themselves on hand-bells, while a troop of mummers performed one of the local Christmas plays.

At Carden Park, too, Frederick Gorst recalled that he and the other servants were presented with a gold sovereign before they sat down to a large Christmas dinner in the servants' hall, which had been specially decorated for the occasion. Dinner was served at four long tables and wooden benches, and it started with a hog's head stuffed with sausage meat and *pâté de foie gras*, and with a shiny red apple in its mouth. Next came cold meats and joints of beef with Yorkshire pudding, and the meal ended with plum pudding flaming with brandy. The feast lasted for most of the afternoon, and by the time everyone had left the servants' hall 'Mr Ling [the butler] and I were almost too tired to serve Christmas dinner for the family and their guests'.

At Welbeck Abbey the celebrations were still grander. Each of the footmen received a five-pound note as a Christmas box, while the servants' ball was held after Christmas, on Twelfth Night. An orchestra from London was engaged and a swarm of fifty waiters arrived so as to free the servants from their duties. It was *their* social event. In all, about twelve hundred guests attended, including the staff, estate tenants and their families, and tradesmen from Worksop and their wives. Frederick Gorst remembered the gaiety and excitement. 'Even the prim head housemaid looked quite chic in a velvet gown, and the head housekeeper, who wore a low-cut blue satin gown, was almost unrecognisable without her stiff black silk dress and her belt of jangling keys.' Champagne was consumed in unlimited quantities, and the dancing and jollifications lasted into the small hours.

In many of the great houses there were also regular weekly junketings organised for the servants. At Longleat dances were held twice a week, on Tuesdays and Thursdays, in the servants' hall. A pianist was engaged from the neighbouring town of Warminister, and a buffet supper was produced by the kitchen and stillroom staff. The outdoor servants attended, too, but the housekeeper kept a careful eye on the younger maids to make sure that they did not behave too frivolously with the unmarried grooms and gardeners.

Nevertheless, stricter employers had doubts about the propriety of parties of any kind; or else, like the disillusioned 'Practical Mistress of a Household', whose pamphlet, *Domestic Servants, As They Are and As They Ought to Be*, appeared in 1859, they considered that care must be exercised to control the celebrations which were permitted.

A day should be selected when the gentlemen of the family are

14 *A Warwickshire hiring fair, 1872.* Some of the girls standing in the foreground are probably maidservants waiting to be hired.

15/16 Domestic servants, their attitudes and habits, were the constant butt of jokes in *Punch* and other humorous publications of the Victorian period. The two illustrations on this page are taken from the Mayhew brothers' novel *The Greatest Plague of Life* (1847). *Left*: 'Oh, ah! Let 'em ring again!' *Right*: The 'scarlet fever'.—'It's my cousin, M'am!' (Maidservants were not permitted unauthorised 'followers').

likely to be absent. The servants should receive permission to invite a limited number of friends, one or two each (according to the size of the establishment . . .). No male guests should be admitted excepting relatives, viz. fathers and brothers, or *authorised* suitors. The company should meet at an early hour, say four or five and separate at ten. The mistress of the family and her female relatives should take an interest in the whole affair, providing suitable amusements which may afford rational enjoyment. The assistance of the cook might be enlisted beforehand to provide a good substantial cake, which with the addition of a few oranges, apples and nuts, and a little British wine, would form a feast at once wholesome and satisfactory. The servants would no doubt cheerfully 'club' together to provide their *tea*, if it did not suit the ideas of the family to supply it, but the whole thing would cost but a trifle, and it is better to do it well. The entertainment might terminate with an hour's dance, if there should be no objection to engage a musician for that purpose.[15]

Despite the author's assurance that the mistress would not wish 'to interfere with' the pleasure of the servants, it is difficult to imagine a really happy party being conducted under these conditions.

Fear of misconduct by the women servants or anxiety that 'undesirable' friendships might be formed lay behind most of the restrictions imposed on their actions. Nevertheless, where servants of both sexes were employed in the same household, misconduct could occur without outsiders being involved. Caroline Clive, wife of the rector of Solihull, noted in her diary, with obvious shock, the birth of an illegitimate child to Betsey, the under-nurse, early in October 1847. 'She so pinched herself in as not to be discovered by us up to the moment of her confession, nor long before by anybody else. The baby was healthy and fat. James, our late footman, is the father.'

Yet perhaps one of the most blatant cases of this kind involved Inkley, who was from 1859 butler to the Charlton family of Hesleyside, Northumberland. He led a number of the women servants astray, but because it was difficult 'to get a sober and efficient butler in such a house for drink as Hesleyside' his employers turned a blind eye to his activities—merely dismissing the

H

women who were the unfortunate victims of his attentions. Mrs
Charlton later discovered that the laundry was another centre of
misconduct.

> It was not in fact till the winter of 1893, when I went down to
> Brighton on the sad occasion of my eldest son's last illness, that
> I really got to know the truth. For he talked much of the olden
> days at Hesleyside when he was but a boy . . . and of the
> scandals in the laundry which, according to him, was nothing
> but a brothel. . . . He gave the names of some of the upper
> servants as among the most licentious, women of whom I had
> no suspicion, believing them to lead blameless lives. It horrified
> me, so long ago as that, to hear about the scenes of profligacy
> he himself had witnessed as he passed the laundry to and fro
> at odd times of the day; and I had no doubt, although he did
> not say so, that he was similarly *au fait* at the indoor servants'
> amours in the [butler's] pantry.[16]

On one occasion, indeed, the jealousy nurtured in the confined
atmosphere 'below stairs' in a small household led to a charge of
manslaughter. In October 1829 Thomas Churchyard, footman in
the family of a Mr Rodwell of Ipswich, was charged with stab-
bing Elizabeth Squirrell, a thirty-three-year-old housemaid in the
same household (and already the mother of an illegitimate child).
Although Churchyard was found not guilty, the account he gave
of life among the servants in the Rodwell household provides an
interesting insight into relationships there. 'He and the deceased
had been in service together for three years, and of late she had
appeared greatly interested in him, and she at times indulged in
violent words and in abuse of his wife, and wished to make a
breach between them.' On the Sunday before her death he had
returned from church and had found her in tears. Soon a quarrel
developed between them over his wife. High words were ex-
changed, and when he called her a whore she came rushing at
him with a knife in her hand. In self-defence he picked up several
knives and threw them at her feet, 'without any intention of
injuring her and solely with the intention of frightening her out
of his pantry'. She left but returned in about three minutes, saying that she had been stabbed. Her condition rapidly deteriorated,
and some hours later the doctor was called, but he was unable to
save her. After lingering for just over twenty-four hours, she died

just after midnight on the following Tuesday. A post-mortem examination revealed a knife buried deep in her body, but as there was a strong suspicion that the injury had been self-inflicted, Churchyard escaped punishment.

It was, of course, only in a tiny minority of cases that tragedies of this kind occurred. For the majority of servants the main problem was not quarrelling with colleagues but rather overcoming feelings of loneliness and isolation. These emotions were touchingly expressed by Ruth Barrow, a young Leicester maid-of-all-work, in a letter to her future husband, written on 23 February 1848 : 'I am allmost ashamed to say it, that I feel very dull and I cannot away with it at all. . . . It is such a great chaing, a chaing that can only be felt by those who have felt what it is to leave all they hold dear, and have sought a home amongst straingers . . . but let us still trust in the Lord and make no arm of flesh our trust.'[17]

Among the worst affected by the isolation of a single-handed place were those young general servants who had been accustomed to living in the rough-and-tumble of a large family at home and who were 'frightened by the loneliness of the long evenings in which they [had] to sit in the kitchen by themselves, or perhaps be left entirely alone in the house'. One girl, who went as a maid-of-all-work to an elderly mother and her daughter in London when she was nearly seventeen, later admitted that she had wondered how long she could remain

> in such a quiet place with no one to speak to except when my mistress gave an order. I felt like a prisoner. Evening dinner was at six o'clock, after which I had nothing to do. I began to feel I must run out of the place and I really believe I should have done so, but just when I felt I could stand the loneliness no longer, my mistress came and asked me if I would like a run out for half an hour as she thought I must feel dull with no one to speak to. I very gladly accepted. It was then 7 o'clock and I was sure to be in by 9 o'clock. . . . All the time I was in that place I was always in to time; in fact it became a recognised thing for me to be in the road when the church clock struck nine.[18]

This girl's employer tried to make her leisure hours more rewarding by encouraging her to read and improve her general education. 'I used to write and my mistress would correct the mistakes in spelling and grammar.' Similar plans for self-improvement were adopted by other mistresses, notably the Countess of Aberdeen, who for a number of years organised the Haddo House Young Women's Improvement Association for girls in service in twenty-four parishes in Aberdeenshire. The scheme was started in the early 1880s, with an annual membership subscription fixed at one shilling. From quite early on classes were organised in singing, wood-carving, drawing and reading, while social evenings were held either weekly or fortnightly. The members were also expected to work at home, and in her address at the annual prize-giving in August 1883, Lady Aberdeen praised the girls for their perseverance:

> It must require some earnestness to sit down when your regular work is done, and when you are probably tired and sleepy, to hunt out the answers to the questions, and to write them down neatly and correctly. . . . People are often afraid that education will prevent girls being good housewives and good servants. If it does, it is the wrong sort of education, for a girl who has been rightly educated . . . will always be the better for it whatever station of life she may be, for she will have been taught to think how to do everything she does as well as possible.[19]

In March 1892 the Countess wrote an article on the subject of 'Household Clubs' in the journal *Nineteenth Century*. In this she called for the experiment to be applied on a wider basis: 'Household Clubs may or may not be one help towards the solution of the problem of how to raise the calling of domestic service to its proper level, but at least they are worth a trial.' Few employers heeded her call, but many did at least provide a kitchen library for their servants or allowed them to borrow books from their own libraries.

On a larger scale, the Girls' Friendly Society, established in 1874, also sought to 'meet needs of *body, soul* and *mind*' of young workers. It was a Church of England organisation, and although its prime concern was with the moral well-being of the girls, it also provided social activities, established at diocesan, ruridecanal and parochial level. Thus in 1877 it was reported that at Dorchester in Dorset a sewing class was held each Friday, with members supplied with material at half-price and taught how to cut out their own garments. At Leamington Spa Bible classes were organised, and it was intended to open a reading-room in the near future. Within ten years of its formation, the Society had a membership of over 100,000, and although it was open to working girls of all kinds, well over half of its support came from domestic servants.[20]

Some girls found warmth and companionship in the membership of chapels or churches which they attended on Sundays. Mrs Lansom of Portland, a former maid-of-all-work, recalled how she joined a young women's Bible class at a Baptist church in the town and made many friends. On Monday evenings she also joined 'Christian Endeavour . . . and became an active member. Later I felt the call to become a Sunday school teacher. No one will ever know the joy I experienced in that community. . . . Had it not been for that fellowship I would never have been able to stand the strain of the "daily round, the common task".' She recalled, too, that no one ever looked down upon her 'lowly estate, though the whole church must have been aware that by "profession" I was a maid-of-all-work'.

Of course, the most valued part of a servant's leisure time were the hours she was able to spend away from her employer's house, either on her afternoon or evening off or during the precious one or two weeks' annual holiday she might secure. But even this was not without its restrictions. Before the girls left the house for their hours off it was common for mistresses to inspect them to make sure that they were quietly and suitably dressed. Most would also try, by advice and exhortation, to ensure that they did not get into bad company while they were away. In this they were supported by such household handbooks as *The Master and Mistress*, issued by the Religious Tract Society in 1842. This warned servants against a 'love of *pleasure*', for in the opinion of the anonymous author, a 'desire to visit fairs, races, theatres, tea-gardens, and similar scenes of low amusement, where they are thrown into bad society, and see and hear things by which their abhorrence of vice is weakened' could prove the first step on the road to ruin. Many girls were prepared to take the 'risk' for the sake of a few hours' pleasure. But others meekly spent their spare time visiting relatives or looking around the shops, in company with a fellow-servant whom they knew.

For those fortunate enough to have a week or a fortnight's

holiday which they could spend at home, this was the high point of the year. And for their family, too, it was a time for general rejoicing. There are entries in school log-books, as at Brailes in Warwickshire, showing that younger children were kept at home in order to be ready to greet brothers and sisters who were returning 'from service' for the holidays.

At Juniper Hill in North Oxfordshire Flora Thompson remembered the generosity that the girls displayed towards their families when they did come home. 'It was said in the hamlet that some of them stripped themselves to help those at home.' And one girl whom Flora knew did this literally. She came for her holidays in her new best frock—a pale grey cashmere with white lace collar and cuffs—and it was much admired in the hamlet. But when she returned to work at the end of a fortnight, she left the dress behind for her younger sister. As she told Flora, her sister had hardly anything to wear 'and it don't matter what I wear when I'm away. There's nobody I care about to see it,' and she went back in her second-best navy serge, while her sister proudly wore the pale grey to church the next Sunday. Many girls managed to give cash to their families, despite their scanty wages.

Flora Thompson also described how a number of girls were engaged to local youths and 'after several years of courtship, mostly conducted by letter, for they seldom met except during the girl's summer holiday, they would marry and settle in or near the hamlet'. But others married and settled away. Butchers and milkmen were favoured as husbands, perhaps because they were frequent callers at the houses where the girls were employed.' Yet such friendships had usually to be struck up secretly, for either the mistress, or, in grander establishments, the housekeeper would intervene to enforce the restriction 'no followers' if relations became too obvious before a formal engagement was announced. That was one of the penalties of being 'in service' and those who transgressed risked immediate dismissal.[21]

7

Employer-Servant Relations

In every household there must be the hands to do the work, the
head to guide and to control the workers.

MRS HENRY REEVE, 'Mistresses and Maids',
Longman's Magazine (1893).

A strict mistress is not necessarily a harsh one, and for the sake of
others as well as herself she should insist upon the daily duties of
each servant being faithfully and punctually performed. Every
mistress should know for herself how long it takes for each household task, and it is then easy to see whether or not time has been
wasted. It would be a good plan for both mistresses and servants
to reckon up the work to be done on each day (allowing a little
margin for interruptions and incidental tasks) and put it against
the time at their disposal for the purpose of the same, and it
would be at once seen whether they might consider that there was
too much or too little work to be done during the day.

MRS I. BEETON, *Book of Household Management* (1888).

THE evolution of domestic service from a system based upon
status to one based almost entirely on contract has been going on
slowly since Tudor times. In nineteenth-century England that
process was certainly not complete and the relation of servant to
employer was still that of subordinate towards superior. Yet within this framework, day-to-day contacts depended very much on
the character of the individuals concerned. Some mistresses were
kind and considerate to their employees; others were harsh. But
for many it was the nature of each of the personalities involved
which determined the nature of the relationship. Thus Jane
Carlyle enjoyed the warmest links with one of her small maids-
of-all-work, Charlotte Southam, and several years after the girl
had left, wrote to her : 'No servant has ever been for me the sort
of *adopted child* that *you* were.' Yet things were very different

with one of Charlotte's successors, 'little Flo', whom Jane first welcomed as 'a remarkably intelligent, well-conditioned girl between fourteen and fifteen', but who was dismissed under a cloud a few months later for slander and lying : 'an incomparable small demon', Jane called her.

Nevertheless, despite these personality differences—which were reflected in the experience of other mistresses and servants—it was a matter of continuing concern to the employing classes of Victorian England to inculcate the correct attitudes of obedience and subservience into their domestic staff. This was a question to which many contemporary writers turned their attention, including the pseudonymous author of *The Servant's Behaviour Book*. She stressed the finer points to be observed. A maid must always get to her feet when 'a lady or gentleman' entered the room in which she was working; if she met her employer or one of his visitors on the stairs, she must either retreat to the landing, so as 'to give room' or else stand to one side. In speaking to her 'betters' she was exhorted to keep her voice low and respectful, and never to reply without saying, ' "Sir", "Ma'am", or "Miss", as the case may be'. Tact was essential : 'Every girl who wishes to live in a gentleman's family must learn, sooner or later, to keep guard over her tongue.' Similarly, *A Few Rules for the Manners of Servants in Good Families*, issued by the Ladies' Sanitary Association in 1901, contained over twenty pages of 'Do's and Don'ts'. Among the suggestions listed were :

> Always stand still and keep your hands quiet when speaking to a lady or being spoken to; and look at the person speaking to you.
>
> Never begin to talk to the ladies or gentlemen, unless it be to deliver a message or ask a necessary question, and then do it in as few words as possible.
>
> Always speak of the children of the family as 'Master'— 'Miss'.
>
> Dropped handkerchiefs, or spectacles, or such small things, should be handed on a salver if possible.
>
> Should you be required to walk with a lady or gentleman, in order to carry a parcel, or otherwise, always keep a few paces behind.[1]

Some writers pointed to the need for the servant to accept his or her station in life without complaint, because the social order had been divinely ordained. The author of *Advice to Young Women on Going to Service* (issued in 1835 by the Society for Promoting Christian Knowledge) noted: 'Had [God] seen that it would have been better for your external good that you should be great and rich He would have made you so; but He gives to all the places and duties best fitted for them.' The anonymous writer of an address to the girls of the servants' training-house in Townsend Street, London, took a similar line: 'Pray that He may teach you to be humble and lowly as Christ's servants should be. . . . Remember, that whatever your situation be, housemaid, or through-servant, or nursemaid, your mistress will expect you to obey her orders. The first and chief of your duties is, *to do what you are desired to do.*'[2] Even the *Servants' Magazine*, a journal founded in 1837 ostensibly to cater for the reading interests of domestic staff, and published by the Female Aid Society, largely confined itself to finding divine justification for the maintenance of the social status quo. Typical of its approach was an article entitled 'A Few Kind Words to Servants', printed early in 1849, in which the writer exhorted her readers to be content with their lot: 'When you think of the improved condition and privileges of servants now-a-days, ought you not to feel contented, and deeply grateful to God who has thus provided for you?' This magazine was still in circulation in the 1860s— though whether the maids for whom it was intended welcomed it as warmly as its publishers hoped is open to question.

Under the influence of these strictures it was all too easy for servants to be regarded as members of a separate race of people, whose only contact with their superiors was through their daily chores. Or as Edward Salmon expressed it, in an article in the *Fortnightly Review* of 1888, 'Beyond the paying of wages or the performance of duties the barrier between the drawing-room and the servants' hall is never passed. Life above stairs is as entirely severed from life below stairs as is the life of one house from another.' This division was underlined by the layout of many houses, with the back stairs, uncarpeted and unlit, giving the servants access to the attic bedrooms in which they slept and the basement in which they spent most of their working hours. These two worlds under the one roof were separated by a door, on one side of which was white paint and a crystal knob and on the other a green baize cover and a plain gunmetal knob.

The social distinctions were neatly summed up in the popular Victorian precept: 'Servants talk about People; Gentlefolk discuss Things.' It is not surprising that even the least vindictive of domestics could feel resentment when brought face to face with the crushing of their human dignity which this approach represented.

One such was Hannah Cullwick, and in an account of her life during the year 1864, she recalled the six months she spent as a maid-of-all-work at Miss Knight's lodging-house at Margate:

> i often thought of myself and them, all the ladies sitting up stairs & talking & sewing & playing games & pleasing theirselves, all so small & delicate. . . . it seems like been a different kind o creature to them, but it's always so with ladies & servants & of course there *is* a difference cause their bringing up is so different—servants may feel it sharply & do sometimes i believe, but it's best not to be delicate, nor mind what work we do so [long as] it's honest. . . . But how often poor servants have to hear the scorn & harsh words & proud looks from them above her which to my mind is very wicked & unkind & certainly most disheartening to a young wench.[3]

In another account of this period of her life, Hannah also described her encounter with one of the guests who 'stood over me as i knelt & was crawling over the floor . . . & instead of showing me . . . with her hand she kick'd me with her foot & pointed. i dare say she thought i shd. feel hurt & vex'd with her but i didn't—i was glad that she thought me humble enough to take it without kicking again.'[4]

It was all part of the same social attitude that servants were warned under no circumstances to 'offer any opinion' to their master and mistress, 'nor even to say "good night" or "good morning", except in reply to that salutation'. Although in many households such rigidities were, happily, ignored and servants were treated as 'one of the family', in other instances they could be regarded, and spoken of, as children by their employers. Typical of this viewpoint was the comment of one unsympathetic employer: 'Servants—as well as children—require to be managed with *kindness* and *firmness*. The greatest "kindness" we can exercise towards them is to endeavour, by a mild rein, to keep

them in the path of duty.'⁵ Barbara Charlton, wife of a Northumberland squire, took a similar line, declaring, 'Servants [are]
like children. . . . [They] have the same distorted sense of fair
play, and a marvellous faculty of secretiveness. They know of all
the wrong things that go on in a household but, otherwise than on
rare occasions vaguely hinting, speak they will not.'

Sometimes, too, even the kindliest of employers thought nothing of changing their servants' names arbitrarily, if they happened
to clash with those of 'the family', while other mistresses gave the
same name to successive holders of a particular position, whatever
their real names might be. One girl from Griston in Norfolk
remembered that her grandmother always christened her housemaid 'Emma', irrespective of the girl's real name.

The law reinforced the subordinate status of the servant,
notably in 1845 in the case *Turner v. Mason.* In this, it was
established as 'a master's province to regulate the conduct of his
domestic servant', and so powerful was that right held to be that
not even a moral duty could justify a servant's disobedience. Ann
Turner, a maid whose mother had suffered a seizure and was
believed likely to die, was refused permission by her employer to
visit the old lady. Notwithstanding this, Ann absented herself and
was immediately dismissed. In the subsequent court case her
employer's action was upheld, as it was considered doubtful
'whether any service to be rendered to any other person than the
master would suffice as an excuse for defying a master's lawful
command'. This decision has remained the basic expression of
subsequent legal opinion on the subject.

Nor did an employer's regulation of his servant's activities stop
with the mere performance of daily duties. Control was, for
example, exercised over dress, both inside and outside the home.
Sometimes, in the case of liveried servants, this meant the provision of suitable clothing by the employer. But female servants
were usually expected to find their own clothes—lilac, blue or pink
cotton working-dresses with white aprons and caps for the mornings, and in the afternoons, at least for housemaids and parlour-
maids, a formal black dress, worn with frilled apron and cap. For
best occasions important people like housekeepers and head nurses
wore black silk dresses. Jewellery was not permitted, and those
who wished to follow the extremes of fashion were firmly re-
strained. During the craze for crinolines, for example, it was quite

common for advertisers for servants to specify 'no crinolines', while Louisa Bain, wife of a London bookseller, recorded disapprovingly in her diary for November 1865, that her new housemaid had 'a large crinoline that almost sweeps one into the ashes. Have suggested to her that it is too large for our small rooms and hope she will reform it, but I fancy people with such crisp, wavy hair as she has are generally obstinate.'

There is little doubt that many girls resented this interference. And when a short-lived trade union was formed among the maidservants of Dundee in April 1872 one of their grievances proved to be the custom in that part of Scotland of demanding that maids wear a large 'fern-shaped headdress' known as the 'flag'. The wearing of the headdress was regarded as a degrading mark of servitude. (However, perhaps more significantly, the union also demanded a weekly half-holiday, one free Sunday every fortnight, and the payment of wages every quarter instead of every six months.) But either through fear of offending employers or through indifference, few girls joined the organisation, and its impact was negligible. By June it had disappeared and *The Times* was able to report complacently : 'The terrors which this movement have inspired may now be shaken off, and the maids of Dundee like many other personages who have created unnecessary commotion are likely soon to suffer a total eclipse.'[6]

But if employers' regulation of dress was disliked by some workers, an equally sore point with others was interference in their religious beliefs. Not only did advertisements of vacancies often specify that applicants must be of a particular denomination but sometimes even when the servants were installed, employers would try to influence their attitude to religion. This was particularly the case where the servant belonged to a different denomination from that of the family he or she served. Henry Mayhew mentions one such case when describing an interview with a Roman Catholic Irish street seller who had once been a domestic servant. She had abandoned service partly because of ill-health and partly because towards the end of her career she had been employed by a family of Methodists who had continually pressed her to go to a chapel. They 'was always running down my religion, and did all they could to hinder my ever going to Mass. They would hardly pay me when I left, because I wouldn't listen to them, they said.'[7]

In this pursuit of religious conformity within the household, it was customary for employers to hold morning or evening prayers (and sometimes both) for members of the family and servants. Attendance was compulsory. Indeed, even at the beginning of the present century, Miss Sharpe of Sandown, Isle of Wight, remembers that in her family it was the practice after tea on Sundays for the whole household to meet in the drawing-room, 'the maids in their afternoon uniform, sitting side by side on a couch, joining in the hymn singing. The gardener was also resident and he would join in, wearing Father's cast-off city clothes.'[8]

On Sundays, too, attendance at church or, in Nonconformist families, chapel, was often obligatory. In the larger households the servants usually went to church in a group and were seated in the pews in order of precedence, according to their status in the household. Concern for social distinctions meant that in many churches servants were relegated to the back pews or the gallery, away from the rest of the congregation. As early as 1846, a reader of *The Times* had deplored the fact that at Rawstone Street Chapel, Brompton, servants in livery were relegated to the back seats of the gallery, 'an extraordinary arrangement which would necessarily exclude all wearers of livery coats from partaking in Holy Communion'. *Punch*, commenting on the situation, suggested that the sign 'Livery servants and Dogs not admitted', which used to hang over the gates of Kensington Gardens, ought to be set up outside the Brompton Chapel.

Within the home itself, this treatment of servants as second-class citizens often extended to their sleeping-quarters as well. These normally fell well below the standard provided for the rest of the house. Mistresses found it convenient to follow the advice of Mrs J. E. Panton, who recommended that although servants should as far as possible be given a separate bed, in other respects their rooms were to be furnished as simply as possible. She declared that while she would like 'to give each maid a really pretty room', she considered it useless to do so, as no sooner was 'the room put nice than something happens to destroy the beauty, and I really believe servants are only happy if their rooms are allowed in some measure to resemble the home of their youth, and to be merely places where they lie down to sleep as heavily as they can'. In houses where more than one servant was kept, it was common for the younger girls to share a room, usually in the attic, a position which was bitterly cold in winter and 'boiling hot' in summer. Sometimes the bedroom would also contain a bell which connected with the mistress's room and which she would ring early in the morning to make sure that the girls did not over-sleep. And at least one mid-Victorian employer had a glass plate inserted in the door of the maids' bedroom so that she could check whether they were wasting a candle by reading in bed. In other cases, where there was only one maid, her room might serve as part storeroom and part bedroom. At a small country house in Herefordshire, for example, the young maid slept in 'a minute bedroom half-filled already with sheer clutter'. Here she had 'the use of two drawers of a huge chest-of-drawers, a tiny mirror on the wall, and a jug and basin on the chest. No bath . . . naturally enough when water had to be carried from outside and up very steep stairs.'[9]

Servants with initiative and character could always respond to inconsiderate treatment either by moving elsewhere, or else, like the fiery Scots maid, Isabella, who was employed by the Carlyles at Cheyne Row in 1846, they could react with defiance and ill-temper. Isabella left after about two weeks, declaring that 'no one woman living' could do the work expected of her and that she would 'never slave [herself] for anybody's pleasure'. Similarly, in Kent the Hall sisters ran into difficulty with their new servant, Eliza Parrott, when she refused to help the housemaid 'as she had engaged to do'. After a brief altercation she gave notice, leaving after a few days and claiming a complete month's wages. Emily Hall refused to pay, whereupon Eliza said she would 'get the lor', and she did. In the subsequent case at Bromley County Court, Eliza's claim was successful. She obtained her month's wages and expenses, to the great disgust of her erstwhile employers.[10]

Cartoons in *Punch* reflect this attitude, especially towards the end of the century, when the servant shortage had further em-boldened the would-be disruptive employee. In its issue of 18 September 1875, for example, *Punch* has a sketch of a family sitting at the breakfast table, with a diminutive page standing before them. The boy is saying: 'Please, 'M, Cook wished me to say when Master'll be done with the *Times*—as she's a waitin' for it!'

The subject of servant independence was also satirised by the Mayhew brothers in their book, *The Greatest Plague of Life: or*

The Adventures of a Lady in Search of a Good Servant by One Who Has Been Almost Worried to Death, which was published in 1847. Typical of their approach is a sketch showing the cook, housemaid, footman and page all sitting comfortably before the fire, with the drawing-room bell ringing agitatedly for attention. Below is the caption 'Oh ah! Let 'em ring again!' (See Plate 15.)

Men-servants were regarded as the greatest villains in this particular employer-servant struggle. The diary of William Tayler, footman, for 1837 indicates that he at least was able to hold up his end in the battle. Thus on 19 May came the entry: 'Been out with the carriage this afternoon with Miss P[rinsep]. She kept me out longer than I thought she aught to of done, therefore I gave her a little row for it. I hope it will do her good. I served the old lady the same way the other day and it did her a good deal of good.'

Like all Victorian footmen, especially in the early part of the Queen's reign, William was always ready to receive vails (see page 10). On 12 January he noted that Mrs Prinsep's son-in-law had called: 'He gave me a sovering for a Christmas box. For which I was greatly obliged to him for, but it's no more than he ought to do as they very frequently dine here.' Similarly, on 26 April he noted that he had got up early to go with the coach 'with a Lady who was going in the country. She gave me half-a-crown and little enough.' In all, Tayler reckoned that he earned between ten and fifteen pounds per annum in this way, but, as he complained in an entry of 4 December, the sum was likely to be nearer the lower amount than the higher 'as service is getting very bad business'.

Although the custom of expecting tips had weakened by the end of the century it had certainly not disappeared. An entry in the Harcourt family accounts for 3 March 1890, for example, shows a payment of 2s. 6d. to 'Castle's man', and there are several similar entries in the accounts. In fact, just before the First World War, Frederick Gorst recalled the contempt with which one of the Duke of Portland's servants greeted a proposed tip of 6d. for sending a telegram: ' "I couldn't possibly accept this," Hales said, drawing himself up to his full six foot three. "I suggest, Count Apponyi, that *you* keep the sixpence. You might want to send another telegram." The Count flushed and said nothing. Then he dug in his pocket and presented Hales with a sovereign.'[11]

Far more common than this studied insolence on the part of discontented servants was, however, the custom of moving to a fresh situation. Although many of the moves were also made for purposes of promotion or a mere desire for a change of scene, an examination of domestic records indicates just how often the junior servants, in particular, did leave their place. Jane Carlyle had no less than ten different maids between February 1849 and July 1853. But even in larger households, where working conditions were likely to be more comfortable, changes were frequent. Between March 1873 and March 1878, the Elwes family of Great Billing, Northamptonshire, had three different kitchen-maids, three scullery-maids and three or four separate holders of the position of first and second housemaid. And at Hardwicke Court, Gloucestershire, the Lloyd-Baker family employed ten different kitchenmaids and four footmen between 1887 and 1893.

To combat this kind of mobility, charitable societies were established to encourage 'faithful service' to one employer—such as the Bath Servants' Friend Society for the Improvement and Encouragement of Good Servants, formed in 1818, and the Norfolk and Norwich Institute for the Encouragement of Faithful Servants, which operated in the 1830s. But many critics considered that the 'good service rewards' they offered were useless, 'whether in the shape of Bibles and hymn-books, or in the more tangible form of gold watches and feather beds'. Indeed, during the 'servant shortage' of the 1890s it was claimed that servants 'would rather have a merry life with plenty of change, and leave gold watches to chance'.[12]

Yet, ironically, despite these generalisations, large numbers of domestic servants, especially the youngest ones, were apparently still either too timid or too ignorant to show their independence by leaving a position in which they were unhappy. Among the most vulnerable in this respect were the young ex-workhouse servants, who had no families of their own to whom they could turn.

In the 1850s the dangers of this situation were pinpointed by two particularly unpleasant examples of brutality on the part of employers towards their young maids. The first involved Mary Parsons, a fourteen-year-old orphan from Bideford workhouse in Devon, who had been engaged by a local farmer, Robert Bird, and his wife as a general servant. Mary took up her new place in

September 1849. By Christmas of that year her mistress was accusing her of dishonesty and was not only depriving her of food but treating her cruelly. The systematic beatings she received proved too much for the child, and early in January 1850 she died from the effects of a blow to the head, sustained, according to her employers, when she fell against the fireplace. A post-mortem examination carried out on 5 January, about three days after Mary's death, revealed the extent of her injuries: 'There was a vast number of wounds and abscesses of some standing on the arms; the nails of the fingers on the left hand had been gone for some time, and the bone of the middle-finger was protruding —the result, probably, of frost-bite and a low state of the system. On the right hip was a slough as large as the palm of the hand. ¸ . . The stomach was perfectly empty.'

Following these disclosures the Birds were indicted for the girl's murder at the 1850 spring assizes at Exeter. But because it was not possible to establish which of the two had actually adminis-tered the fatal blow, the judge declared in his summing up that they must be acquitted on the murder charge. 'On this direction the jury returned a verdict of "Not Guilty".' Needless to say the decision caused a tremendous outcry, and later in the year the Birds were indicted again on three charges of assault arising out of the same facts. This time they were convicted, but their sentence of two years' imprisonment hardly matched the gravity of the crime they had committed.

The second case involved Jane Wilbred, aged about fifteen, who had been educated at the West London Poor Law Union School, and who was engaged as a general servant in July 1849, by George Sloane, a well-to-do member of the legal profession, and his wife. From Christmas 1849 the couple embarked on a campaign of cruelty towards the girl, depriving her of food and bed coverings. Like Mary Parsons, Jane was also beaten and was forced to walk about the house half-naked; most seriously, she was deprived of food to such an extent that even after twelve days in hospital she weighed only just over four stone. The Sloanes also forced her to eat her own excrement.

But Jane was fortunate in that sympathetic neighbours ob-served her plight, and her life was saved. Both Sloane and his wife were later charged with assault and were sentenced to two years' imprisonment. But public indignation was running so high

I

that when Sloane first appeared before the magistrate he was in danger of being lynched by an infuriated mob.

The shortness of the term of their imprisonment was roundly condemned by both press and public. *The Times* criticised the inadequacy of the penalty for a crime which it called 'almost unexampled in the annals of English crime', while the *Morning Chronicle* of 6 February 1851 pointed out :

> For a series of deliberate, cold-blooded and fiend-like cruelties, practised towards an unprotected orphan girl . . . for this brutal and obscene tyranny the law of England has no other punishment than two years' compulsory seclusion within four walls. . . . A mere pickpocket would fare worse at the bar of an English Criminal Court than those heartless monsters who have all but killed a helpless orphan child. . . . So enormous a discrepancy between law and opinion is an evil which calls for the deliberate attention of the Legislature.

The response of parliament to this call for action was gratifyingly prompt. Within months the Apprentices and Servants Act of 1851 was on the statute book. It laid down that the master of any servant or apprentice under the age of eighteen was to supply 'necessary Food, Clothing, or Lodging', and failure to comply could be punished with three years' imprisonment. In addition, where any 'young Person under the Age of Sixteen' was hired out as a servant from a workhouse, 'so long as such young Person shall be under the Age of Sixteen' he or she was to receive at least two visits a year from the local relieving officer or other official appointed by the Poor Law Guardians. Unfortunately, these regulations with regard to regular visiting were not properly observed, either because of the inertia of the Poor Law authorities or because of the failure of a mistress to notify the authorities when a girl left her employment for a fresh place.

Nor, sad to say, did the act prevent a recurrence of the brutality displayed in the cases of Mary Parsons and Jane Wilbred. Even at the end of the century lapses still occurred, as when Mrs Camilla Nicholls of 14 Pitt Street in fashionable Kensington was charged with the manslaughter of her young servant, Emily Jane Popejoy. Jane, the daughter of a carpenter from Bagshot in Surrey, entered Mrs Nicholls's service in October 1896 at the age of sixteen. She and her fellow-servant were kept short of food.

and by means of a variety of subterfuges Jane was deprived of some of the inadequate meals which were supplied. Evidence was also given of beatings endured by the girl, her fellow-servant claiming to have seen her with a black eye and broken nose.

Eventually, fatally weakened by the treatment she had received and suffering from pneumonia, Jane was sent home in December 1897. Shortly after her arrival there she died. But just before her death she was examined by Dr Osburn, a local doctor, who was shocked at her 'extremely emaciated' condition. Although 5 ft 5 in. tall, she weighed only 65 lb. He also found extensive bruising on her legs and body and 'the cartilage of the nose was broken'.

A detailed coverage of the trial of Mrs Nicholls in late April and early May 1898 was carried by *The Times*; the newspaper applauded her eventual conviction and sentence of seven years' penal servitude. Significantly, in an editorial on 3 May 1898, it gave as its grounds for so doing the fact that the verdict had helped to safeguard the interests of 'the large class whose rights and personal security . . . would undoubtedly have been menaced by a verdict of acquittal . . . the large class of female servants . . . who are often, through ignorance or poverty, as unable to protect themselves as was Jane Popejoy'.

In the twentieth century the growing opportunities for women to obtain employment outside the ranks of domestic service, as well as the increasing awareness among young people of their legal rights, led to a disappearance of these cases of spectacular cruelty. Nevertheless, instances of petty tyranny and harshness certainly persisted up to the First World War. The short-lived *Domestic Servants' Advertiser*, which appeared between 20 May and 8 July 1913, contains several examples involving the beating of teenage servants by their employers and their deprivation of food or non-payment of wages. The cases were too well documented to be dismissed as mere sensational horror stories. Indeed, as late as 1930, Miss Isambard-Owen of Llandudno remembers meeting a seventeen-year-old Welsh orphan who was employed in a 'tall, gaunt' London boarding-house and was 'harried and bullied by a shouting landlady. She dared not leave, having been told, most untruthfully, that if she gave notice she would be liable to instant dismissal with no wages. This was actually against the law, but how would she know? and many were the bitter tears which she shed.'[13]

Yet if a small minority of young servants were treated in this harsh fashion, at the other end of the scale there were many more who enjoyed an extremely happy relationship with their employers. A former maid from Broomfield, Essex, who entered her first job at the age of eleven in a local farmhouse, recalled the kindness she received from the family : 'I was well cared for just as if I were their only child. I went to Market in the pony trap with them. . . . I did not have to buy any clothes. The lady had some of hers cut down for me for which she paid the dressmaker herself.' Similarly, Flora Thompson in *Lark Rise to Candleford* describes the friendliness with which most of the local tradesmen, schoolmasters and other employers greeted the Juniper Hill girls who entered their households as maids-of-all-work. Indeed, one eleven-year-old girl from the hamlet, who went as a maid to an elderly couple, remained with them throughout her teens. In the end she was 'adopted as a daughter by the people to whom she had become attached'.

Countless other servants enjoyed close links with the families they served, and especially with the children of the household. As one girl remembered, to her and her two sisters and brother the maids were much-loved companions, ready to join in their fun : 'Who else would help us to make an April Fool of my Father? Who else would help us with the organisation of the Christmas party we gave to our Parents? Who else, if both parents happened to be out, would be pressed into playing card games in the Nursery? And, where else could one hope occasionally to pick up the illicit mouthful of bread and cheese except in the kitchen at elevenses?' Some servants remained with one family for years, like an eleven-year-old orphan, Annie Jones, who was taken into service by the Cook family of Bristol in 1864. She remained with the family until she died, at the age of ninety-one, in January 1955—a total of eighty years. She was buried in the family grave at Canford Cemetery, Bristol, and a headstone records the fact that she was 'the faithful servant and friend of the Cook family'. Likewise, Harriet Sizeland, who became nurse to the Chorley family in 1867, was still nominally employed by them over sixty years later. She then went into retirement with an annuity and a cottage to her native Leeds, where she remained until her death at the age of about one hundred. One of her young charges also recalls that even at the age of seventeen he was 'not allowed, in my grandmother's home, to get a glass of water from the pantry sink without Nurse's permission'.[14]

Similar records of lifelong attachment by servants to a particular family can be found elsewhere; indeed, in Victorian England it was not uncommon for masters to commemorate the loyalty of their staff by ordering the erection of suitably inscribed tombstones over their graves when they died. Arthur J. Munby, the London barrister who secretly married Hannah Cullwick, made a collection of many of the inscriptions and they were published in 1891 in a book entitled *Faithful Servants*. Among those mentioned was the nurse of Charles Lowder, 'who, when her master's family were reduced to poverty, gave them her savings, and remained with them without wages, until she died, at the age of 84, in January 1859'. She, at least, was taking literally the advice of the anonymous butler in *Hints to Domestic Servants* when he declared : 'We are to be *benefactors* to our masters . . . to make their welfare our object, and to contribute in every possible way to promote their interests. And this is the duty of every servant, whatever rank he may hold in the family.'[15]

Wise mistresses recognised, for their part, that there were certain rules of commonsense and courtesy to be observed when dealing with staff, if they wished to win their loyal and wholehearted co-operation. Mary Ames, wife of a Norwich stationer, was one such employer, and she advised her newly married daughter in the following terms :

> You must make all allowances for servant being slow. . . . You have often heard me say, long before you thought of being a Minister's wife, that a good servant would never stop in a Methodist preacher's family for this reason—they have so much running about and their errands are so unjudicially planned. In the midst of a dirty job, or when washing a floor or linnen, they are sometimes called off 3 or 4 times. Consequently there is to tie on apron, change shoes, bonnett and shawl, sometimes cap—all this a lot of times. They are out of temper, saunter along, dont care to return nor turn to when they come back so the work is always about. These errands should be all planned as you can before you begin to wash, clean a room or iron, and do not disturb them for any time till they have done, or at least not send them out. It is a common

remark that Met. preachers wives are never good mistresses because they dont know how to manage them nor their work, dont let this be said of my dear Mary.[16]

Apart from these day-to-day personal matters, however, one of the most sensitive areas of employer-servant relations was that involving wages and allowances. Throughout the nineteenth century servants' wages were, unlike those of most other workers, paid at lengthy intervals—perhaps every half-year or every quarter and occasionally at still longer intervals if the employer were short of money. Even in the first decades of the twentieth century few received a monthly payment, and it will be remembered that one of the aims of the abortive Dundee Servants' Union in 1872 had been to secure more frequent wage payments. It was also customary for employers to require their staff to sign a formal receipt, acknowledging that the money had been paid. This applied even to the humblest members of the household, such as scullery-maids and stable-boys. Thus at Englefield House, Berkshire, Henry Barnes, stable-boy, signed a statement that he had 'Received this 29 of Septr. 1866 of Richd. Benyon Esqure. four pounds for half a year's Wages.' All his more senior colleagues followed a similar practice.

Any consideration of wage changes over the nineteenth century must, of course, take into account the wide variations which existed between one household and the next, and between one servant and another. Although normally the upper servants, such as cooks, housekeepers, ladies' maids and butlers, earned more than those employed in junior positions, this was not invariably the case. The wages of a cook in a small household might be equivalent to those of a housemaid or laundry-maid, or even a general servant (or maid-of-all-work), in a more impressive establishment. *Jackson's Oxford Journal* for 6 April 1872 contains an advertisement for a 'plain cook' at a wage of £9 a year, and another for a 'general servant' at £12 per annum. Similarly, on 16 March in the same year, there were advertisements for a housekeeper at £20 per annum, a 'plain Cook, in a small family' at '£16, all found', and a 'thorough good Cook' in a 'Gentleman's Family' at £25 a year. Although the position of housekeeper was normally considered the highest in the female hierarchy (except, occasionally, for the lady's maid) in these particular examples, the cook in the gentleman's household commanded the more remunerative situation. Yet if 'there was no limit to the amount to be paid to the most skilled and modish ladies' maids, the most reliable and honest housekeepers at the top end of the scale', there was equally no limit, at the opposite end of the spectrum, to what might (or might not) be paid to the maid-of-all-work. As late as the 1890s some ex-workhouse girls were being paid a mere 1s. a week or £2 10s. a year as general servants of this type, although in London at least the Poor Law authorities appear to have insisted on a minimum annual payment of £5 to the girls for whom they were responsible.[17]

A second problem associated with estimates of national wage changes is the wide geographical variations which occurred in rates of pay. In London, Charles Booth discovered, perhaps not surprisingly, that while the average earnings of servants in the West End were £20 4s. per annum, those in the North were £17 18s., and elsewhere in the capital only £15 10s. He also concluded that the earnings of cooks varied from about £24 in the West End to £18 in the South, those of housemaids from £17 in the West End to £13 in the East, while general servants obtained nearly £17 10s. in the more prosperous West End and only £12 10s. in the East. Similar variations existed between London and the provinces, with wages in the capital at least ten per cent above comparable provincial situations in most cases.

Another point to be borne in mind is that, at least in the short term, the experience of the holder of a particular position could affect the level of wages paid, even when the general trend of remuneration was upwards. A few examples will illustrate this. At Lamport Hall, Northamptonshire, Joseph Hutchinson, footman, entered service in September 1842 at a wage of £10 per annum; this had been raised to £20 per annum by October 1845, when he left. His successor, Frederick Wetherell, was recruited in October 1845 at £10 a year and by 1849, when he resigned, was earning £16. The third holder of the position came to Lamport in 1847 at £15 per annum and left a year later at the same wage. Yet despite the fluctuations, by the middle of the 1850s the rate of pay of the then footman had risen to £24 per annum.

Physical appearance also played a part in the appointment and remuneration of liveried men-servants. According to Charles

Booth, for footmen especially, height and appearance were more important than efficiency. A second footman of 5 ft 6in. could command £20 to £22 per annum in London during the 1890s, while one of 5 ft 10 in. and over would secure £28 to £30. 'Again, a short first footman could not expect more than £30, while a tall man would command £32 to £40.'

On the female side similar short-run variations occurred, as can be shown, for example, in the wages books of the Lloyd-Baker family of Hardwicke Court, Gloucestershire, in the late nineteenth and early twentieth centuries (Table 1).

Table 1 : Annual wages of kitchenmaids and upper- and under-housemaids appointed by the Lloyd-Baker family of Hardwicke Court, Gloucestershire, 1887-1913

	Kitchen-maids		Upper-housemaids		Under-housemaids	
	Wages		*Wages*		*Wages*	
	1887	£11	1887	£23	–	–
Jan.	1889	£10	–	–	–	–
Apr.	1890	£11	–	–	–	–
Dec.	1890	£9	–	–	–	–
Jan.	1891	£14	–	–	1891	£14
Nov.	1891	£12	–	–	–	–
Apr.	1892	£18	1892	£25	1892	£12
Dec.	1892	£17	–	–	–	–
Jun.	1893	£19	–	–	1893	£13
	–	–	1894	£25	1894	£14
	–	–	–	–	1903	£19
	–	–	–	–	1904	£16 & £17
Jan.	1906	£16	–	–	–	–
Dec.	1907	£18	–	–	–	–
	–	–	1908	£30	1908	£19 & £20
	1910	£17	–	–	1910	£17
	–	–	1911	£31	1911	£18
	–	–	–	–	1913	£19

The servants' book of a small middle-class household at Bodicote, near Banbury, Oxfordshire, reveals that the wages paid to cooks over the period 1852-62 varied between £9 and £14 per annum. Almost forty years later, from 1891 to 1901, the range had increased to between £14 and £20 per annum. Housemaids in the same family earned from £7 10s. to £10 per annum in the earlier period and from £10 to £14 a year in the later. In each case the abilities of the worker concerned were a prime factor in the wage she obtained. Thus Elizabeth Slaney, the cook engaged in October 1857 at £9 per annum, was told that her mistress would 'give her one Pound more if she would keep good order and Tidy habits in the kitchen with a young Girl to help but no promise made for that extra Pound and no better performance'. Elizabeth's annual rate consequently remained at £9.[18]

Age was another significant factor in determining the wages a servant could command, and this was illustrated in Miss C. E. Collet's *Report on the Money Wages of Indoor Domestic Servants*, which was published in 1899 by the Labour Department of the Board of Trade. The information for this report, which covered the wages of female servants, had been collected between 1894 and 1898, and Table 2, taken from its pages, indicates both regional variations and the wage differentials attributable to age.

Table 2 : Average wages of female domestic servants classified according to age

	London	England and Wales
Under 16	£7·9	£7·1
16	£9·3	£9·0
17	£10·6	£10·6
18	£12·8	£12·2
19	£14·1	£12·7
20	£15·7	£14·4
21–24	£17·5	£16·5
25–29	£20·6	£19·5
30–34	£23·2	£21·5
35–39	£27·0	£23·1
40+	£27·8	£24·7

More detailed analyses of individual household wage rates over the years can be found in Appendix A. But the *overall* level of change for the various grades of servants can perhaps best be indicated by extracts from the 1861 and 1906 editions of Mrs Beeton's *Book of Household Management* and by the figures provided by the 1899 Board of Trade survey. One writer has, indeed, estimated that between 1850 and 1870 alone 'average' wages for female servants rose by about thirty per cent; but this of course excludes the many young servants who were still earning £5 per annum or less at the end of the century.[19]

In addition, in the early and mid-Victorian period the high cost of tea and sugar affected the level of wages paid, since servants who supplied these items for themselves obtained appreciably more cash than those who did not. In fact, in at least one Gloucestershire household in the 1830s, gifts of tea and sugar were seen as rewards for good conduct. The account book of the small landowner, William Cother of Longford, shows that on 28 September 1832 he gave his two maids 'half a pound of Tea and a pound of powder Sugar, by way of encouragement to good Behaviour and as a present on Barton fair day. N.B. They had a present of the same amount on the Barton fair day preceding, and a pound of Tea and two pounds of Sugar on Christmas day.' Similarly, cooks who were allowed such perquisites as dripping, fat, bones, old tea-leaves and rabbit skins, or, more rarely, commission on tradesmen's bills, would expect lower cash wages than those for whom these 'extras' were forbidden. 'Beer money' was a further perquisite allowed in some of the larger households—a survival of the days when servants drank beer instead of tea. As late as 1908 even the female servants at Taplow Court, Buckinghamshire, were paid 2s. per week 'beer money', and a similar sum was given to the early twentieth-century maids at Hatfield House, seat of the Marquis of Salisbury.[20] At Hackwood House, Hampshire, payments for beer for staff amounted to around £4 10s. per quarter in the early 1870s; but it is not clear in this case if 'beer money' was provided or merely the drink itself. Even washing money was allowed by some employers.

All these factors influenced the amount of cash wages actually paid. As to which was the better alternative for the servant, *Beeton's Domestic Service Guide* had no doubt. It declared:

> If you are offered two places equally promising, choose the one where everything is found, even at less wages. If you work hard

Table 3: Wages of male servants as quoted in the 1861 and 1906 editions of Mrs I. Beeton's
Book of Household Management

1861	When not found in livery	When found in livery
House steward	£40–£80	–
Valet	£25–£50	£20–£30
Butler	£25–£50	–
Cook	£20–£40	–
Gardener	£20–£40	–
Footman	£20–£40	£15–£25
Under-butler	£15–£30	£15–£25
Coachman	–	£20–£35
Groom	£15–£30	£12–£20
Under-footman	–	£12–£20
Page or footboy	£8–£18	£6–£14
Stable-boy	£6–£12	–

In most establishments such men-servants as coachman, footman and page are provided with livery by employers. This does not affect the question of wages.

1906	
House steward	£60–£100
Groom of the chambers	£45–£55
Valet	£35–£50
Cook	£100
Head gardener (not in house)	£70–£120
Under-gardener	£40–£45
Butler	£55–£90
Under-butler	£35–£45
Footman	£18–£40
Under-footman	£18–£34
Second footman	£18–£34
Coachman	£40–£70
Coachman (not in house)	£70–£90
Groom	£25–£35
Under-groom	£18–£25
Page	£12–£18
Stable-boy	£6–£12
Servants' hall boy	£6–£12
Steward's boy	£8–£15
Head gamekeeper	£100–£150
Under-gamekeeper	£50–£70

Table 4: Wages of female servants as quoted in the 1861 and 1906 editions of Mrs I. Beeton's Book of Household Management

1861	When no extra allowance is made for tea, sugar and beer	When an extra allowance is made for tea, sugar and beer
Housekeeper	£20–£45	£18–£40
Lady's maid	£12–£25	£10–£20
Head nurse	£15–£30	£13–£26
Cook	£14–£30	£12–£26
Upper housemaid	£12–£20	£10–£17
Upper laundry-maid	£12–£18	£10–£15
Maid-of-all-work	£9–£14	£7½–£11

1861	When no extra allowance is made for tea, sugar and beer	When an extra allowance is made for tea, sugar and beer
Under-housemaid	£8–£12	£6½–£10
Stillroom maid	£9–£14	£8–£12
Nursemaid	£8–£12	£5–£10
Under-laundry-maid	£9–£14	£8–£12
Kitchenmaid	£9–£14	£8–£12
Scullery-maid	£5–£9	£4–£8

1906	Everything found, or an allowance for the same
Housekeeper	£30–£60
Lady's maid	£25–£40
Cook	£20–£60
Kitchenmaid	£16–£28
Scullery-maid	£14–£18
Stillroom maid	£18–£28
Head nurse	£25–£35

1906	Everything found, or an allowance for the same
Under nurse	£12–£18
Head laundry-maid	£22–£30
Under-laundry-maid	£12–£20
Parlourmaid	£20–£35
Head housemaid	£20–£28
Under-housemaid	£14–£18
General servant	£12–£28

you require good beer, tea, and sugar, and you will probably spend more on these requisites in buying for yourself than the money allowed by your master will cover. And when everything is 'found' for you, you know that your wages are all your own, and can be spent on your clothes, or put by for the rainy day that is sure, sooner or later, to come to us all.

It is against this background that the suggested wage payments for male servants put forward by Mrs Beeton (Table 3) have to be seen.

It can be seen from Table 3 that not only had the number of different positions within the household increased over the years but sharp wage rises had occurred, particularly among the senior staff members. Perhaps the principal beneficiary was the butler, whose wage range had almost doubled over the period. The male cook and the gardener had also achieved substantial increases, but at the lower end, the stable-boy earning £6-£12 at both dates had not advanced his position at all. The livery question had ceased to be the point of issue in the early twentieth century that it had been in the middle of the nineteenth.

Table 4 presents the comparable wage rates for the female

Table 5 : Average wages of female domestic servants according to class of work

Class of work	Age in years	London wages	England & Wales (excl. London)
Between maid	19	£12·4	£10·7
Scullery-maid	19	£13·7	£13·0
Kitchenmaid	20	£16·6	£15·0
Nurse-housemaid	21–24	£14·9	£16·0
General	21–24	£14·9	£14·6
Housemaid	21–24	£17·5	£16·2
Nurse	25–29	£21·0	£20·1
Parlourmaid	25–29	£22·2	£20·6
Laundry-maid	25–29	£27·3	£23·6
Cook	25–29	£21·8	£20·2
Lady's maid	30–34	£28·1	£24·7
Cook-housekeeper	40+	£41·6	£35·6
Housekeeper	40+	£34·3	£52·2

servants. As with the men, the main gains had come at the upper end of the household hierarchy, with the lady's maid, the cook and the housekeeper making considerable progress; but the wages of the kitchenmaid and scullery-maid had also advanced sharply.

The wages quoted by Mrs Beeton were *suggested* levels only. By contrast, the figures collected by the Board of Trade in the 1890s (Table 5) were based on actual returns made from over two thousand households, and they relate to the average wages earned at selected (i.e. most frequently stated) age periods.

The unexpected variation in wages of cook-housekeepers and housekeepers as between London and the rest of England and Wales is not explained in the report. It may be due to a difference in terminology in different parts of the country (see page 53), or to the small size of the London housekeeper sample.

Finally, in the larger households, 'board wages' were paid to servants left behind when the employer and his family were travelling or at another residence. With care, money could be saved out of the sum allowed, as a former maid from Dedham, Essex, remembered. She entered service with the Mulholland family in 1900 at the age of fifteen, and shortly after she and two other servants were left behind 'to caretake and keep tidy the house'. Board wages were 10s. or 12s. 6d. a week, 'and we had Veg. from the garden and could buy Milk, eggs etc. from the home farm. We all managed to save a few shillings out of that and got our shoes mended, pair of stockings and stamps etc.' At Taplow Court, Buckinghamshire, early in the twentieth century, the senior women staff members were paid 14s. per week board wages and the junior ones 12s. By contrast, on the Drummond estate at Cadland, Hampshire, a more complex system existed. Board wages for the senior staff (housekeeper, lady's maid and butler) even in 1860 were 15s. a week; for the coachman, under-butler, footman and groom they were 14s. per week; for the middling female staff (upper housemaid, stillroom maid and kitchenmaid) they amounted to 11s. 6d.; and the lowest grade of all (under-housemaids and under-laundry-maid) were expected to live on 10s. 6d. each per week, in the belief, presumably, that the more junior their position, the smaller their appetite. As they were probably young, active girls performing a heavy day's work, the reverse is likely to have been the case. But that was just their misfortune.

8

Misdoings and Misdemeanours

Maid-servants live well, have no care or anxiety, no character
worth speaking about to lose, for the origin of most of them is
obscure, are fond of dress, and under these circumstances it cannot be wondered that they are as a body immoral and unchaste. . . .
There are a great number of felonies committed by servants over
the metropolis. . . . Some respectable looking young women, in
the service of middle-class and fashionable families are connected
with burglars, and have been recommended to their places through
their influence, or that of their acquaintances. Some of these
females are usually not a fortnight or a month in service before
a heavy burglary is committed in the house, and will remain for
two or three months longer to prevent suspicion.

HENRY MAYHEW, *London Labour
and the London Poor*, IV (1861).

DESPITE Henry Mayhew's sweeping charges as to the immorality of Victorian maids, the vast majority of servants were neither
criminals nor lawbreakers, but spent their days working honestly
and diligently for long hours and little pay. Yet for the small
minority who *did* stray from the path of virtue, as his comments
indicate, prostitution and petty theft were the commonest offences
committed. The most serious crimes, particularly murder, affected
but a tiny number, and, in the case of murder at least, very often
accompanied theft or attempted theft.

The alleged immorality and casual prostitution among servant
girls (or 'dollymops' as they were sometimes christened) were
attributed by Mayhew partly to the fact that maids had little
opportunity to meet respectable men of their own class in the
course of their everyday duties, and partly to the fact that their
love of dress encouraged them to add to their income in any way
they could. 'Vanity is at the bottom of . . . this, and is one of the

chief characteristics of a class not otherwise naturally vicious', he sternly remarked. Policemen and soldiers were the usual objects of the maids' affections, with soldiers particularly 'notorious for hunting up these women, especially nurse-maids and others that in the execution of their duty walk in the Parks, when they may easily be accosted. Nurse-maids feel flattered by the attention that is lavished upon them, and are always ready to succumb to the "scarlet fever". A red coat is all-powerful with this class, who prefer a soldier to a servant, or any other description of man they come in contact with.' The soldiers, for their part, were only too anxious to take advantage of the situation, for the average ranker could not 'afford to employ professional women to gratify his passions, and if he were to do so, he must make the acquaintance of a very low set of women, who in all probability will communicate some infectious disease to him. He feels he is never safe, and he is only too glad to seize the opportunity of forming an intimacy with a woman who will appreciate him for his own sake, cost him nothing but the trouble of taking her about occasionally, and who, whatever else she may do, will never by any chance infect.'[1]

Yet if some girls did temporarily become prostitutes for the apparently frivolous reasons mentioned by Mayhew, most moved in that direction only because of hard necessity, when they were out of a place and had no other means of earning their living. The London barrister Arthur Munby, for example, describes in his diary a meeting in February 1859, with an eighteen-year-old servant girl who had just run away 'from her place by reason of ill-treatment; didn't know London—didn't know what to do. Knew her danger, but verging towards it from sheer idiotic insouciance.' Munby tried to save her from herself by engaging a room for her in a respectable coffee house, but his efforts proved in vain : 'She . . . never slept there after all.' Three years later he mentioned his meeting with another maid out of employment, who also became a prostitute. She was 'delicate with . . . a refined face', and her father was respectably employed as a gamekeeper in Hampshire. Nevertheless, necessity had driven her onto the streets, and according to Munby she would have 'prostituted her virginity' with him, had he been prepared to accept her.[2]

Dr William Acton in his classic study of *Prostitution*, published in 1857 and reissued in an enlarged form in 1870, confirmed that

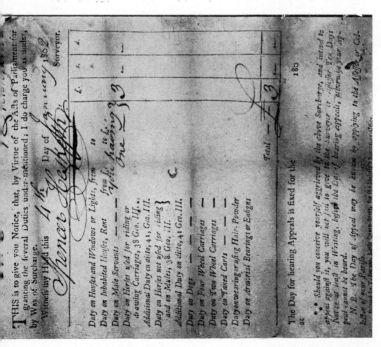

THE SERVANT AS TAX LIABILITY

17/18 Receipts for male servants' tax, 1802 and 1911. The 1802 receipt relates to the tax rate for a male householder living alone, under the servant duties legislation of 1798. These duties were further increased in 1808. The tax remained in operation until it was repealed by the Finance Act of 1937, but from 1869 to its repeal it remained at the modest level of 15s. per servant.

THE MIDDLE-CLASS HOUSEHOLD: FEMALE SERVANTS

19 A lady's maid from Charlbury, Oxfordshire, c.1880. Ladies' maids and governesses occupied an ill-defined position in the servant hierarchy. Most of them came from middle-class families in reduced circumstances, and their efforts to preserve the gentility appropriate to their station frequently caused them to be regarded as snobs by the other servants. *(left)*

20 Nurse with her mistress and children, 1911. (above)

although some women fell 'through vanity and idleness, love of dress, love of excitement, love of drink . . . by far the larger proportion are driven by cruel biting poverty'. He concluded that prostitution was 'a transitory state, through which an untold number of British women are ever on their passage'.

But many servant girls, like the eponymous heroine of George Moore's novel *Esther Waters*, fought hard against a step which they considered the final degradation. In describing Esther's plight, after she had made several vain attempts to find fresh employment, Moore wrote:

> She felt that she could struggle no more, that the whole world was against her—she felt that she must have food and drink and rest. All this London tempted her; the cup was at her lips, for a young man in evening clothes was speaking to her. His voice was soft, the look in his eyes seemed kindly. . . . There was a lightness, an emptiness in her head which she could not overcome, and the crowd appeared to her like a blurred, noisy dream. And then the dizziness left her, and she realised the temptation she had escaped.

Soon after Esther met another maid, named Margaret Gale, with whom she had once been in service. Margaret had become a prostitute after 'one of her masters had got her into trouble' and his wife had turned her out.[3]

Margaret's fate was typical of many who were seduced by their employer or by a relative of his but whose misfortune, if they were found to be pregnant, was to be 'dismissed from [their] employment without a character', while their seducer escaped scotfree from 'the consequences of his wrong-doing'. Dr Acton wrote with bitter contempt of the 'gentlemen whose délassement is the contamination of town servants', but it is unlikely that his censure carried much weight with sexual adventurers like the anonymous author of *My Secret Life*, who openly admitted that 'one of the charms . . . of intrigues with servants is the odd, out of the way places, and times in which I tail them'.

Yet, as Acton's researches confirmed, by no means all 'fallen' women remained fallen for life. Many managed to overcome their difficulties and to marry respectably, becoming 'the wedded wives of men in every grade of society, from the peerage to the stable'. Indeed, he claimed that in the home counties, even when

K

they did not marry, women with children to support were often thought to make the best servants. Yet this did not prevent him from condemning as 'paltry, peddling scratches on the surface of the evil', the various maids' protection societies which were springing up to try to prevent women suffering the social stigma and economic deprivation of unmarried motherhood.

Disapproval of extra-marital sexual relations did not, of course, apply with equal force in all parts of the country. In Wales the vice of 'bundling' was widely tolerated up to the third quarter of the century. The Rev. J. W. Tevor, chaplain to the Bishop of Bangor, complained, for example, that the householders of Anglesey tacitly agreed, when hiring servants, to provide facilities for fornication. And in Glamorgan the superintendent of police admitted that farm servants of both sexes often slept in the same room; it was also claimed that in South Wales generally the unmarried men-servants ranged the countryside at night demanding admission to the female servants' quarters.[4] The Archdeacon of St David's even declared at the end of the 1860s that 'bastardy was common, unchastity . . . the rule' among farmhouse servants in South Wales.[5]

Yet if, as Acton maintained, many women were able to work hard and respectably to bring up their illegitimate children, sometimes the financial burden proved too great—as in the case of Sarah Drake, a cook-housekeeper of Harley Street. Sarah was brought to court in December 1849, charged with murdering her two-year-old son, who had been farmed out since birth. It transpired that she owed the woman who had looked after him between £11 and £12; she could not pay the debt and was afraid that if the truth came to light she would lose her place. After strangling the boy, she packed his body in a box, handed it to the butler to address and then sent it by a footman to be despatched by rail to her sister in the country. Although there was no note with the body, the origin of the parcel was traced to Sarah and she was charged with murder. During the trial it was revealed that this was not the first time she had been in the dock, for in 1842 she had been tried for the wilful murder of another illegitimate child, but had eventually been convicted of 'concealment of birth only, and sentenced to six months' imprisonment. In that case the child was also packed up in a box, which was addressed to the porter of the Knutsford Union.'

Elsewhere the records of assizes show a steady trickle of cases involving maids charged either with concealing the birth of a child or with infanticide. At Oxford assizes, for example, during the period February 1867 to February 1869 there were four cases involving young servants charged with wilful murder or with 'endeavouring to conceal' a birth. All were aged between nineteen and twenty-two, and all were found guilty. Their sentences varied between one month's and eighteen months' imprisonment with hard labour. A decade earlier, at the assizes heard at Oxford during February and July 1858 and March 1859, no less than seven servant girls, between nineteen and twenty-five, were similarly charged. Five were found guilty and were imprisoned.

Some of the bolder or more desperate girls risked discovery by giving birth to their babies secretly in their employer's house—as Jane Carlyle discovered to her horror. She confided in a letter to a friend that during her absence at St Leonard's-on-Sea in 1864, her cook, Mary, had given birth to a child 'in the small room at the end of the diningroom'. While she was in labour Mr Carlyle had been taking tea in the dining-room with a friend, and 'the child was not born till two in the morning when Mr C. was still reading in the *Drawingroom*!' Mrs Carlyle's second maid had then fetched 'two women—one of whom took the child home to be nursed—need one ask where all my fine napkins went, when it is known that the Creature had not prepared a rag of clothing for the Child!' The charwoman who enlightened Mrs Carlyle as to these happenings also revealed that this was Mary's second illegitimate child and that she had stolen butter, tea and china to give 'to her man and her friends'.

But the most common resort of a maid in this situation was either to return home to her parents or to enter a workhouse, which at least provided shelter during her confinement. In London servants were said to come 'in very large numbers' to the lying-in wards of the workhouses. In April 1871, at the time of the census of population, Kensington Workhouse had about thirteen unmarried servants with their young babies within its walls—nearly one in ten of all the servant inmates. But at Fulham and St George's Workhouses at the same date there were only two or three maids in this situation. According to a former chairman of the Kensington Poor Law infirmary, it was quite common for the girls to have their baby 'without their parents in the country knowing anything at all about it'; they then made arrangements for the child to be farmed out, but babies so disposed of were 'sometimes deserted and sometimes die'. Occasionally the infants were allowed to stay in the workhouse infirmary, and were then left to the tender mercies of the Poor Law.[6]

A small number of girls brought actions in the petty sessional courts to obtain a maintenance order for their child against the putative father. It was not until 1844 that the mother was allowed to apply to the magistrates in this fashion, and even then, the provision authorised was extremely meagre—£1 a week towards the baby's maintenance for the first six weeks after birth, and 2s. 6d. a week thereafter until the child was thirteen years of age. Under the 1872 Bastardy Laws Amendment Act the upper weekly limit was raised to 5s., but this sum was still far too small to support a child. Nor did all of the girls obtain the maximum permitted amount. One who did not was Sarah Streak of Goring, Oxfordshire, who charged 'John Butler of Reading, Berks, a servant' with being the father of her illegitimate child, born on 27 June 1869. Although her claim was upheld by the Henley bench, the maintenance order was made for only 1s. 6d. a week, plus 17s. 6d. costs. In a similar case heard by the Henley magistrates about two years earlier the award had also been for 1s. 6d. a week, but the costs in that instance amounted to only 12s. Other applicants had much the same treatment.

Yet if prostitution and suits involving the paternity of children were two matters which could bring domestic servants before the courts, a far more common cause of their downfall was petty larceny—for males and females alike. In many cases, as Mayhew pointed out, the offence involved the theft of small items which the employer was not likely to miss, such as tea, sugar and other provisions, which were 'frequently given to acquaintances or relatives out of doors'.

The complaints of employers on the subject were many and varied, like those involving Jane Carlyle's 'old Treasure' who was found to be not only incapable of cooking a meal or telling the truth, but who 'finished off by stealing eight bottles of ale'. Then there was Lady Elizabeth Spencer Stanhope's discovery at one country house in which she was staying, in the middle of the century, that the housemaids were stealing feathers from the pillows 'and butlers and housekeepers carrying off even the best china—'in this apparently most admirably regulated house where I am sure no eye of vigilance is wanting, but I believe all houses are alike'. Some erring maids used guile to cover their tracks, like the parlourmaid employed 'with the highest references from Prince Albert's Model Office in Marlborough Street' by Louisa Sherrard, in 1851. Mrs Sherrard was horrified to discover that not only did she steal the brandy 'but emptied it into half empty wine bottles to escape detection'.[7]

The records of petty and quarter sessional courts confirm the wide variety of objects stolen, although by no means all employers took the extreme step of taking an errant servant to law. In most cases they preferred, like Mrs Carlyle, immediate dismissal of the offender rather than the unwelcome publicity of legal action. Nevertheless, at Oxford quarter sessions during the years 1875-76 alone, seven cases were heard involving thefts by servants from employers, ranging from the removal by one girl of £4 and '1 jacket and 1 dress' to the stealing by another of '1 chemise of the value of 10s.' Six of the seven accused were found guilty, the most serious offence being the theft of £30 0s. 9d. by a groom from Caversham near Reading, and he also received the stiffest sentence: '9 calendar months' hard labour in the House of Correction'. The other offenders (all girls) received one or two months' imprisonment with hard labour. Sometimes the punishment appeared excessive in relation to the crime. Thus at the Oxford Trinity quarter sessions in 1853 a twenty-year-old maid from the village of Piddington was sentenced to twelve months' hard labour for stealing two pairs of stockings and other small articles, while about a decade earlier an eighteen-year-old servant from Somerton was sentenced by the same quarter sessions to 'three calendar months at hard labour' for stealing 'a piece of ribbon'. A case heard at Warwick quarter sessions in October 1874 also proved that Lady Elizabeth Stanhope's acquaintance was not the only victim of the petty crime of feather stealing, for a middle-aged servant employed by a Stratford-on-Avon brazier and greengrocer was found guilty of removing a blanket and four ounces of feathers without her master's consent, and was sentenced to one calendar month's imprisonment with hard labour.

It was the prevalance of this type of minor theft which caused the writers of books on household management to stress the importance of keeping a strict eye on domestic staff. *Beeton's*

Domestic Service Guide warned of the tendency of servants (especially cooks) to entertain policemen in their kitchens, declaring : 'Should a too-confident policeman, or any other clandestine visitor of a domestic servant, be so indiscreet as to "pocket", or otherwise carry away, any food, drink, or other property of the servant's employer, so that the same might be found upon the departing visitor's person . . . both the indiscreet visitor and the servant would be liable to be given into immediate custody, and prosecuted for theft.' One has an irresistible vision of the errant policeman being forced to arrest himself!

Some writers appealed to the honesty of the servants themselves, like the anonymous author of the *Address to Young Servants*, which was published in 1863 : 'The beginnings of dishonesty is very often just the taking a little tea or sugar, or some other trifling thing which would not be missed; but remember, God's eye sees through the darkest night, and if man cannot see you it is impossible to hide from Him.'

Alongside this problem were disputes over the exact quantity and value of perquisites to be allowed to servants—especially cooks. In about 1825 this was made the subject of a satirical handbill, announcing that a servants' union had been formed in Edinburgh to demand, among other things :

> That mistress's old clothes have ever been, and must continue to be, the property of maid-servants, and that when a gown or any other piece of dress has been worn a sufficient time, it must be considered as old clothes.
>
> That in case of any difference of opinion between the mistress and the maid about the condemnation of the dress— the servants of the house and those of the two adjoining houses to be appointed Judges.
>
> That hare and rabbit skins, kitchenfee, fat, dripping, shall continue to be considered the property of the cook, and no skinned hare or rabbit to enter the house.[8]

But the whole question was viewed more seriously by 'A Practical Mistress of a Household'. She did not mince her words, stating that 'about sixty per cent of the servants in and out of place would properly belong to the criminal class, if their antecedents as well as their present doings were known. . . . Numbers of servants, who are going on—as they say—"swimmingly" in service at this day, have previously *lost their character*, and have obtained their present position through false representation.' She then went on to justify these exaggerated claims by warning employers against the perquisite system : 'This opens the door to a larger system of robbery than many people dream of. . . . The term "perquisite" is so comprehensive, so elastic, and accommodating, that it is made to embrace and signify almost everything in the various departments of the house.'

Her complaints of servant dishonesty would certainly have had the support of 'M.P.', an anonymous correspondent to *The Times* of 9 April 1879, who had discovered he was being defrauded by the tradesman who supplied his coachman's liveries. The coachman had two suits of liveries and two of stable clothes each year, and in October 1878 'suits of each were sent home in the usual course. These clothes I marked, owing to a vague suspicion that tricks were being played. When lately the spring liveries and stable clothes arrived, on opening the parcel I recognised my old friends of last autumn, and found that coats, waistcoats and trousers had all been again sent to me as new. I need not add that I was charged on both occasions for new clothes.' When taxed with the fraud, the coachman admitted that he had saved his October liveries, keeping them as good as new, and had then arranged with the tailor for the provision of 'some private clothes in exchange'. But although *he* expressed suitable sorrow for his transgressions, the tailor was made of sterner stuff. In response to a letter from 'M.P.', he declared that he had provided private clothes to the full value of the liveries, and that he assumed the coachman 'had as much right to save his liveries as his wages, and to buy my goods with the one as with the other. . . . I can assure you that this is an every-day practice between tailors and their customers' servants. The only persons who gain by it are the servants, for it would be more profitable to the tailors to supply the liveries of the price paid by the masters than the private clothes at the same price.' It was this latter statement which aroused the especial ire of 'M.P.', and he called upon tradesmen to 'set their face, as a body, against the dishonest connivance with servants to defraud masters which is only too common'.

Samuel and Sarah Adams in *The Complete Servant* (published 1825), for their part, warned servants against forming friendships with tradesmen who probably had ulterior motives for their actions, and 'mostly [sought] only their own interest and profit in everything. If any proposal that is new, or unexpectedly profitable, force itself on your notice, do not act on your own opinion, nor hastily, but, confidentially, consult your mistress, or some relation, else you may be as hastily ensnared to your utter undoing.' There were dangers, too, in conniving at the dishonesty of others for '*you are defrauding* a master or mistress, whose property you are bound to watch and protect; and you incur the guilt and shame of the fraud, though you may not participate in the gain'.[9]

Yet, as Frederick Gorst reveals in his reminiscences, servants themselves felt very differently over the question of informing on the misdeeds of their fellows. On one occasion when Gorst was serving at a large dinner party attended by Edward VII, a big bunch of prize grapes provided for the dessert disappeared before it could be placed on the table. Later Gorst discovered that one of the extra footmen on duty from Buckingham Palace had concealed the grapes in a cupboard and had then walked out with them. Gorst recalled that the day after the incident the steward 'posted a notice of a five pound reward for any information about the theft of the grapes, no questions asked. But for no price would I denounce a fellow servant.' These are sentiments which he expresses more than once in his book.

Another cause for concern for the householder anxious to check waste and dishonesty was the buyer of kitchen-stuff, grease and dripping, who appeared regularly at the area door offering to buy on liberal terms the cook's or maid-of-all-work's 'perquisites' of dripping, etc. 'In this traffic was frequently mixed up a good deal of pilfering, directly or indirectly. Silver spoons were thus disposed of. Candles, purposely broken and crushed, were often part of the grease; in the dripping, butter occasionally added to the weight; in the "stock" (the remains of the meat boiled down for the making of soup) were sometimes portions of excellent meat fresh from the joints which had been carved at table; and among the broken bread, might be frequently seen small loaves, unbroken.' In view of the range and size of these secret purchases, it is not surprising that the women traders were described as 'well-cloaked'. The items would later be sold in the rag and bottle and marine-store shops found in the poorer areas of most large towns.[10]

Yet no matter how infuriating and costly this petty larceny

might be, it was the theft of major items which aroused real anxiety in the breasts of most householders. Mayhew warned of servants who plundered the 'wardrobe of gold bracelets, rings, pearl necklace, watch chain, or other jewellery, or of muslin and silk dresses and mantles, which they either keep in their trunk, or otherwise dispose of'. The worst offenders, in his view, were 'Irish cockneys, connected with . . . thieves', who had been trained by them from their infancy. 'In these robberies they are always ready to give the "hue and cry" when a depredation has been committed.' Another problem arose when men-servants, such as butlers or footmen who had charge of the household plate, turned to gambling. 'They go and bet on different horses, and pawn a certain quantity of plate which has not the crest of their employer on it, and expect to be able to redeem it as soon as they have got money when the horse has won.' But the gamble might not come off.

> [The servant] bets again on some other horse he thinks will win—perhaps bets to a considerable amount, and thinks he will be able to redeem his loss; he again possibly loses his bet. His master is perhaps out of town, not having occasion to use the plate.
>
> On his coming home there may be a dinner-party, when the plate is called for. The butler absconds, and part of the plate is found to be missing. Information is given to the police; some pawnbroker may be so honourable as to admit the plate is in his possession. The servant is apprehended, convicted, and sentenced possibly to penal servitude. Cases of this kind occasionally occur, and are frequently caused by such betting transactions.[11]

A dishonest coachman, by contrast, might use his master's carriage as a get-away vehicle following a robbery, as did Tom, coachman to Sir Henry Halford of Leicestershire. As we saw in Chapter 5, in 1830 he was accused of assisting 'some woman to carry off the furniture of Lodgings to the value of 30s.' Another wrongdoer might use the carriage for his own private excursions; the Earl of Athlone was a victim of this type of coachman. When the Earl wrote to warn a prospective employer of the coachman's misdemeanours, the catalogue of faults was a long one:

> He behaved to me in a most insolent & rascally manner & ill-

treated my horses by driving them about the Streets for his own amusement at a time when they ought to have been in the stable, having ordered the Carriage home. The Evening previous to my turning him out of my house he bid me be Damned & drive my own Carriage, & because I would not pay him a months wages & Board wages he sent me an Attorney's letter, he has contracted Debts in this neighbourhood for which he will be arrested, & robbed me of a pair of fustian Small Cloaths, which he took with him. A wish to prevent you or any other Gentleman from being imposed upon by such fellows makes me inform you of this man's bad conduct.[12]

In a few cases, greed or anger at an employer's treatment might lead a servant to go a step further and commit the far more serious crime of murder. One of the best known of these cases occurred in 1840, when a young Swiss valet, François Courvoisier, murdered his elderly employer, Lord William Russell, an uncle of the future Prime Minister, Lord John Russell. The motives appear to have been a mixture of avarice and resentment at his master's unreasonable demands—but with the latter predominating. Among the items stolen in the course of the crime were £10 in money, some silver spoons and forks, and a pair of gold auricles for assisting the hearing. However, on the day in question Courvoisier had been reprimanded on three separate occasions for neglecting his duties and for other faults. Then, at about midnight, Lord William rang the bell in his bedroom, and the valet, thinking this was for a warming-pan, took one up on his own initiative. When he entered his master's bedroom, the latter reproved him for not coming up first to see what was required. He ordered Courvoisier to take the warming-pan away, but about twenty minutes later rang again, asking for it to be returned. Shortly after Lord William came downstairs, and seeing Courvoisier in the dining-room, charged him with having 'no good intentions'. He declared the valet must leave his post the next day. This combination of circumstances proved too much for Courvoisier, and about an hour later, when his master was asleep, he crept upstairs and stabbed the old man to death. Afterwards Courvoisier claimed that he had stolen the money and other items only to make it appear that the crime had been committed by a burglar.

The valet's trial aroused great interest; indeed, the *Morning Chronicle* declared that Lord William's murder had created a 'greater degree of excitement and consternation' than any event which had occurred in the metropolis for a 'considerable number of years'. Among those who attended the trial were the Duke of Sussex, the Earl of Mansfield, Lord and Lady Arthur Lennox, and many other 'people of rank'. And following Courvoisier's conviction and sentence to death, his hanging at Newgate attracted another great crowd of about twenty thousand people, including not only members of the nobility but such people as the writers Thackeray and Dickens. According to the *Annual Register* there was also a large number 'of men-servants present . . . evincing the fearful interest taken in the culprit's fate by the class to which he had belonged'. Charles Greville claimed that the event had 'frightened all London out of its wits. Visionary servants and air-drawn razors or carving-knives dance before everybody's imagination and half the world go to sleep expecting to have their throats cut before morning.'

In 1872 a similar incident involving murder in fashionable Mayfair took place, when Madame Riel, a difficult and exacting employer, was strangled by her Belgian maid, who was under notice to leave. The maid then helped herself to travel funds and jewellery from her mistress's possessions and departed for France. 'She was pursued, arrested, returned, tried, convicted and sentenced to death, but her punishment later was reduced to penal servitude.'[18]

A sprinkling of such cases occurred in the years that followed, but one of the most gruesome mistress-servant encounters involved Kate Webster, an Irish maid-of-all-work and her employer, a Richmond widow in her middle fifties, named Mrs Thomas. After only a month in service, Kate's sloppy methods of working led Mrs Thomas to give her notice to leave. Then on 2 March 1879 a row developed between them because Kate had returned from her Sunday afternoon off late and noticeably the worse for drink. Mrs Thomas attended a Sunday evening church service, but when she returned home alone, Kate was waiting for her. She bludgeoned her employer to death and then proceeded to cut her into small pieces. 'Having reduced Mrs Thomas to manageable portions, she put them on the stove and boiled them.' Kate then decided to sell the furniture in the cottage; this proved her undoing, for it aroused the suspicion of neighbours and her crime was discovered. Although she escaped to Ireland, she was brought back and was tried and found guilty. She was later hanged at Newgate. And as Richard Altick points out, 'Kate Webster's butchery simply intensified the effect already produced by Britain's succession of murderers from the servants' quarters. It was with good reason that many a nervous Victorian householder worried less about his staff's professional expertise than about their good will. The effect of Webster *et al.* undoubtedly was to make such householders scrutinise their prospective employees' credentials with extra care.'[14]

Against this sombre background, such relatively minor servant offences as drunkenness or impersonating an employer—or even the presentation of a false character reference, appear as light relief. Most employers accepted that among their men-servants, in particular, there was an over-fondness for drink which they could only curb by maintaining a strict vigilance over the distribution of liquor supplies within the household. Hence the need to maintain careful control over the wine cellar and to keep records of the quantity of alcohol consumed. Nevertheless, both family correspondence and court records show that these restraints were often inadequate. Thus at the petty sessions held at Henley, Oxfordshire, on 26 July 1869, Elizabeth Milchen, a servant at Rotherfield Greys, was charged with being unlawfully drunk and riotous; her case was dismissed with a caution. A coachman found drunk in the Market Place at Henley on 19 March 1880 was less fortunate. He was fined 3s. and had to pay 6s. costs. Public houses often proved the servant's Achilles' heel; in April 1864, 'A Suffering Mistress' wrote to the *Cornhill Magazine* calling for a reduction in 'the numbers and the flaunting attractiveness of the innumerable public-houses which make drunkards of nearly half the cooks in England, in various degrees of inveterateness'.

Most employers tried to ensure that the drinking habits of their servants did not reach the publicity of the courts, either by accepting the occasional lapses with resignation or by dismissing the servant concerned before the situation got out of hand. Yet the heartsearching to which this latter solution could give rise is illustrated in the letters of Richard Huddleston of Sawston Hall, Cambridgeshire, and his friend Kenelm Digby. On 27 September

1861 Digby wrote to say that his man-servant, 'poor Harris', was leaving that day.

> We part with him more for his own sake than for ours. Had he continued with us he would not have had strength to stand against the temptations of our service : for he had too much liberty : & therefore he would have settled into a sot. As it is I hope & believe he will quite recover himself & we have promised to give him an excellent character & that for four years & a $\frac{1}{4}$ will enable him to do well. . . . A golden bridge should be left for every one who seeks to return to himself; & in every other respect he conducted himself always well. We offered to keep him if he would promise to drink only in the house, where he was not stinted, & not go to a public house : but I think he refused this from having the mania of seeing a little of the world.

Harris eventually obtained a place as ship's steward, but Digby noted anxiously that although the position was 'excellent', there would be plenty of opportunity for drinking. The temptations open would be 'awful as he would have wine brandy &c. *ad infinitum* at his disposal. We did our best to keep him from it.'

The offences of impersonating employers and of embezzlement were, like drunkenness, more common among male servants than female, since the latter usually had little freedom to go out in circumstances which made impersonation possible, while their chances of handling money were few and far between. The social aspirations of some of the vainer men-servants made them vulnerable to the temptation of impersonation, as did the opportunity for gain that this might also bestow. One typical example was provided in 1865 at Warwick quarter sessions, when a forty-two-year-old servant was charged with embezzling £1 2s. and with receiving 'in the name and account of his master' a further sum of £3 7s. 6d. He was sentenced to six months' imprisonment in the House of Correction.

On a slightly different note, Lady Dorothy Nevill was obliged to dismiss her German lady's maid when she discovered that the woman's 'love of the stage . . . had led her to undertake different parts at some low theatre or penny gaff. The worst part of the business was that, being cast for the part of Marie Stuart, this Teutonic Thespian annexed a very handsome black velvet dress of mine in which to impersonate Scotland's ill-fated Queen.'

Even Jeames Plush, the archetypal caricature footman of Thackeray's humorous sketches, who eventually both made and lost a fortune in railway speculation, was not guiltless of this weakness for impersonation. When he began his money-making ventures he wrote his letters as from his master's residence in Berkeley Square—and was taken at his face value, so that

> Day by day, share after share,
> Came railway letters pouring in,
> J. Plush Esquire in Buckley Square.

Yet despite these examples of misconduct and lawbreaking by domestic staff, it must be remembered that they involved only a small minority of the vast servant army, and that most workers were more sinned against than sinning. For, as was seen in Chapter 7, the mistress was as capable of depriving her dependant of her rightful wages or food (as in the cases of Mary Parsons and Jane Popejoy) as the servant was of stealing food and other items from the household, or of committing other wrongful acts.

YEARS OF DECLINE: THE NEW CENTURY

21 Nannies at a children's party, c.1903. The nanny on the far right remained with the Buckley family for about fifty years.

22 Nannies at a children's party in Berkshire during the mid-1920s. They are just getting ready to take part in the nannies' three-legged race.

23 *A London maid-of-all-work, 1856*

24 *A London kitchenmaid, 1870.*

9
The Winds of Change, 1900-14

A very independent spirit is a marked characteristic of the lower classes of servants. Even when seeking a place, after arranging with a mistress, they not unfrequently fail to appear on the specified day. They have changed their mind, thinking the work too hard, or the neighbourhood too far from their friends, or what not.

CHARLES BOOTH and JESSE ARGYLE,
'Domestic Household Service' in *Life and Labour in London,* ed. Charles Booth, 2nd Series (1903).

ALTHOUGH in many ways domestic service between 1900 and 1914 continued the traditions of its Victorian heyday, with the employment of a resident maid still regarded as the hallmark of middle-class respectability, in other respects attitudes were changing. Even in the 1890s writers on household affairs had commented on the increasing reluctance of younger girls to become 'skivvies' or 'slavies', especially in small households, when they could obtain work in shops, factories and offices. And among those who did become maids, as Charles Booth noted, a more independent spirit often prevailed. One manifestation of this was a revival of trade unionism among servants just before the First World War, but still more significant was the greater willingness of girls to change jobs than even in late Victorian times. Thus Lilian Westall, who obtained her first place as a servant in about 1908, when she was nearly fifteen, had, within six years, been employed in six different domestic situations in addition to working for a short time in a factory.[1] Similarly, at the Brassey family's estate at Apethorpe, Northamptonshire, there were, between 1903 and 1911, five first kitchenmaids, four second kitchenmaids, and *ten* third kitchenmaids (some of whom stayed for a few weeks only), although among senior staff in the household changes were few.

L

Indeed, although in 1911 domestic service was still far and away the biggest employer of women and girls in the country, with a work force of about 1·3 million, the rate of expansion of that labour force was falling well behind the growth of demand. Not only were there fewer servants in proportion to the number of families in the 1900s than there had been in the 1880s (see Chapter 2), but, as the 1911 census report declared, the number of domestic indoor servants was growing 'at a much lower rate since 1901 than . . . the general population'. Even the decision of Queen Alexandra in 1901 to recognise the importance of domestic service by inviting ten thousand London maids-of-all-work to attend a series of 'Queen's Teas' to celebrate her husband's accession to the throne could not make housework popular. But for those who did attend the teas, held in about thirty different districts of London, there was the pleasure of drinking tea and eating buns and strawberries and of being waited on 'by ladies, wearing the finery appropriate to their station'.

Nevertheless, it was in conditions of growing 'servant shortage' that a number of Edwardian householders were reluctantly forced to economise on their resident domestic staff. Some overcame their difficulties by the introduction of labour-saving appliances; others by the use of part-time helpers. The number of daily charwomen was rising steeply: by 1911 it had reached 126,061, an advance of between 12 and 13 per cent over the previous decade. The performance of the heavier cleaning duties became increasingly the province of part-time employees, while, according to one writer, as early as the 1890s the family washing was 'consigned to a company or to individuals . . . almost as universally as it was formerly done at home'. The 1911 census report confirmed the large increase in the number of workers employed in powered laundries over the preceding ten years.

We have already noted in Chapter 2 two further means by which the servant-keeping classes had attempted to alleviate the shortage of staff in the closing years of the nineteenth century: the recruitment of servants from abroad and the employment of 'lady helps'. Neither practice had been widely adopted, though because of the increasing deficiency of ordinary servants in the new century, these two groups continued to feature as minority elements in the domestic work-force.

Despite the enthusiastic claims made on their behalf by employers who had enlisted staff from overseas, there were in 1911 only 10,827 foreign women and girls and about 1,750 men employed in England and Wales out of a total domestic staff of around 1·3 million females and around 54,000 males (including those engaged in hotels, lodging-houses and eating-houses). French, Germans and Swiss predominated, the French and Swiss being mainly engaged as ladies' maids or valets.

The difficulties surrounding the employment of 'lady helps' (outlined in Chapter 2) had made the idea generally unpopular and it had been largely abandoned during the 1890s. Yet in the conditions of shortage in the early 1900s it was revived, with the establishment of such organisations as the Guild of the Dames of the Household at Cheltenham in 1902, the Guild of Aids at Bath, and the Central Bureau for the Employment of Women in London. Each of these organisations provided a modicum of training for those seeking domestic work, and, as the Central Bureau declared in 1909, although they made a feature of supplying lady servants, they did 'not recommend applicants unless they had received at least three months' training'.[2] But despite all the preparations, 'the most successful and contented lady helps were those who secured posts as companions to tolerant old ladies employing no other domestic help'. Such positions were comparatively rare and were clearly outside the general run of staff shortages.

More hopeful than this method of alleviating the servant scarcity, therefore, were schemes devoted to economising on the number of staff employed. These took two principal forms. Firstly, there were revolutionary proposals to reorganise domestic and social life so as to introduce communal catering and service flats. Secondly, and more practically, there was the use of labour-saving appliances, such as washing-machines, vacuum cleaners, and other similar devices. It was in this latter area that the servant question was eventually to find its main answer in the twentieth century.

Throughout the period the most important labour-saving device of all, a conveniently constructed and fitted-out house, was not achieved. Rooms were cold and draughty, heated only by open fires, and this involved the servants in the daily cleaning of grates and the repeated carrying of scuttles of coal from the basement to the ground-floor and first-floor living-rooms. In the kitchen the large range or cumbersome gas-cooker required endless cleaning, while floors had to be scrubbed and kitchen tables kept in a state of pristine whiteness. However, thanks to the advances of technology, a variety of minor devices came along to ease the load, including the vacuum or suction cleaner. The key invention here was attributable to H. Cecil Booth, who in 1901, patented a device for drawing air through a cloth on which the dust was deposited. Booth founded the British Vacuum Cleaner Company, which used 'pumps, electrically or petrol driven, mounted on horse-drawn carts. For domestic cleaning the cart stopped outside the house and a hose was passed through a window.' So fascinating did it appear to London society that teaparties were given so that guests could watch the cleaning operations taking place around them.

Smaller domestic cleaners appeared around 1904, and the Army and Navy Stores Catalogue for 1907 contains a number of advertisements for various 'suction cleaning machines and dust extractors'. The 'Atom' Suction Cleaning Machine was one example which could be purchased for £11 17s. 6d. It not only cleaned carpets, hangings and covers but was 'equally efficient in freeing coats, dresses and old wearing apparel' from dust. Then there were the Bissell Carpet Sweepers, some of which were specifically recommended 'for ladies' use', presumably in families where no full-time servants were kept.

Self-acting polishing pads and heavy wood and iron washing-machines were also designed to satisfy labour-saving needs. Washing-machines, in a rather crude and heavy form, had become available from the middle of the nineteenth century; they 'usually consisted of a wooden tub corrugated on the inside and with a lever or "dolly", set into the lid, which could be moved with a handle'.

A few advertisers, like the makers of Stephenson's furniture cream, concentrated on the approach of making the servant's life an easier one. The caption to their advertisement, showing a housemaid working busily away at a table with a broad smile on her face, was 'Polishing a Pleasure'. In the same vein, the 'Servants' Friend' knife cleaner of 1880, which was produced by Messrs Spong & Co., promised not to 'belie its name' but to impart a 'lasting polish to knives' with, presumably, minimal effort on the part of the servant. Each machine could clean three, four and sometimes more knives at a time. Mr J. W. Fleming, whose used one such device when he worked as a part-time knife-boy and general help at the age of ten, describes how it operated. It consisted of 'a wooden frame mounted on cast iron, with slats into which the knife blades were pushed between two leather bands. Emery powder was put in between the leathers, the handle was turned and the blades cleaned. . . . To finish the job a flat board covered with linoleum with a sprinkle of Oakey's powder cleaned the shoulders, followed by washing, of course.'[3]

But for those anxious to achieve fundamental changes and to sweep aside the petty cares of household management, more ambitious plans were put forward. In an article entitled 'A Reformation of Domestic Service' which appeared in the *Nineteenth Century* during January 1893, the writer, Elizabeth Lewis, called for the provision of a 'culinary depôt in every street from which meals could be sent out'. She pointed out that in Nice, Rome and many other places 'the dinner is brought in to the apartments by a man from the restaurant, in a tin case containing a number of dishes', and she maintained that the same system could be adopted in England 'with ease and punctuality'. Once this reform had been achieved, the problems and wastefulness of running a family kitchen would be eliminated and a modification of the whole domestic system could be aimed at. A 'noble army of certificated day-housemaids' would appear to carry out their duties 'with promptitude, regularity, and thoroughly trained skill', and would then depart in the evening as quietly as they had arrived. The number of resident servants would be drastically reduced, and as a result there would be an overall amelioration of employer-servant relations. 'Left to each other, mistresses and maids would alike and together grow more simple and natural in their requirements and ways, to the great advantage and elevation of their nobility of character, and the jarring words "It's not my place" would be less and less spoken.'

These ideas were further developed in an article appearing in the same journal during the following month. It was entitled 'The Doom of the Domestic Cook', and in it the writer extolled the virtues of a system which would make 'the distasteful morning visit' to the kitchen a thing of the past. His plan was to establish a restaurant which would cook meals for several blocks of houses in the West End of London. According to his calculations the building and fitting-out of a centralised kitchen to cater for 3,500 people, including 'administrative offices, manager's residence, stabling, etc.', as well as cooking equipment, refrigerators and other necessary items, would amount to £43,300. (£6,000 of this would be spent on fifty carts and a hundred horses for delivery and similar purposes.) The dwellings supplied from the kitchen would all be within a quarter of a mile radius of it. And he considered that while the 270 or so households in his sample area were currently spending about £50,000 per annum 'for the privilege of having their food cooked in their own homes', they would, if they followed his 'principles of co-operation', save approximately two-thirds of this. He admitted that technical problems remained, such 'as the nature of the heated carts and vans which would have to be used, the porterage of light and cold viands by boys on carrier tricycles, the necessity of hot closets in the houses heated by gas for keeping warm the various courses', but claimed that they were as nothing compared to the 'miseries to which we have hitherto submitted. The Domestic Cook is dying out. What is to take her place if it be not some such system as the one I have attempted to describe?'

His readers were not convinced, and although the ideas were again canvassed in the new century (so that in November 1910 the Countess of Aberdeen opened a home at Letchworth Garden City from which day servants could go out to work in nearby middle-class households), nothing worthwhile came of the plans.

Yet if staff shortages were causing heartsearching on the part of employers, they also had their effect on the workers. In particular, they encouraged the formation of unions among domestic servants for the first time since the abortive efforts of 1872, when for a short period the maidservants of Dundee and the menservants of Leamington had each tried to combine in order to improve their working conditions.[4] These fresh attempts at organisation began before the turn of the century, when in June 1891 the London and Provincial Domestic Servants' Union was formed, with the slogan: 'By our Industry we Live. Unity is Strength.' Its secretary, Richard Redman, was a former butler, and a number of its twelve-member committee were butlers, cooks and ladies' maids. According to its first balance sheet, covering the period 23 October 1891 to 25 March 1892, its total income amounted to £136 15s. 0¾d. (of which about £40 had been obtained from entrance fees, subscriptions and the sale of membership cards), while expenditure had amounted to £108 16s. 0½d., of which just over half had been in respect of the half-yearly rent of the office, while £8 had been the secretary's half-yearly salary.[5] The first annual meeting of the union was held in the following June, when much time was devoted to a discussion of 'the ills from which its members' suffered. 'The old notion that a maidservant is a chattel to be enumerated along with a man's horses and oxen has not altogether disappeared,' declared the *Weekly Dispatch* of 12 June 1892 in its account of this first assembly.

When the union's rules were registered in November 1892 they showed that, in addition to the usual demands for higher wages and a reduction in working hours, there were proposals to establish *bona fide* servant registry offices and to improve 'the present unsatisfactory' system in the matter of characters. An entrance fee of 1s. was levied, in addition to 1d. for a membership card, and a weekly subscription of 1d. 'payable quarterly in advance on the usual Quarter Days'. Yet in a preface to the rule book, the union leaders made clear their belief in a pacific policy to achieve their aims :

> It is the desire of this Union to work in an educational way to raise the standard of domestic servants, and to endeavor to bring back the good feeling which formerly existed between servants and employers, and further wish it to be thoroughly understood that the Committee do most strongly object to the strike policy of ordinary trade unions.

During the months that followed, meetings were held to try to increase membership, but in spite of the efforts made, the union failed to attract more than a tiny minority of the metropolis's servants. In 1892 membership was estimated at 326, and this rose to a peak of 562 in 1895, before falling back to 244 in 1897; the union was finally dissolved in 1898.[6] It enjoyed the patronage of a number of eminent clergymen, including Dean Farrar, but despite this and despite its avoidance of the militant approach of its Dundee predecessor, it failed. The diffused nature of domestic service and the unwillingness of upper servants to join in agitation organised by lower servants, or *vice versa*, partly explained this outcome, as did the fear of servants of losing their places and being deprived of good character references if they appeared too active in the wrong cause.

However, the setback seemed only temporary when in 1910 a new union for domestic servants was established in London, under the title of the Domestic Workers' Union of Great Britain, and with a young servant named Grace Neal as secretary. Shortly afterwards a similar organisation was formed in Glasgow under the leadership of Jessie Stephen, the daughter of a Socialist tailor and cutter in the city. Miss Stephen was employed as a cook, and when in the autumn of 1911 there was a good deal of correspondence in the Glasgow press from dissatisfied domestic servants, she decided to organise a meeting in the Christian Institute, Bothwell Street, to discuss grievances. This meeting led to the formation of a union, to demand higher wages, two hours' free time each day, and regular rest days each month. Thanks to the publicity gained, the claims for two hours' free time and for wage advances were agreed by many employers.[7]

But despite the energy expended by Miss Stephen and her friends, membership remained small. She herself attributed this to the fact that the majority of servants in the area were drawn 'from the Highlands of Scotland or Southern Ireland and it would have been a great risk for a lonely servant to become militant by joining a trade union'. Her own experience certainly bore out the dangers of victimisation, for she was eventually blacklisted by employers and servant registry offices in Glasgow, and so she decided to come to London to join the Domestic Workers' Union there. This union also ran its own registry office, and through it Jessie was able to obtain a fresh post with employers who had 'no objection to engaging a trade unionist'. She recalled: 'I became very active in propaganda and educational work for the union in my spare time. Later the family moved to Herne Bay and asked me to accompany them but I was so deeply involved in my work for the union I had to refuse. We parted on the best of terms.'

The union registry office, for its part, made it clear that employers seeking staff through its agency must promise:

A minimum wage; sufficient food and decent sleeping accommodation . . . minimum hours of leisure out of house; fortnight's holiday per year on full pay; a true and fair written character to be given on leaving a place; no cleaning of out-

sides of upstairs windows etc. We earnestly appeal to all
Domestics to whom these concessions and others may be made
to show their appreciation of them by rendering willing and
efficient service in return.[8]

The organisation, like its predecessors, encountered difficulty
in breaking through the inertia of the domestic servant towards
industrial combination, and membership had reached only about
245 by 1912 and slightly less in 1913. When war broke out, the
union continued its work for a time, but as more and more
domestic servants took up employment in munitions factories and
elsewhere, it lost its remaining support. It was wound up in
1918.[9]

The formation of servants' unions did not lead to any spectacular improvements in their conditions, but served rather as a
barometer of discontent. Thus, while there is no record of unionism between 1872 (a year of general industrial unrest) and 1891,
from that year until 1914 there were no less than three separate,
if largely unsuccessful, attempts at combination by domestic staff.

So far parliament had taken little note of the position of the
domestic servant, beyond passing such measures as the 1851
Apprentices and Servants Act, which was discussed in Chapter 7.
An Englishman's home was still his castle, and there were no
'Home Acts' to match the Factory Acts which had earlier improved the lot of factory workers. Even in May 1911, when
Horatio Bottomley, Liberal M.P. for South Hackney, sponsored
a bill 'to regulate the hours of work, meal times and accommodation of domestic servants and to provide for the periodic
inspection of their kitchens and sleeping quarters', the measure
never progressed beyond the first reading. But in two areas at
least the period 1900-14 saw an advance for domestic servants—
as for other workers—in the passage of legislation to provide for
old-age pensions and sickness benefits.

Before the passage of the 1911 National Insurance Act the
treatment accorded to a servant when he or she became ill
depended very much on the attitude of the individual employer.
According to *Beeton's Domestic Service Guide*, mistresses were
'not bound to provide medical attendance or medicine for any of
their servants nor to pay for it unless ordered by them. . . . Should
the illness of a domestic servant appear likely to incapacitate her

for her duties permanently, or for a considerable time, her employer is not bound to continue the contract.' Indeed, the reaction of all too many mistresses was summed up by Mr E. Haviland-Burke, M.P., in a debate in the Commons on 28 November 1911: 'There are exceptional women as there are exceptional men but . . . the ordinary idea of the average woman who employs a servant is that if her servant becomes ill, she gets rid of her before she gets too ill to be moved.'

Of course, some employers adopted a far more sympathetic stance—like Charlotte Brontë, who despite her own precarious health, insisted on nursing both of her servants when they were ill, as well as carrying out the household chores. Furthermore, even when employers declined to allow their servants to be nursed in their own household, they might send them along to a hospital to which they regularly subscribed. According to one observer, in the 1890s, a number of donors to the voluntary hospitals in London looked upon these institutions as provident dispensaries, to which, if they gave a good subscription, they had 'a right to send all their dependants for hospital treatment'. St George's Hospital, Hyde Park Corner, was particularly singled out as 'a hospital for gentlemen's servants'; according to its secretary in the year 1890, about sixteen per cent of its patients fell into the servant class—although by no means all of them were employed by subscribers to the hospital.[10]

For those who could not rely upon the goodwill of employers or the support of their family, charity and self-help were two other alternatives available. One organisation which combined both principles was the Servants' Benevolent Institution, which was first established in 1846 and is still in existence in the 1970s. The initiator of the scheme was a servant named William Ashwell, and in appeals to his fellow-domestics 'and the public in general' he called for the building of almshouses to assist the aged and also pointed out that 'in the four workhouses of St Marylebone, St Pancras, St George, Hanover Square, and St James, Westminster, there [were] not fewer than 1,659 adult paupers who [described] themselves as having been domestic servants. Let not servants, any more than men of any other class, think that help worth anything is to be got save for themselves. . . . The true patriot spirit is self-help.'[11] But in spite of Ashwell's advocacy of the principles of self-help, his organisation quickly became heavily dependent on charity, and by the middle of the Victorian era was providing not only pensions for over a hundred aged former servants but also temporary relief to those who had fallen on hard times due to sickness or unemployment.

But for many domestic workers who became ill, the Poor Law and the workhouse remained the only resort. At Kensington Poor Law Infirmary in 1871, for example, fifty-five of the 130 female inmates recorded in the census were domestic servants; and at St George's Workhouse, Hanover Square, there were 133 female domestic servants out of a total of 434 female inmates. The position was summed up in 1911 by David Lloyd George during a debate on the 1911 National Insurance Act: 'The majority of . . . servants are employed in houses where there is only one servant. . . . The mistress cannot keep a sick servant, not because she has not got the means, but because she has not got the accommodation; she has not got the time for nursing and for attendance.'

For workers faced with such unattractive alternatives when they became ill, it might have seemed that the Liberal government's National Insurance Act, with its promise of free medical treatment and cash benefits during sickness, would have been warmly welcomed. Yet, at least in the bill's early stages, many servants viewed it with suspicion. Thanks to a campaign, organised largely by the *Daily Mail* newspaper, fears were aroused that the threepence per week contribution required from mistress and female servant alike would undermine the existing good relations between employer and dependant, and would also represent a 'tax' on the servant's already scanty income. The *Daily Mail* claimed in a leader on 20 November 1911 that although both maid and mistress would pay 13s. a year towards the fund, with the mistress acting 'as the collector of a thoroughly unpopular impost', the servant would gain little thereby.

Her position is positively changed for the worse. In present circumstances, if she is ill her mistress provides her with medical attendance, pays her wages, and cares for her till she is well. Under the Bill the servant will run the risk of being required to shift for herself in illness. She will be granted medical attendance by an overworked and underpaid insurance doctor, and given a wretched pittance of 7s. 6d. a week to meet the cost of her maintenance. Nor is this all the mischief that will be caused by these clauses of the Bill. There are thousands of families too poor to pay the new tax of 26s. for a servant; and thus will be obliged to do without a domestic. A great increase in the number of unemployed servants is therefore a certainty.

In making these statements the *Daily Mail* conveniently ignored the many employers who made no formal provision for their servants during illness. And in raising the bogy of unemployment, it failed to recognise that *scarcity* of servants was the great talking-point of the Edwardian and early Georgian middle-classes—not a superfluity.

Other alarmists warned that mistresses were not only being turned into tax-gatherers but might also have to endure the invasion of their drawing-room by inspectors anxious to check that the legislation was being observed. In fact Lloyd George had already tabled an amendment to remove any threat to the 'sanctity of the drawing-room', but it was an effective argument while it lasted.

As early as July 1911 rumblings of discontent over the position of servants under the National Insurance Bill were heard, with Lloyd George receiving several deputations on behalf of women workers. But it was at the end of October that the campaign really gathered momentum. The *Daily Mail* opened its columns to opponents of the measure, and soon letters were pouring in. Some, like 'Rita', a well-known Edwardian novelist, 'called for a strike of mistresses against the tax' and received many promises of support. Another employer, writing from Berkeley Square, similarly expressed her willingness 'to start a protest league against this obnoxious clause in the Insurance Bill (the servant stamp). . . . I have no intention of paying the 6d. per week and my maid also refuses to have anything to do with it. If every household flatly refuses to pay what will happen? Let the women of England strike against the clause, and at once.'[12]

Some of the letters proved to be bogus—like the missive written 'on behalf of forty-seven servants employed at Hamblin's Hotel, Old Brompton'. As the Attorney-General informed parliament, in answer to a question, 'no such hotel exists and . . . the forty-seven servants are purely imaginary'.

Letters of protest were meanwhile arriving at the House of

Commons by the sackful, and the campaign of opposition only reached its peak at the end of November with the holding of a meeting of over twenty thousand women at the Albert Hall, under the leadership of the Dowager Lady Desart. However, on the day immediately preceding this Lloyd George invited a party of mistresses and maids to discuss the measure with him at the Treasury. Some, though not all, of the Albert Hall meeting organisers attended, and after explaining the details of his proposed measure, Lloyd George claimed to detect a change of heart among the servants present : 'I observed a great deal of enlightenment appear on [their] faces . . . not unmixed with surprise, when I told them accurately what the benefits were. They were not so loud in their protests at the end . . . as they were at the beginning.' The Liberal *Daily News* triumphantly heralded the meeting as the 'Death-blow to the Protest League'. Consequently, despite the impressive size of the Albert Hall gathering, the vigour of the campaign was already abating, as the benefits of the legislation percolated through to the class most concerned—the servants. In any case, when it came to the point, few employers were prepared to risk prosecution for defying the law, while among the domestics there had always been a number who had refused to join the protest, believing that any proposal 'which roused their mistresses to such a pitch of fury must be fundamentally a sound idea'.[13]

When the scheme came into operation in July 1912, every insured woman worker became entitled to medical attendance from a doctor of her own choice; free treatment in a sanatorium or other institution 'when suffering from Tuberculosis'; a weekly sickness benefit of 7s. 6d. a week for twenty-six weeks; and a disablement benefit of 5s. a week, should she still be unable to work after this period had elapsed. Men were covered on similar terms, except that in their case the weekly contribution was 4d. and their sickness benefit amounted to 10s. a week for twenty-six weeks.

Yet if ill-health was one major hazard for the servant with no home of her own to fall back upon, unemployment and old age were two other problems. Even when demand for servants was at a high level, there were always some who were too old or too shabby to get employment, while others were affected by the seasonal demand for their labour. In 1910 the Royal Commission on the Poor Laws discovered that on the east coast, women servants who were busy in July and August were under-employed for the rest of the year. 'The workers get into debt and receive poor relief or beg. The tradespeople in these seaside resorts suffer greatly from the fact that their customers are always indebted to them.' Similar comments were made with regard to south coast resorts.

Old age was an even greater difficulty for servants who had no families of their own, and here at least the early twentieth century brought improvement to many. Traditionally, butlers and footmen would try to save enough money in their working life to set themselves up as publicans on their retirement, while other servants would seek to become small shopkeepers or proprietors of lodging-houses. The dependants of the largest households could hope to receive a small pension and perhaps a cottage on the family estate or a room of their own in their employer's house where they could spend their last years. Thus on the Brassey family's Apethorpe estate, Northamptonshire, a financial statement prepared in 1911 reveals the regular expenditure of 8s. per week each for pensions to several retired long-serving employees, often with the benefit of a free cottage as well. Sometimes the pensions were followed by legacies to old and valued retainers. There must have been many country squires who felt as Horace Walpole did when, in his old age, he wrote : 'I know . . . how pleasant it is to have laid up a little for those I love, for those that depend on me, and for old servants.'

Unfortunately for most servants, these opportunities did not exist. For those who neither married nor became trusted retainers in a comfortable household, old age meant loneliness and, at the end, perhaps entry into a workhouse. According to Joseph Chamberlain, in evidence before the Royal Commission on the Aged Poor in 1893, no one would employ a servant 'past 50 years of age and accordingly, almost by the necessity of the case, they will have to go to the workhouse'. He claimed that in Birmingham Workhouse there were 438 female inmates over the age of sixty-five, and that more than one in three of them had been 'directly connected with domestic service'. Evidence from other workhouses tends to bear this out. At the time of the 1871 census approximately one female inmate in three at the St George's Workhouse, Hanover Square, was a domestic servant, and those aged sixty or over comprised nearly half of the total. At Fulham and Kensington Workhouses similar proportions operated. This situation can be better appreciated if it is realised that in 1911, when the female indoor work-force had risen to around 1·3 million, those aged sixty-five or over only numbered 17,131; among the men the figures were about 54,000 and 742 respectively. Despite the 'servant shortage', employers did not wish to risk employing older staff who might fall ill or who were perhaps too stiff to rush around in response to commands.

Nor was it only the general staff among former domestic servants who were likely to end up in the workhouse. Of the sixty-three female servants aged sixty or over in Kensington Workhouse in 1871, three were former cooks, two were housekeepers, and one was an ex-governess. At Kensington Hall Infirmary, which catered for the sick only, of thirty-five inmates over the age of sixty, nine were cooks, seven were ex-housekeepers, one a former governess, and one a lady's maid. The fate of Mrs Everest, Winston Churchill's devoted childhood nurse, was a warning that it was not only the employee of the small household who could find herself redundant after many years' service. Despite the young Winston's appeals to his parents for a reprieve, Mrs Everest was abruptly dismissed on economy grounds, with a small pension, in 1893. In *My Early Life* Churchill has described how two years later he travelled up from Sandhurst to attend her last illness and to pay for a doctor to attend her. Years later he wrote of the fate 'of poor old women, so many of whom have no one to look after them and nothing to live on at the end of their lives'.

The Old Age Pensions Act of 1908 mitigated this unhappy state of affairs. For the first time those aged seventy or above, whose income from other sources did not exceed £21 per annum, were entitled to a weekly payment of 5s. as of *right*. Although the amount appears pitifully small to modern eyes, it was a first step towards helping to independence old people who would otherwise have had to rely on the uncertainties and petty restrictions of the Poor Law. Of the approximately 88,000 female pensioners whose former occupations were recorded in the census of 1911, over one-quarter had been in domestic service.

10

The Final Phase

With the spread of education and of modern ideas combined with
alternative forms of employment, domestic service entered a new
phase. Women and girls in the years between the wars showed—
even during the period of heavy unemployment—a growing reluctance to enter the profession. The perfunctory and casual work
of untrained and unwilling entrants did nothing to ease the
situation. . . . The younger generation in the years between the
two World Wars was inclined more and more to think that the
domestic worker held an inferior place in the labour market and
to despise her accordingly. To live at home, to be free agents in
the evening after factory, shop and office had closed, became
increasingly desirable.

VIOLET MARKHAM and FLORENCE HANCOCK, *Report on
Organisation of Private Domestic Employment* (1944-45).

Only since the 1st War did things change. The wealthy then
realised we were worth more than they paid us. When the call for
women came thousands 'joined up'. I went into a High Explosive
factory. We filled a gap, which has never been really recognised.

A former cook in a letter to the author.

THE First World War represents a watershed in the history of
domestic service. Girls who had felt there was no alternative but
to take a job as a maid now found themselves acting as factory
workers, bus conductresses, canteen assistants, land girls, nurses
and shop assistants—often replacing men who had been called up.
During the course of the war the number of female domestic
servants fell by about a quarter, while female munitions workers
increased from 212,000 to over 900,000. And in 1917 about half
of the 2,500 women tram and bus conductresses were said to be
former domestic servants.[1] For most men-servants, too, there was
little alternative but to join the armed forces or a vital war

industry, and sometimes they had the active encouragement of their employers to do so. Thus Colonel Borton of Cheveney, Kent, noted in his diary on 17 August 1914 that he had taken 'Albert Pattenden (my footman) and Reiss my cowman to the Maidstone Barracks to enlist'. A week later he drove 'that gallant old soldier Sammy Johnston (my butler) to the Barracks to enlist although 43 years of age'.[2] Reiss, like many thousands of other men in this murderous conflict, was killed in action, while Pattenden and Johnston were both wounded.

But for those workers who did remain in service, the demand for their labour was so great that they could pick and choose their employers. One middle-class family in Essex, who had recruited only two different house-parlourmaids between 1903 and 1914, had four changes between that year and 1918; two of the four stayed for weeks only.[3]

With the coming of the armistice many former servants returned to their old jobs, but for others the prospect now seemed narrow and limited. A former butler recalled that although he went back to his previous employers in 1919, he left shortly afterwards as 'the job was too restricting'. He went into business on his own and, despite the difficulties of the inter-war years, prospered.[4] A number of women felt the same, and among the permanent legacies of the war were increases in the scope of female employment and a still further reduction in the status of domestic service. 'Servant-keeping was never again easily available to the middle classes as a whole, and in the post-war world it increasingly became a privilege of upper income-levels. In the commuter area of London the number of servants per 100 families fell from 24·1 in 1911 to 12·4 in 1921, while in the West End it declined only from 57·3 to 41·3.'[5] By 1931 about half a million households, or just under five per cent of all private families, employed resident domestics (rather more than three-quarters of them being one-servant households); by contrast, in 1911 there were estimated to be '800,000 families in this country with servants'.[6]

The war was barely over when, in December 1918, the Ministry of Reconstruction, mindful of the 'servant problem', appointed a Domestic Service Committee to look into the whole question of the distribution, training and conditions of servants and to consider why the occupation was failing to attract the necessary

M

number of recruits. The committee's findings were not unanimous —a fact perhaps scarcely surprising, since its members varied from trade unionists to titled ladies—and several dissenting memoranda were issued by individual members who found themselves unable to support the general conclusions. The Marchioness of Londonderry, for example, opposed several recommendations, including one for the adoption of local joint committees of employers and workers to decide conditions of employment along the lines of the Whitley Councils which were being adopted in other industries. She felt that such ideas would 'produce a spirit of hostility on the part of the employer and lack of co-operation on the part of the worker'. But the force of her arguments was rather reduced by the fact that 'pressure of work' prevented her from attending any of the meetings in person.

Yet despite the disagreements, the report did identify several reasons for the unpopularity of domestic service. These included the 'loss of social status' encountered by those entering the occupation. It was felt that the distinctive dress they wore marked them out 'as a class apart, the cap being generally resented'. There was also resentment at the custom of addressing domestic workers by their Christian names or surnames instead of Miss ——, and the attitude of the press and the stage in representing servants 'as comic or flippant characters' was condemned. Other unfavourable aspects were the long hours of duty and the lack of companionship in small households.

Among the remedies put forward were the provision of properly organised training centres; a reduction in the hours which workers spent on duty; the provision of regular meal-time and holiday breaks (including a fortnight's holiday with board wages each year); and the allowance of two hours' free time daily, when servants should not have to answer bells and do other work, or a day off at regular intervals in lieu. For non-resident staff a maximum working week of forty-eight hours was proposed, exclusive of meal breaks. It was suggested that there should be a night's rest of at least nine hours for the youngest servants and that if uniforms were required, they should be provided by the employer.

At the end of the report came a memorandum on wages prepared by Miss Jessie Stephen, who was one of the committee members. In this she drew up a minimum scale of pay which she considered should form the basis for 'fixing a National Standard Wage for Domestic Workers'. (See Appendix A for a copy of this.) Needless to say, it was not adopted.

So, despite the efforts made, the committee's findings had little practical effect. One small concession made by the government was to provide free uniforms for those prepared to take jobs as resident domestics but who lacked suitable clothes or money to buy them. According to the Central Committee on Women's Training and Employment in its report to the Minister of Labour in 1923-24, nearly 4,000 women were provided with clothing under the scheme, at a total cost of £12,470.

There was also a campaign to persuade demobilised, out-of-work soldiers to go into service, and although a number of ex-soldiers did drift into domestic work, they largely moved into clubs, hotels or restaurants rather than private houses. In 1931, out of total of 70,409 males in domestic service, only half—35,693 —were in private service.[7] They included batmen who had accompanied their demobilised masters into private life, but whose loyalty was often tested in the transfer from the shared dangers of war to a world of unshared privilege in upper-class society.

In addition, in 1920 the Central Committee on Women's Training and Employment, which had been given the task of dealing with post-war unemployment among women, launched 'homecraft' and 'home-maker' courses with a domestic bias. Although the 'home-maker courses were not regarded as vocational training', being aimed solely 'at giving unemployed women some instruction in elementary home duties', those taking up the homecraft places were required, from 1921, to give an undertaking that they would enter residential domestic service when their training had ended. For women with a regular trade to go to when economic conditions improved, this was unacceptable, and many refused to sign. Eventually under pressure from women's organisations, the government in 1924 agreed to amalgamate the two courses to form a 'home training' course, and to end the requirement to enter domestic service. But in any case, the contribution of the schemes to the home work-force was small. At the end of 1924 only 25,000 had been sent on the courses by the Central Committee, at a cost of £400,000, and by no means all of these candidates had gone into service. (For nannies, private training colleges had been established in the later nineteenth century, for example the Norland Nursery Training College, but even in the inter-war period they contributed only a few hundred recruits to the total of domestic nurses.)

During the depression of the early 1930s the number of state-supported training centres for servants was again increased, and by 1934 there were twenty-four of them, mainly in the distressed areas. They were each attended by up to forty day pupils, aged around fifteen, and with courses lasting thirteen weeks. There were also six residential centres in which girls underwent a more intensive course lasting eight weeks. And in 1937 a further centre was opened to train Welsh lads as houseboys and kitchen assistants, 'work for which they were said to have a natural aptitude and which was rewarded by a wage of 10s. to 15s. a week'. A state-aided Roman Catholic training centre 'helped to staff the servants' hall at Arundel Castle, the Archbishop's Palace at Westminster and Beaumont College'.

In their first fifteen years of life these various centres trained and placed about 67,000 girls—at a time when there were between 300,000 and 400,000 women unemployed. 'The training centres drew in only a trickle of these and the least hint of a trade revival caused a run-down in the number of applicants.'⁸ In fact, as Elaine Burton discovered while employed as a social worker in the Rhondda Valley in 1935-36, despite the lack of jobs in the area, the girls simply refused to enter domestic service because they felt their friends would look down on them 'and you never knew when your day was finished'. Miss Burton added: 'I remember many of these youngsters accepting jobs in shops which carried lower wages and much worse working conditions than domestic work in the majority of private houses. But somehow you kept your independence—and your evenings!'

So, despite the varied efforts at official level, by 1921 the number of women and girls in domestic service in England and Wales had only recovered to just over 1·2 million after the wartime decline. But with the deepening of economic depression and the growth of unemployment from 1921 onwards, more girls were reluctantly forced to enter service because other avenues of employment were closed to them. In 1931 there were 1,332,224 female servants, of whom 1,142,655 were in private service.

Yet among those driven into domestic work by adverse economic conditions, a critical attitude often prevailed, and a readiness to question the validity of the subordinate status they were expected to occupy. Violet Firth, who had worked as a lady gardener for three years during the First World War and who 'knew the servant's position from personal experience', pinpointed this in her book, *The Psychology of the Servant Problem*, published in 1925 : 'A mistress does not demand of her servant work only, she also demands a certain manner, a manner which shall clearly indicate her superiority and the inferiority of the woman who takes her wages; there is nothing derogatory in performing the work, but there is something very derogatory—something which is hurtful to human dignity—in assuming the required attitude.' In the inter-war years fewer and fewer girls were prepared to adopt the deferential attitude which had been demanded of their Victorian predecessors; as one employer remembers, 'Noise was continuous, shouts of laughter, loud singing. . . . Older maids looked in dismay and contempt at half-done jobs and offhand lasses who demanded latch-keys.'[9]

One reluctant recruit to the servant ranks during the 1920s was Jean Rennie of Greenock in Scotland, who went into service in 1924 as a third housemaid in a country house in Argyllshire. In the previous years, at the age of seventeen, she had been awarded a scholarship to Glasgow University but had been unable to take it up because her father was out of work. She obtained a job as a parceller at a worsted factory, but within a short time she was made redundant because of depression in the woollen industry. She then spent three months searching the newspapers for a fresh post before applying, with great reluctance, for the Argyllshire job. She later wrote : 'My greatest horror was the knowledge that *I* would now have to submit to the bondage of servitude—a cap and apron.' She was to remain a domestic servant for sixteen years, but her dislike for her job never waned. Indeed, in her first place she bitterly compared the waste of food in that large country house (even by fellow-servants) with the plight of hungry children in her native Greenock.[10]

Another girl who became a servant under economic pressure was Esma Berte, whose father lost his job as a chartered accountant in 1931. She answered an advertisement which encouragingly spoke of 'Lovely garden; other help kept.' But, as she recalled,

'I never got into the garden! And the other help was a lad who helped with the horses they kept for riding. I had 15 shillings a week, of which I managed to send home five, and I had one afternoon and evening off a week—after I had washed up and washed the kitchen floor, and I had to be in at ten.' She was allowed one weekend off in four to visit her family, but eventually the hard work proved too much for her and she had to leave.[11]

The deep distress in London's dockland in the 1920s is remembered by Mrs Dora Duncan, who went with her mother to recruit a general maid.

> We went to a Hall which was lined with girls and women waiting for work. Mother engaged a nice girl, about thirty years old, who stayed with us several years until she married, and paid her I think about 27s. 6d. a week to live in. What I shall never forget was that girls crowded round us as we left, and plucked at our sleeves, asking if we had friends who would give them work. I don't think I had ever come across desperate poverty before.[12]

Nevertheless, for those who still had a choice in the matter, domestic service remained low on the list of desirable occupations. Middle-class families unable to get staff wrote embittered letters to the press claiming that girls preferred to live on the dole rather than take up domestic work. (The complaint was rather wide of the mark in that private domestic servants had been deliberately excluded from the extension of unemployment insurance in 1920. Girls receiving insurance payments when they were out of work were therefore not former servants, who were not to be included in the insurance scheme until 1938.) Yet so shrill did the complaints become that in 1923 the Ministry of Labour appointed a committee, under the chairmanship of Mrs E. M. Wood, to investigate the charges.

The committee found no justification for the allegations that girls had refused work as servants because they preferred to draw the dole. One typical complaint investigated was that produced by a Chester reader in a letter to the *Daily Mail* of 12 April 1923: 'It is a crying disgrace that all these women and girls should have the dole when domestic servants are wanted in great numbers. I had to give up curing my own bacon and am thinking of giving up my dairy and poultry simply because I cannot get an experienced cook.' But when the case was taken up with the manager of the Chester Employment Exchange he was unable to trace any appeal for staff from the woman in question. Most of the other complaints yielded a similar result.

However, the committee did discover other reasons for reluctance to enter service. Largely they followed the pattern of those put forward four years earlier in the report of the Ministry of Reconstruction's Committee on Domestic Service. There was, in particular, continued resentment at the low status of servants, which was apparent even among other members of the working class. A parlourmaid giving evidence to the committee declared : 'Invitations out start : "Be sure and don't let it be known you are a domestic. We shouldn't like our friends to mix with servants." It is the snobbery of our own class.' A housemaid similarly observed : 'If two girls come from the same family and one went as a domestic servant and the other as a clerk, the servant would be looked down on much more than the clerk.'

Other girls disliked the loneliness of small households, and the committee concluded that there was 'little difficulty, even now, in obtaining domestic workers for big private establishments maintaining a large staff'. Leisure time was usually more generous in larger households than in small, and there was often a better spirit of teamwork and camaraderie.

Under these conditions of scarcity the bargaining position of those who did take up household work was greatly increased. Employers were prepared to snatch at anyone who *said* she could clean the house or cook meals. Monica Dickens in *One Pair of Hands* has amusingly described how she obtained a succession of jobs as cook-general in London, even though she had had no real training in domestic work or the culinary arts. Similarly, a young North-country maid who moved to London and registered for temporary work with a large agency in the late 1920s often had a choice of over fifty jobs at any one time. Some employers economised by requiring one servant to fulfil a number of different roles. Thus Mrs Stratton-Brown of Hampshire remembers that when she lived at Chatham in 1936 she had a young girl 'who started the day wearing a pink linen dress to do all the house work; after lunch she added a stiff white collar and became the Nannie taking my young son out for walks with the other Nannies; then for tea she changed into a brown dress and coffee

coloured apron, and became the parlour maid. We gave her 12/–
a week, which later went up to 14/–.'

But many mistresses were far less fortunate, as the following
extracts from the servants' book of Mrs Collier of Crowell in
Oxfordshire indicate :

> September 1918 After many struggles and employing a variety
> of charwomen, I heard Annie Strange would be shortly
> requiring a situation as house-parlourmaid, engaged her to
> come on September 24 at £25 a year, to be raised to £26 in
> January 1919.
>
> 27 November 1924 At present no suitable cook has applied,
> advertising & registry offices seem useless.
>
> 20 October 1929 Advertised for another house-parlourmaid in
> the *Oxford Times* and *Thame Gazette*—received six appli-
> cations. Finally settled with Winifred Kiddy aged 16,
> daughter of a gamekeeper at Tythrop. Rather too young,
> but appears to be keen on her work. Wages £20 to start.

The last-named servant left in April 1931 due to ill-health; she
was then earning £26 per annum. In all, over the period 1914
to 1924, Mrs Collier had ten different house-parlourmaids and
ten cooks, whereas over a comparable period from 1903 to 1913
the changes had been two and six respectively.

Yet, despite the tendency for servants to move more frequently
and perhaps to worry less about obtaining good references than
their Victorian and Edwardian predecessors (a number of girls
simply ran away from jobs they did not like), for those who remained in employment, the daily chores had changed but little.
Admittedly, labour-saving appliances were becoming more common : houses now usually had water laid on in the upper floors,
so maids did not have to struggle upstairs with cans of hot water
for baths; gas fires were often installed in bedrooms; and rooms
tended to be more simply furnished, thereby easing problems of
dusting and polishing. But the account of one girl's introduction
to the duties of 'between maid' for a comfortably-off family in
Lancashire in 1925 would not have been out of place fifty years
earlier. Perhaps the only difference was that she felt free to leave
after six months and had little difficulty in obtaining a fresh
place. She had three fellow-servants : Daisy, the cook, Maud, the
parlourmaid, and Mabel, the housemaid, the two latter being

friends who had worked in several places together. As between maid she had to help both cook and housemaid, and her pre-breakfast duties were as follows :

> Do kitchen range and light fire.
> Fill kettles and put cook's tools ready on table.
> Sweep floor. Do maids' sitting-room fire.
> Sweep maids' room, dust and lay breakfast table.
> Scrub front steps.
> Clean taps and basins in cloakroom.
> Scrub cloakroom floor, polish lavatory seat.
> Scrub vestibule floor.
> Make early morning tea and carry up to maids.
> Take cans of hot water up to maids.
> Do fires in dining-room, drawing-room, library, and morning-room.
> Sweep first landing, front stairs and hall.
> Wash, and put on clean apron for breakfast.[18]

She had to rise by 5.30 each morning in order to complete her labours, and the rest of her day continued in much the same fashion :

> After breakfast Mabel claimed me for help with bed making and other upstairs work. At twelve thirty she sent me down to Maud for half-an-hour's silver cleaning, or lessons in table and tray laying. Lunch over, up I went again to do the staff bathroom, back stairs, housemaid's cupboard, and the top landing; also to wash dusters and clean all the copper hot water cans. By 2.30 Daisy would be growling up the back stairs, 'Isn't that girl coming down yet? She's supposed to be between maid, not under-housemaid.' If Mabel felt like it, she would let me go, if not she made me finish the last little job. What a scene I went down to! Daisy would have died rather than wash one basin. In addition to breakfast and dinner dishes every pan, spoon, sieve, and dish used by her were piled on the table, in the sink, on the draining board and on the floor. She was an excellent cook, but a messy worker, and on my way to the sink I often slithered on gravy, milk and other greasy liquids. Daisy retired to wash and change and have a little rest, while I tackled the mess. After scrubbing the kitchen and larder floors,

I washed our sitting-room floor, and prepared our tea. After tea, out to the kitchen again, to prepare vegetables, and wait on Daisy. Fetch and carry for her, stir or beat mixture, wipe up her spills and chop parsley. . . . When the gentry were at dinner I carried some of the dishes as far as the dining-room door, and if we had guests staying in the house Mabel collared me to help turn the beds down and put out night clothes. Not until our evening meal was over was I able to tackle another mountain of washing up, another sea of spills. This I did while my sisters-in-service sat by the fire with a tea tray. If we had no dinner party, I finished about 9.30 p.m., but guests meant that I chanted my Good Nights as late as 11.30.

This girl had little contact with her employers, and it was her fellow-servants who proved the real taskmasters. The cook, in particular, treated her harshly : 'Daisy was the last straw which broke this camel's back. Never once did she give me a kind word. How one woman could think out so many ways of making another person's life hard is incredible.' In the end she left the job.

Of course, by no means all young maids were as unfortunate as this. Indeed, in her own later career this girl had pleasant employers and fellow-servants as well as ill-tempered and thoughtless ones. Mrs Meadows, an elderly lady for whom she worked in Kent and who kept a chef, housemaid, parlourmaid, daily woman and four gardeners, had an extremely happy household.

My dusting and silver cleaning were finished by twelve o'clock when I dressed to wait at table. I stood in the room throughout lunch and dinner, while the mistress sat, just discernible, at the far end of a massive table. . . . Afternoons were quiet and pleasant. I read, knitted, and talked with Olive [the housemaid]. Sometimes Mrs Meadows would send me out for a walk, saying I must not shut myself up with old people. The old gardeners were sweet, I only had to appear at my pantry door with a small mat to shake, and one of them would toddle up and do it for me.

Countless other servants enjoyed happy relations with their employers. Some stayed with one family for years, just as their Victorian predecessors had done, and even when they married or retired they continued to keep in touch with their old employers. Thus a former butler, who only retired in 1973, when his last employer died and left him a house, remembers that even if hours were long 'there were always compensations. I may have been a lucky one. I always met good employers.'[14] Similarly, Mrs M. Jenner of Thornton Heath has happy memories of domestic service in the 1920s and 1930s:

> I had quite a few different jobs, some as cook and some as housemaid, and quite happy in most of them. The best and happiest one was the last one about 1928. My friend . . . was the cook, my sister was the parlourmaid and I was the house-maid. The family that we worked for were wonderful people, always so kind and friendly that work was a pleasure. Food was the same that was served in the dining room and at Christmas bottles of drink would come out, including cham-pagne. We three worked together so well everything went like clockwork. I don't think I have any regrets.[15]

For Mr Tuckwell of Oxford, on the other hand, the pleasantest side of his career as hall-boy, footman and butler was the en-couragement he was given to play cricket and football by his employers. Sometimes his subscriptions to the relevant clubs would be paid, and he was allowed additional time off to permit him to compete in various inter-club events. He also enjoyed the visits made with his employers to Scotland for the grouse-shooting (where he acted as loader) and to Wales for the fishing.

For those employed in the largest households the formality and hierarchical structure of domestic life largely persisted. As in Victorian times, 'each department was a law unto itself' and no one lightly interfered in another domain. As the *New Survey of London Life and Labour*, published in 1931, noted, 'The vitality of "demarcation disputes" is illustrated by the fact that, as we are assured, the ancient quarrel as to whose duty it is to lay the cloth for the servants' meal when the servants' maid is out still goes on.' Certainly, Mrs D. King, who was in service from the age of fourteen in 1927 until she left to be married in 1934, recalls that it was 'the Butlers or Cooks who made or spoilt a place, they really had so much power'. And Albert Butler, who worked as a gardener in a number of stately homes during the inter-war period, notes: 'In all the places where I worked, it was the head servants that made life hard for the under-dogs. The gentry affected us not at all. I remember with amusement (now) the ludicrous attempts of some of them to "ape" the master and the mistress, in speech and manners.'[16] But in his experience, easily 'the most hated servant of all was the lady's maid. This was so in most big houses. *Nothing* escaped her eyes and her tongue wagged unceasingly.'

If some servants were contented with their lot, many others retained to the end of the inter-war period that dislike of domestic work which had been noted in the official reports of 1919 and 1923. There was disgust at the petty restrictions imposed and the inferior treatment accorded. Mrs Hilda Rickard of Devon recalls that when she and her husband were employed by a naval captain's wife as cook-general and chauffeur respectively, during the 1930s, they 'lived on kedgeree and rice pudding. The store cupboard was kept locked, so that I had to remember each morning what I needed, and I'm afraid that very often I forgot something, which worried me quite a lot. In the end I discovered a door key that fitted the store, which was a great relief.' But she also remarks bitterly : 'This locking things up makes people dishonest; it's as though because one is working class one is not to be trusted !' Likewise another girl, although remaining with the same employer for nearly eighteen years, can remember the many minor humiliations of her position. She had wanted to learn to play the piano and to play tennis, 'but it was frowned upon by my employer who said, "Whoever heard of a domestic servant wanting to do such things?".' When this girl finally left domestic service to become housekeeper to her uncle, she felt that at last she 'was really alive, able to get out in God's beautiful world whenever I wished'.[17] Similar views are expressed by a man who spent the first fourteen years of his life as a footman in private service until he moved into a factory during the Second World War. In the late 1960s he was made redundant, and 'the labour exchange learning of my previous experience in private service offered me a job in Buckingham Palace. But now I had tasted freedom I had never known and all overtime paid'—so the offer was rejected. He adds : 'I have never regretted leaving private service.'

Some dissatisfied workers, like Ethel Beaumont, wrote of their experiences to the press. In an article in the *Evening Standard* of

9 March 1933 Ethel described her first place as cook-general:

> The . . . house was exceptionally nice—for the owners. The rooms were well furnished in good taste to give the greatest possible comfort. But the kitchen—there was only a wooden table and two wooden chairs, one backless. There was no fire to sit by, merely a coke boiler and a gas-stove. . . . All the washing, barring sheets was done at home—even heavy bath sheets. There was no wringer, so that everything had to be wrung by hand, a task far too heavy for the average young girl.

Her second place, as a chauffeuse, was still worse. During the first week the cook fell ill, and she had to do the cooking, housework and shopping as well as her own job. Then after a few weeks her employers decided they did not want a chauffeuse, and asked Ethel if she would stay as a 'help'. She agreed, but after a time was 'accused of being rude; in fact, "The way you enter a room is rude!" I remarked that they really couldn't talk of manners, never having said either "Please" or "Thank you" since I had been in the house. The reply to this was, "Of course not! You are paid to do the work!".' As she added: 'To my knowledge these last people have had eight cooks and four chauffeurs in twelve months. Twelve dissatisfied people telling others!' More and more girls were prepared to stand up for themselves in this fashion, and to refuse to accept what they felt was inconsiderate behaviour from employers.

These feelings were intensified by the social changes of the Second World War and its aftermath. By 1951 about 350,000 women were employed in private domestic service in England and Wales, as compared to the 1·1 million so recorded in 1931. Over the same period there was a dramatic increase in the number of clerks and typists, who had by 1951 reached 1,271,000 and now constituted the largest single occupation for women.[18] Almost twenty years later, in 1969, the total number of those engaged in private service in the whole of Great Britain had shrunk to 118,000; 12,000 of these were men, and 106,000 women.[19]

In the post-war world the old traditions of personal service and obedience of one class to another have proved unacceptable. The 'home help' and the *au pair* have gone some way to bridging the gap, while in 1946 the government-sponsored National Institute of Houseworkers was set up to train domestic workers. However, for most women it is 'self-help' which has provided the solution to the 'servant question' since 1946. Some former employers have found the transition not unwelcome, like the Elstree householder who wrote to the author in August 1974 : 'I am a good butler, my wife is the best cook I've ever met. We both of us drive a car very much better than my grandmother's old chauffeur—who was a very poor hand at it. Now that we do all these things for ourselves we *do* them much better.'[20] But for those with large houses, some help remains necessary, and even the stately homes have begun to feel the pinch. For example, the Marquis of Bath, in an interview in 1973, could boast a resident staff of only two— a man and wife, both Spanish. In 1905 there had been forty-three indoor servants in the then marquis's establishment at Longleat. Similarly, at Beaulieu Abbey the Montagu family are now reduced to three staff members only. 'If they left, I don't know how I would replace them,' Lady Montagu admitted.

In bringing about this change domestic trade unionism has had only a minor part to play. As before 1914, so in the inter-war and immediate post-war period the impact of trade unionism has been small. There was a domestic section of the Workers' Union, for example, which in 1928 merged with the Transport and General Workers' Union. The small Domestic Servants' and Hotel Workers' Union, in which Jessie Stephen played an active role, catered primarily for those in commercial employment. And at the end of the 1940s the servants at Buckingham Palace joined a union. According to Gabriel Tschumi, a royal chef, 'Every royal servant joined the Civil Service Trade Union, and union meetings were held in the servants' quarters.'[21] Nevertheless, these organisations have had a negligible influence, and the most significant expression of workers' views on domestic service has been the way they have voted with their feet—abandoning the sweeping-brush and the kitchen sink for the typewriter and the factory machine.

This changing relationship of servants and employers has been reflected in variations in wages. During the First World War pay had risen, along with prices, and as the latter collapsed in the depressed post-war world, so some wages were cut as well. Nevertheless, levels tended to remain above the pre-war situation, save for the youngest girls, who as maids-of-all-work might still be receiving only 5s. a week or less in the mid-1920s.²² This is demonstrated in the servants' book of Mrs Collier of Oxfordshire, which runs from 1903 to 1932. In what was primarily a two-servant household, the maximum paid to a cook before the First World War had been £24 per annum, and to a house-parlour-maid £23. Yet by the early 1930s the cook was receiving £50 per annum, and an experienced house-parlourmaid £38. Even a sixteen-year-old trainee house-parlourmaid engaged in November 1929 for the low wage of £20 per annum had by the time she was eighteen managed to secure £26 a year. Among the male workers similar trends developed. Mr E. G. Dollymore of London remembers entering service as a hall-boy at the age of fourteen in 1927 for a wage of £20 a year. Two years later he had been appointed second footman in another landed family at £36 per annum; and by 1937, as first footman to Lord Willingdon, a former viceroy of India, he was earning £60 per annum. Although some of the increase was due to Mr Dollymore's promotions, a good deal was also attributable to the advance in servants' wages during the inter-war period.

In London a *New Survey of London Life and Labour* was undertaken in 1930 to match the work carried out by Charles Booth in the 1880s and 1890s. The wage ranges payable to domestic servants in the capital at that date are set out in Table 6.

Table 6 : Annual wages of adult female resident servants, 1929-30

Cook	£54–£63	Housemaid	£40–£50
Cook-general	£45–£52	Nurse	£50–£68
General	£40–£52	Parlourmaid	£45–£52
Working housekeeper	£45–£52		

In addition, the *New Survey* compared its findings with those produced by the Board of Trade between 1894 and 1896; the comparisons are given in Table 7.

The *New Survey* concluded that, taking into account all servants employed in private domestic service, wage rates since 1894-96 had increased least for the older workers; their rates had gone up

Table 7 : Comparative average annual wage rates
at three age-groups

	21–29	*30–39*	*40+*
1894–96			
Cooks	£20 8s.	£25 6s.	£28 0s.
Generals	£15 12s.	£17 12s.	£17 12s.
Housemaids	£18 6s.	£21 14s.	£25 16s.
Nurses	£18 18s.	£27 16s.	£29 0s.
Parlourmaids	£20 18s.	£23 4s.	£24 12s.
1929–30			
Cooks	£49 14s.	£59 18s.	£60 4s.
Generals	£45 6s.	£53 12s.	£46 12s.
Housemaids	£43 0s.	£48 14s.	£50 18s.
Nurses	£52 10s.	£62 16s.	£83 6s.
Parlourmaids	£47 12s.	£51 10s.	£55 4s.

by 87 per cent. By contrast, for the girls under 21 years of age, the increase in basic rates had been 150 per cent. Over this same period the average cost of living had perhaps risen by 70 to 80 per cent, so that in real terms the younger servants at least had achieved a considerable improvement over their late Victorian predecessors.

Of course, in the provinces wages tended to be lower, as is shown by the Collier figures above. But much depended on the age and skill of the servant and the status and size of the household in which she worked. Mrs Peter Black remembers that in her parents' country house in Sussex, with a large indoor staff, the cook received £75 per annum; the parlourmaid £50; the housemaids £30-£48; and between maids and kitchenmaids £20.[23] On the other hand, Mrs May Murray, also of Sussex, noted in a letter to the author: 'In 1938 one could still get a General Servant at £36 a year, House-Parlourmaid at £45, and a single-handed Cook at £60—not to mention married couples at a joint wage of £100.' But, she adds, 'then came World War II, when everything changed'.

Certainly the picture has altered fundamentally since 1945. As late as 1931 nearly five per cent of private households had a full-time resident servant; by 1951 it was a mere one per cent. At the same time wage rates have also risen. For example, one

26 *Out on an errand, c.1890.*

25 *Parlourmaid on duty, c.1901.*

27/28 Housemaid, c.1906. In spite of the many dirty tasks they had to perform, housemaids were expected to be immaculately dressed at all times of the day. *Above:* in morning dress. *Below:* the same housemaid dressed for the afternoon.

writer suggests that women servants were probably earning on average £255 per annum in 1955 and £310 per annum in 1960; this represented more than a sixfold increase over their estimated earnings in 1906 and was well ahead of the average increase in retail prices over the same period. By the early 1970s the situation was such that resident servants were earning more in a week than many of their Victorian predecessors had earned in a year. According to Massey's Employment Agency of Baker Street, London, in 1973 a first-class butler would expect £20 a week or more, a good cook at least £18, a lady's maid £14, and a parlourmaid £12, with 'everything found'. All the advantages of country house living or an expensive address in Mayfair or Belgravia were available in return for living-in service. But even they were not sufficient attraction. 'Apart from providing the whole range of domestic labour-saving machinery . . . employers have to take on daily help to relieve the resident servants of the more tedious and time-consuming chores.'[24] Very often, too the servants are recruited from overseas—from Spain, Portugal and even Asia. Thus the Marquis of Bath's man-servant comes from Spain and in 1973 earned more than £20 a week, together with a free cottage with all modern conveniences. But even so, candidates for living-in posts are comparatively few and far between.

In Victorian England the employment of a resident domestic servant was the legitimate ambition of every middle-class family. During the inter-war years that aim became increasingly difficult to achieve; now, in the Britain of the 1970s, the resident servant has become the ultimate social symbol—the prerogative of the wealthy few. In other words, servants, who were once taken for granted as essential but customary appendages to any respectable household, have acquired the irresistible lure that comes from being almost unattainable. In the future that position seems unlikely to change, and at least one former servant is 'overjoyed' that it is so. To her it marks the end of a very 'lonely and depressed form of employment' in which she was reluctantly forced to 'waste' the earliest years of her working life.[25] Fortunately, not all have such unhappy memories as these of their life 'in service'.

Appendices

APPENDIX A

DOMESTIC SERVANT WAGE RATES

(1) Annual wages of domestic servants employed at Milton Manor, Berkshire.
[*Wages book preserved at Berkshire County Record Office.*]

	1845	1846	1847	1848	1849	1850
Housekeeper*	£25	£25	£25	£25	£25	£20
Lady's maid	£16	£16	£14	£16	£16	£16
Cook	£11	£12	£13	£14	£13	£13
Housemaid	£12	£12	£13	£14	£10	£11
Butler	£40	£40	£35	£35	£35	£35
Coachman	£18	£65†	£65†	£65†	£65†	£65†
Boy in house	–	–	£8 11s.	£5	£5	–
Gardener†	£39 10s.	£39 10s.	£39 10s.	£39 10s.	£39 10s.	£39 10s.
Stable-boy	£11 8s.	£10 8s.	£12 8s.	£14 8s.	£14 10s. 4d.	£8

N.B. A sudden fall in wages for a particular post indicates a staff change.
  * The housekeeper made periodic payments to her employer for tea for the servants, e.g. in 1847 the payment was £1 4s.; in 1849 £1 17s. 4d.
  † Non-resident. The coachman (from 1846) and the gardener each rented a cottage at £3 18s. per annum.

(2) Wages paid at Lamport Hall, Northampton.
[*Wages book preserved at Northamptonshire County Record Office.*]

	1830	1837	1841	1848	1851
Lady's maid	£15	£15	£18	£18	£18
Cook-housekeeper	£40	£34	£30	£36	£40
Upper housemaid	£10	£10	£11	£11	£14*
Under-housemaid	£9	£9	£9	£9	£9
Dairy-maid	£9	£9	£11	£9	£9
Kitchenmaid	£8	£8	£8	£9	£10*
Laundry-maid	£11	£11	£11	£11	£15*
Nurse	–	–	–	–	£21
Nursemaid	–	–	–	–	£7
Butler	£45	£60†	£60†	£25	£47
Footman	£15	£18	£14‡	£16	£17*
Coachman**	£52	£52	£52	£52	£52
Groom	–	£20	£16	–	–

* Wage rate raised by £1 per annum to this level in October 1851.

† Between 1837 and 1848 Dodson, the butler, also acted as house steward; but in 1848 he reverted to being butler only. He left Lamport early in 1851.

‡ Footman aged only fifteen in 1841, hence the lower wage.

** The coachman also received each year one suit of livery and two stable jackets.

(3) Wages paid by the Elwes family of Great Billing, Northamptonshire.
[*Wages books preserved at Northamptonshire County Record Office.*]

	1873	1875	1877
Lady's maid	£20	–	£30*
Second lady's maid	–	–	£10
Nurse	£25	£30	–
Cook	£45	£45	£45
First laundry-maid	£20	£22	£20
Second laundry-maid	£14	£12	£14
First housemaid	£16	£18	£18

(3) continued

	1873	1875	1877
Second housemaid	£12	£12	£14
Third housemaid	–	–	£10
Kitchenmaid	£16	£18	£16
Nursemaid	–	£16	–
Scullery-maid	£8	£10	£10
Butler	£60	£65	£55
Coachman	£40	£40	£40
First footman	£28	£30	£30
Second footman	£22	–	–
Hall-boy	£12	£8	£10
Groom	–	£20	£20

* Jane White, the former nurse, was appointed lady's maid. In 1881 she became housekeeper at £40 per annum.

(4) Wages paid to resident servants at Englefield House, Berkshire. [*Wages books preserved at Berkshire County Record Office.*]

	1875	1885	1886	1887	1888	1891
Housekeeper	n.a.	£60	£60	£50	£50	£65
Cook	n.a.	£40	£40	£50	£50	£50
Upper laundry-maid	£22	£24	£24	£24	£24	£25
Second laundry-maid	£16	£18	£18	£18	£18	£18
Third laundry-maid	£13	£14	£14	£10	£14	£14
Fourth laundry-maid	–	£11	£10	£10	£10	£10
Upper housemaid	£20	£22	£22	£22	£24	£24
Second housemaid	n.a.	£18	£18	£18	£18	£18
Third housemaid	£14	£14	£15	£15	£15	£15
Fourth housemaid	£10	£12	£10	£10	£10	£14
Kitchenmaid	£14	£19	£19	£18	£18	£18
Scullery-maid	£10	£10	£10	£10	£10	£12
Butler	n.a.	£80	£70	£70	£70	£70
Valet	n.a.	£55	£55	£55	£55	£50
Under-butler	£34	£40	£38	£38	£40	£40
Footman	£30	£32	£32	£30	£28	£30
Second footman	£14	£28	£28	£28	£26	£26
Second coachman	£24	£24	£26	£26	£26	£24
Groom	£18	£20	£20	£20	£18	£18
Helper	n.a.	£18	£18	£18	£18	£18
Odd man	n.a.	£30	£30	£35	£30	£28
Odd man	n.a.	£28	£28	£28	£30	£30

N.B. The coachman seems to have been non-resident. One coach-man stayed with the family for about twenty years, leaving in 1886; his wage rate was not mentioned. His successor, who stayed for a short time only, received £36 per annum, as did the next man, who remained with the family to the end of the period.
n.a. = not available.

(5) Scale of wages suggested by Miss Jessie Stephen in the Ministry of Reconstruction's *Report . . . on the Domestic Service Problem, Parliamentary Papers*, 1919, XXIX, 35.

Scale of wages per week with food

	£	s.	d.
Housekeepers	1	2	6
Assistant housekeepers		18	6
Cooks with kitchenmaids and scullery-maids	1	2	6
Cook-housekeepers	1	5	0
Cooks with kitchenmaids		19	6
Cooks with between maid		17	6
Cooks, single-handed		17	6
Cook-generals		15	0
General domestic worker, unskilled		12	0
General domestic worker, skilled in all duties		15	0
Head kitchenmaid of two		15	0
Kitchenmaid with scullery-maid		12	6
Kitchenmaid, single-handed		12	6
Second kitchenmaid		10	0
Scullery-maid		7	6
Between maid		7	6
Head housemaid		15	0
Second housemaid		12	6
Under-housemaid		7	6
House-parlourmaid		12	6
Head parlourmaid	1	0	0
Second parlourmaid		15	0
Head nurse	1	0	0
Second nurse		15	0
Under-nurse		10	0
Under-parlourmaid		10	0
Lady's maid	1	0	0

(5) continued

Scale of wages per week with food

	£	s.	d.
Young ladies' maid		15	0
Head laundry-maid		18	0
Second laundry-maid		12	6
Laundry-maid, single-handed		15	0
Head stillroom maid		18	6
Second stillroom maid		12	6
Stillroom maid, single-handed		15	0
Head dairy-maid		15	0
Second dairy-maid		10	0

A sliding scale of wages for workers from 14 to 18 years of age ranging from 6s. 6d. to 10s. per week, if absolutely unskilled. These wages include food; where no food is given £1 must be added to the weekly amount. For daily workers a minimum of 9d. per hour is recommended where the hours worked exceed four per day. If a worker works less than four hours, she should be paid at the rate of one shilling per hour.

APPENDIX B

THE DUTIES OF SERVANTS

(1) Conditions of service of a cook employed by William Cother, landowner, of Longford, Gloucestershire, 14 January 1837.
[*Preserved at Gloucestershire County Record Office.*]

Hired Elizabeth Freeman at nine guineas a year. To enter on her Service February first. She says she can undertake to Cook, Roast and Boil Meat, Fry & Boil Fish, Make Pastry, Curry &c. &c.—Will obey orders without grumbling. Cut and leave Meat fit to come to Table when cold—make no waste, leave no fat &c. &c. Use economy on all occasions. Ask leave whenever she goes from home. Never leave the House after night. Has no followers. Dinner sometimes to be got at short notice. Assist the other Servant on all occasions, particularly at Washing, Ironing &c., W.C. informed her that he often was in the kitchen giving directions &c. &c. She is generally to go to Church every other Sunday morning—when she wished to go to see her Friends (say once in three months) she might do so by asking 2 or 3 days previous, at the time she wished, or a day fixed for that purpose.

Elizabeth Freeman lived the last 4½ yrs. with Miss Strickland of Apperley Court as Housemaid, who has given her a character, and 3½ years as Cook, with the late Mrs Dyer of Nailsworth—Mrs Hawkins of Minsterworth, where her mother lives, has also given a good character.

(2) Duties of male servants at the Newdigate home in Blackheath, London, 1836.
[*The Newdigates were Warwickshire landowners. Preserved at Warwickshire County Record Office.*]

Black Heath, April 15 1836.
Regulations to be observed in the Family & the particular duties of the House Servants each separately though it is hoped that every

member of the Family will at all times be ready & willing to promote the welfare & comfort of the whole, & that they will be ready & willing to assist each other.

No Servants are allowed to go out without leave first obtained. For fear of accidents by fire or otherwise Mr Newdigate wishes it to be understood that when a bell rings more than once it *must* be answered, & that it is the duty of every Servant both male & female hearing a bell ring more than once, to ascertain that it be answered immediately. Also that it is the duty of every Servant finding the great Doors left open to shut them.

*Butler.** Is answerable that all Men Servants perform their duties with alacrity, care & diligence. He is to see that the Great Doors at the Entrance are kept shut, & that the Wicket is off the latch before dusk. That all the Doors & Windows are fast & the fires safe at night—That all is quiet below stairs & that the Men Servants are in bed before him every night. He has the care of Mr Newdigate's clothes and waits on him. He keeps the cellar Slate & the inventories.

He has the care of the Cellars Plate & Glass & is answerable that the plate & glass are kept particularly clean.

He lays the Cloth & takes up the Parlour Breakfast & Waits— He must hold himself in readiness to answer the House & Door Bells without delay. He attends the fires on the ground floor till 2 o'clock P.M. and when the Footman is out on duty—He sees that the Coal Box in the School Room is filled in the morning to last the day. He attends to the Cisterns & Fountain when the water comes on, & observes that the supply comes in regularly, & that none of the ball cocks are fast. He also attends to the Hot Water Pipes & keeps them supplied with water (about once per Week) when required &c. He observes that the circulation of Hot Water is regular throughout in about $\frac{1}{2}$ an hour after the fire is made.

Both Servants take up & attend Luncheon & at the Parlour dinner. They both take away & clean up the glass &c.—They both attend with Tea & Coffee. The Coachman or Groom or both *when required* will assist at the Parlour dinner that the other Servants need not be obliged to leave the Room. Mr Newdigate earnestly hopes that all the Servants will pay particular attention to their language and manners it being quite Impossible that a Servant can be agreable [*sic*] without a civil & obliging manner particularly where Ladies are concerned.

Footman. Trims the Lamps, rubs the Dining Room and Drawing Room Tables, Cleans the Glass, Plate and Silver hafted Knives. He prepares for the Children Dinner & Luncheon at which both Servants attend.† He answers the bells & attends to the fires on the

Ground floor after 2 o'clock—He attends the carriage & lays the Cloth for the Parlour Dinner, assists in Waiting & cleaning up after. He brushes & cleans the young gentlemen's clothes & takes them up. He assists to clean the Windows of the ground floor & is expected to be civil & to make himself generally useful. On no account is he to be absent without leave previously obtained.

Boy. Makes & attends to the fire in the furnace of the Pipes— Cleans the Young Gentlemen's Shoes, the Servants' Hall passages & half the Yard. He riddles Cinders & takes them for Laundry & Pipes—He must carry coals for the Nursery fires. He goes on errands and must make himself generally useful. He must always be civil & on no account to go out without leave previously obtained.

* When a similar list of duties was prepared in 1833 it was noted : 'The Butler in all things connected with the Establishment is considered the representative of the Master, and is to be obeyed as such. He is to keep order & Regularity in the Family, & is answerable that all the servants perform the duties allotted to them with care & diligence.' No doubt these provisions also applied in 1836.

† In 1833 it was noted that the footman was expected to 'dress' himself ready for his luncheon duties at 12 noon. He then prepared 'the Table for Children's Dinner & Luncheon which both Servants attend'.

(3) List of duties in a small household in Devon, 1896.
[*Presented in the form of instructions to a mistress. Kindly provided by Miss C. Chichester of Exeter.*]

Cook's work is to turn out kitchen, larder, pantry, hall, dining room —steps; brass work; & has to help Housemaid with large beds.

Housemaid (get them up early). Before breakfast the housemaid must do the stairs & dining room if this is not done by the cook. Must see there is a good fire & should do the door & step before breakfast. Kitchen breakfast at 8 if house breakfast is at 9. Directly the lady leaves her bedroom the servant must run up & open out the bed & window & after that must help cook with the knives & boots. When dining room breakfast is over, it must be cleared away at once. If the cook doesn't help the housemaid with beds, she must wash up while the beds are being made & then the housemaid goes on with her work till lunchtime.

The housemaid should dress before lunch if possible, if not, before three. The housemaid should then do the housework or clean the silver on its day. Caps should be found by the mistress.

After tea should get dinner ready. Cook should tell the maid how many courses there are so that she knows how many knives to put on. Mistresses should not go down after dinner because then the servants expect a rest.

If possible bring up the servants not to have a night out in the week. If they have friends they take morning or evening in turn on Sundays. Always be punctual, if the mistress is not punctual the servants will be unpunctual. Always make the servants as punctual as possible.

The housemaid should have 4 dusters weekly, 2 soft & 2 common ones.

The cook should have 4 also; if she wants more give her 5.

If you go out directly after breakfast order dinner overnight. Go down about 10 o'clock & order it. Always tell the cook how many extra there will be for dinner.

If possible have a boy in from 7.30 till 9 to clean knives & boots & carry up coals if necessary.

(4) Duties of a house-parlourmaid.
[*Instructions written out by one maid for her successor in 1913. The family consisted of four people living in a three-storey house with six bedrooms and two living-rooms in Bedford. Kindly provided by Miss East of Devon.*]

6.30	Take hot water to Mrs East, draw up blinds etc.
6.35	Do sitting room.
7.00	Call Miss East.
7.05	Dust drawing room.
7.15	Clean ladies' boots.
7.30	Call Master East, brush clothes & put them ready.
7.45	Lay breakfast.
8.00	Own breakfast.
8.30	Strip beds, do washstands & tidy bathroom.
9.00	Make beds.
9.30	Sweep, dust & tidy bedrooms.
10.00	Special day work.
12.00	Clean knives, rub up table silver & tidy pantry.
12.30	Dress for luncheon.
12.45	Lay table for lunch.
1.30	Own dinner.
2.30	Clear away luncheon : wash up table silver.

Special day work

Mondays. Count dirty linen. Sweep & dust stairs. Clean bedroom silver & drawing-room silver alternately.

Tuesdays. Turn out Miss East's and Mrs East's bedrooms alternately.

Wednesdays. Sweep & dust stairs. Clean dining room silver.

Thursdays. Turn out sitting room & Master East's bedroom alternately.

Fridays. Sweep & dust stairs and landings thoroughly, polishing furniture & clean brass. Clean bathroom & lavatory.

Saturdays. Wash hair brushes, clean pantry & count clean linen. If any time to spare in afternoon, rub up silver, clean windows, or help with mending if required. Tidy sitting-rooms, sweeping up hearths & making up fires two or three times a day.

APPENDIX C

REMINISCENCES OF DOMESTIC SERVANTS BETWEEN THE WARS

(1) Domestic service in a preparatory school in the 1930s.
[*Information provided by Mrs Betty Dingle of Leatherhead.*]

In the early '30's I was the Matron of a boys' prep. school and as such classed as an 'upper domestic servant'. By today's standards the living conditions were primitive beyond belief.

All drinking water was fetched from the village. It was the whole time job of one of the 'house boys' to fill and light all the oil lamps in the school. My boys went to bed by candlelight which I lit by carrying round a small oil lamp and a taper.

Clean sheets were provided for staff and pupils at the beginning of term and again at half term—we could not bath more than once a fortnight because of the shortage of water. Guess what the boys' beds were like!

I did the boys' mending, was responsible for them when they were not in class—taught them when a master was absent—made the butter by hand when there wasn't anyone else to do it. Played bridge at least twice a week and was expected to lose as the Rector got very angry if he didn't win. I set mouse and rat traps, entertained the Rector's guests. For all this and much more I received 10s. a week—this of course for only 36 weeks of the year. The rest of the time I was expected to keep myself.

In spite of all this I enjoyed the life. I was lucky enough to have a family to go home to.

The 'house boys' lived together in an attic with just their beds—no carpet on the floor and neither had I. When the Rector found out that I was being brought a cup of tea from his pot wasn't I told off!

(2) A day in the life of a kitchenmaid in 1919.
[*Information provided by Mrs Helen M. Iles of Wallington.*]

It was in the year 1919, a lovely house just off Portman Square, where it needed twelve servants to look after the house, the family consisting of a middle-aged couple. I was kitchen maid—lowest of the low in the household and expected to be at the beck and call of ALL Servants, though Cook had first priority.

This period of time was one of 'Shortages' with rationing still the order of the day, but not as austere as the aftermath of World War two.

However, the house was elegant with fourteen rooms, plus basement, which comprised still room, butler's pantry, an enormous kitchen and scullery, store room, wine cellar, and a room for the 'boots' as the master went riding (in Rotten Row). The kitchen had an enormous kitchener (two ovens with a fire in the centre). There was also a large iron gas stove, but in the fifteen months I was there it was forbidden to use it, and the gas was sealed off. As a result of this the fire was the only means of cooking, and also heating the water.

My first task in the morning was to light the fire and make tea for the staff (12) by 6.30 a.m., a problem as of necessity, the kettle was large and dampers on the stove had to be manipulated so that the heat went on to the water tank as well as the kettle, as the 'master' had to have shaving water at 6.45 a.m. and his bath at 7 a.m.

I had to hurry my cup of tea and make my way to the front of the house and clean the brass and scrub the steps.

The house had double doors and two of everything outside, plus an elaborate burglar proof system of brass rods inside—all of which were cleaned daily.

The steps numbered six and were very wide and *white*, attained by scrubbing with shale oil soap.

The lady of the house did not approve of hearthstone, or whitening, and this task, which I can assure you was no easy one, had to be completed by 7.45 a.m.—the local byelaws were such that 8 a.m. was the time limit for this job to be completed.

I then had to get back to the kitchen and help cook prepare staff breakfast, lay up table, clear, wash up all pots, pans, and china etc., then prepare breakfast for 'upstairs'.

By that time I was already preparing vegetables, etc., for staff lunch, or would be making sauces in readiness for cook, under her direction.

Every day the kitchen and scullery had to be washed, table

scrubbed, and stove blackleaded, and in addition to this, copper pots had to be cleaned, and knives went through the machine, which had bath-brick or emery powder placed inside, before a vigorous hand turning.

In addition to the general daily duties, one of the other rooms in the basement was cleaned weekly by the kitchen maid, also the stairs from the main floor to the basement, and the long passage that led from the area front door to the back of the house.

By the time lunch for staff and family was over it was about 3 p.m., when I was allowed to go to my room to change from a 'cleaning' uniform to an afternoon dress and apron.

By 5 p.m. I was getting tea for staff, which they came down to the kitchen for, as I had to lay up the table in the servants' hall—before the preparation of dinner.

The family did a lot of entertaining despite shortages, but staff had to keep to their own rations, so that when laying the table I had twelve small dishes of butter and twelve small bowls of sugar to place around the table; all were named.

My day finished at 10 p.m. The last job was filling the big coal scuttle and getting the wood ready to start the fire in the morning. I was allowed one bath a week and used to set my alarm for 5.30 a.m.

I had alternate Sunday afternoons off, but as I had to prepare all vegetables for the evening, lay up supper for staff, etc., it was about 3 p.m. to 3.30 p.m. before I left the house. I had to be back again by 10 p.m. and still remember the awful telling off I got because the butler had to let me in at 10.15 p.m. when I had had to wait for a bus.

Once a month I had a whole day off (after breakfast) and alternate Sunday mornings I was allowed to attend church, which left me enough time for preparation of lunch, provided vegetables, custards, etc. were ready before I went.

For this I got £18 per year, a good wage for a girl 14 years plus. I left when I was 15½ years, having found a post in a shop near my home.

APPENDIX D

THE SERVANTS' HALL

Rules and orders in Wasing Place servants' hall to be observed by the servants of this household and other people who may occasionally happen to be there.

[Wasing Place, near Reading, was the seat of Sir William Mount, Bt, for many years M.P. for South Berkshire. These rules were in operation at the beginning of the twentieth century. I am indebted to Mrs M. Keal of Oxford for a copy of them. She joined the Wasing Place staff in 1905.]

First. That the hall shall be cleaned every day by one of the servants who shall take his turn weekly, and observe that a fire be made in due time, the cloth laid, and after meals to put everything in its proper place.

Second. That any servant who shall have the management of the hall agreeably in the aforesaid article, shall at the expiration of the week deliver to his successor all things belonging to it, clean and in good order.

Thirdly. That if anyone shall take anything belonging to the hall out, or displace anything, cut more bread than is necessary, make unnecessary waste, wipe their knives and forks on the table cloth, or hand towel, say anything indecent at meal times, give the lie at any time, shall forfeit the sum of two pence, or receive six strokes with the boot on their breech.

Fourthly. That if anyone shall leave dirty boots or shoes, or make any dirt whatever without immediately cleaning it, or shall be guilty of any indecency whatever, shall be subject to the punishment mentioned in the foregoing article.

Fifthly. That if anyone be heard to swear he shall forfeit for every oath the sum of one penny.

Sixthly. That if anyone shall by accident, or otherwise, break any utensils, it shall be left to the decision of our mistress, whose decision shall be final.

APPENDIX E

THE EMPLOYER'S POINT OF VIEW

(1) Extracts from the diary of Mrs Henry Williams of 22 Hanley Road, Hornsey Rise, North London, for 1866-67.

[Mrs Williams employed a general servant, but staff changes were rapid. In the period September 1866 to September 1867 she had five different servants, as well as two charwomen and a 'stand-in girl'. Mr Williams came of a fairly well-to-do family but was himself a traveller for a firm selling and hiring marquees, tarpaulins, flags, etc. The servants were each allowed every Sunday afternoon or evening off, and one other evening each week as their free time. I am indebted to Mrs H. Jones of London for the extracts.]

1866

Aug. 28   A servant girl called after the situation. Went after the girl's character at Mrs Colds 15 St John's Villas. In evening engaged Margaret Simmons as my servant, £10 a year, to commence from next Thursday, Sept. 5th.

Oct. 18   Margaret a day's holiday, gave her a sovereign.

Dec. 1   Gave Margaret a row et cetera yesterday.

Dec. 11   Margaret Simmons has given me notice that she will leave me on the 6th of next month, should I be suited with another servant.

Dec. 29   A servant called. She is too old.

1867

Jan. 9   A servant Harriet Harris called, I wrote for her character to Clapham.

Jan. 10   Received the character of Harriet Harris from Clapham, have written to say I will take her.

Jan. 14   Busy in the kitchen all morning, found Margaret had left many things dirty. Margaret left about 7. New servant, H.H. came at nearly 9.

Jan. 15   Found Harriet very slow in her work. Dear Harry came home to dinner, badly cooked, and late.

29 Domestic Servants' Training School at Headington Hill Hall, Oxford, 1913. The school was financed by charity. (*above*)

30 Maid-of-all-work, London, 1911. This servant was aged only 13. She was employed by an artist and his wife at a wage of £5 a year. (*right*)

31 Junior servants at Cokethorpe Park, Oxfordshire, 1938. Standing (*left to right*): second parlourmaid, kitchenmaid, scullery-maid, third parlourmaid. Seated: second and third housemaids. Not shown are the cook, head parlourmaid, head housemaid and lady's maid who were also employed by the family. (*left*)

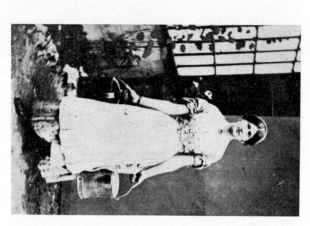

32 The servant as criminal. Lucy Ellis (aged 35) was sentenced to death at Bedford assizes in July 1876 for the murder of her illegitimate baby at Stagsden, Bedfordshire. The sentence was later commuted to life imprisonment.

33 Hannah Cullwick (1833-1909). The photograph was taken in 1864 when Hannah was temporarily employed as a maid-of-all-work at a Margate boarding-house. She later entered the service of A. J. Munby, the author and barrister, whom she married in 1873. The marriage was carefully kept secret until after Munby's death in 1910, when its disclosure caused a sensation. (See page 112.)

34 Miss Jessie Stephen, 1957. Miss Stephen led a trade union for Scottish servants before the First World War. She was an active campaigner for improved working conditions for servants in the inter-war period. (See pages 158 and 168-9.)

Jan. 17   Came down in morning, found nothing ready, had to bring up breakfast. Went with Lizzie [sister] inquiring for servants as Harry gave this servant warning this morning.

(2) Extracts from the servants' book of Mrs Collier of Essex and Oxfordshire.

[*When the extracts commence in 1911, Mrs Collier employed three resident servants. Emma Pierpoint, cook, had been employed since 1908 and was earning £22 per annum; Laura Gibson, house-parlourmaid had been employed since 1903 and was earning £23; Eva Watts, nurse, had been employed since 1906 and received £24, out of which she had to provide her 'own dresses etc.' I am indebted to Mr M. T. U. Collier of Reading for the use of this book.*]

1911
Jan. 2   Paid Emma Pierpoint up to Jan. 26 and she departed.
Jan. 3   May Thompson (Mary) arrived at £23, to be raised. Had been kitchenmaid at Writtle. Paid her travelling expenses 10s. 3d.
June   Allowed cook to have a girl one day a month to clean her bedroom and help her.
Oct.   Gibson not being well, went home for a rest; decided not to have her back again. Wrote and gave her notice on Oct. 10th, paid her wages up to that day and a month's wages and a present of £3, having been with us 8 years.
Oct. 9   Lucy Roberts came as stop-gap at 1s. a day.
Oct. 17   Lucy Roberts left, gave her 10s. washing, travelling, etc. Ada Wilson, aged 19, arrived at £16 a year for a month on trial. Had a good deal to learn, but willing, good tempered and remained.

1912
Jan. 21   Raised May Thompson (cook) to £24 a year.
March 6   Went to see Mrs Hyde and told her we should not require her daughter Annie (nursemaid) after about April 10th, as children older and going to make rather different nursery arrangements.
April 15   Annie Hyde (nursemaid) left. Had Mary Lawrence 3 days a week as char to help in all departments, from 9 a.m. to 3 p.m. at 3s. 6d. a week and her lunch.
Oct.   About Oct. 1st, M. Lawrence came at 7.30 a.m. instead of 9 a.m. as nursery fire has to be done. This is during

o

winter months and she receives 4s. 6d. a week breakfast and lunch.

Oct. 21 Raised Ada Wilson's wages to £17.

1913
Aug. Raised Ada Wilson's wages to £18.

1914
Feb. Eva Watts (nurse) having been with us 7 yrs. and 3 months, gave notice. To leave on March 26th. When the 26th arrived she was in bed with influenza. Betty also in bed—arranged she shd. leave on Mar. 31. Engaged Annie South, aged 34 as nurse at £29 a year; had been cook for six years with the Hamilton Gepps— very fond of children and some experience with them.

March 31 Eva Watts left. Annie South arrived, paid her 3s. 7d. journey money. Promised to pay her wages from Mar. 26th.

Dec. Mary Thompson (cook) became so nagging to the others and relations so extremely strained in the kitchen we mutually agreed she should leave January 5th 1915. I advertised in Essex Papers on Dec. 4th. Girl from Epping came to see me the same morning. Bertha Fewell—had been in a situation at Loughton. Got a good reference and engaged her to come on Jan. 5th 1915. Age 24. Wages £22—to be raised if satisfactory at the end of 1915.

1915
Jan. 1 May Thompson left, having been with us four years. Bertha Fewell arrived, paid her travelling expenses from Epping, 7½d.

Jan. 11 She gave notice to leave at the month. Reason given her young man was leaving Epping and wanted her to find a situation near him!

Jan. 21 Raised Ada Wilson's wages to £19.

Jan. 28 Bertha Fewell announced she would like to stay!

June 12 Received a letter from Mrs Hamilton Gepp, saying she would much like my Nurse, Annie South to go back to her, which after some conversation and tears Annie decided to do, as her sister much wishes her to get a place near her.

June 25 Bertha Fewell (cook) gave notice; cannot get on with Ada and wants an evening out.

Notes

[*Complete bibliographical references to the published sources cited in short-title form will be found in the bibliography.*]

CHAPTER 1 (pp. 1-13)

1. Marshall, *English Domestic Servant*, 7.
2. Stuart, *English Abigail*, 2.
3. Elton, *England under the Tudors*, 58.
4. Laslett, *World We Have Lost*, 1.
5. Laslett, *World We Have Lost*, 12.
6. For an example of an eighteenth-century apprenticeship document, dated 18 December 1759, involving Mary Sutton, 'a poor child' of the parish of Harrington, Northamptonshire, see Harrington Parish Record, 58. (Northamptonshire Record Office.)
7. Thomson, *Life in a Noble Household*, 119-20.
8. Marshall, *English Domestic Servant*, 17-18. Also information from Mrs J. Knowles of Chelmsford on Wissman family.
9. Hecht, *Domestic Service*, 54.
10. Colquohoun, writing in 1806, suggested there were perhaps 110,000 men-servants in the country, as opposed to 800,000 females, but these and other figures put forward were little more than guesses. See Hecht, *Domestic Service*, 34.
11. Hecht, *Domestic Service*, 161.
12. Marshall, *English Domestic Servant*, 20.
13. [Leigh Hunt], 'The Maid Servant', 482.

CHAPTER 2 (pp. 17-31)

1. Banks, *Prosperity and Parenthood*, 71.
2. Lady Cynthia Asquith, 'In Front of the Green Baize Door' in Streatfield, ed., *Day Before Yesterday*, 101. Lady Cynthia Asquith was the daughter of the 11th Earl of Wemyss and March; she married Herbert Asquith, the second son of the Liberal Prime Minister, in 1910.
3. Beeton, *Book of Household Management*, 1001.

4. Moore, *Confessions of a Young Man*, 132-6. A correspondent to *The Times* of 6 November 1878 similarly wrote of 'Domestic Slavery in the West End' when he described the working day of a seventeen-year-old servant girl of his acquaintance 'in a fashionable lodging-house near Piccadilly'.

5. Dawes, *Not in Front of the Servants*, 116. Before his children were sent off to boarding school, the bank manager also employed a living-in nursemaid or governess.

6. Ruth M. Packe, 'Life in a Country Parsonage 1890', essay submitted for a competition organised by the Leicestershire Local History Council in 1969 and preserved at the Leicester County Record Office.

7. Gorst, *Of Carriages and Kings*, 132; Huxley, *Victorian Duke*, 137.

8. Account book of Edward William Harcourt for 1883-91 (Harcourt MSS). The variations in expenditure were attributable to staff changes and to the periodic recruitment of less experienced (and thus cheaper) replacements. Servants' liveries cost £61 13s. 11d. in 1883 but £83 7s. 9d. in 1886, the year when total expenditure stood at £1,025 6s. 6¼d.

9. Peel, 'Homes and Habits', 81-2.

10. Lady Cynthia Asquith, 'In Front of the Green Baize Door' in Streatfield, ed., *Day Before Yesterday*, 102.

11. Thompson, *English Landed Society in the Nineteenth Century*, 195. The 'agricultural depression' was responsible for the situation Professor Thompson describes.

12. Booth, *Life and Labour in London*, 2nd Series, 4, 212.

13. *Hansard*, 5th Series, XXXI, 1911, 541.

14. Best, *Mid-Victorian Britain, 1851-73*, 103.

15. *Ibid.*, 81; Banks, *Prosperity and Parenthood*, 132.

16. Belley, 'Domestic Service', 178.

17. *General Report of the 1881 Census*, 33.

18. Miss C. E. Collet, *Report on the Statistics of Employment of Women and Girls*, 22, based on the 1891 census.

19. Jones, *Outcast London*, 138.

20. One of the earliest advocates of the 'lady help' was Rose Mary Crawshay in her book, *Domestic Service for Gentlewomen*.

21. Turner, *What the Butler Saw*, 238; *Times*, 24 and 28 Sep. 1875.

22. Verney, *The Passing Years*, 5.

23. *General Report of the 1901 Census*, 95, for comment on the increase in the number of foreign male domestics over the previous ten years.

CHAPTER 3 (pp. 32-48)

1. 'Hannah's Places'.

2. Information provided by Mrs D. M. Brookes of Tetsworth in a letter to the author.

3. For example, the Rev. W. C. Risley noted in his diary for 12 November 1868 : 'Widow Robbins of Clifton came begging, relieved her to purchase her Son some clothing on going to Service.'

4. Davenport-Hill, *Children of the State*, 25. One detailed tract for young servants was *Instructions in Household Matters, or The Young Girl's Guide to Domestic Service, Written by a Lady with an Especial View to Young Girls Intended for Service on Leaving School*, London, 1844. Reminiscences of a former servant now living at Brighton.

5. Rich, *Education Act, 1870*, 79.

6. *Housekeeping in Northamptonshire, 1600-1900*, Document 24.

7. Dawes, *Not in Front of the Servants*, 109.

8. *Report of the Women's Advisory Committee on the Domestic Service Problem*, 8.

9. 'A Servant's Life, 1866-72', 62-3.

10. W. T. Layton, 'Changes in the Wages of Domestic Servants during Fifty Years', 516; *Jackson's Oxford Journal*, 20 Jan. 1872. This last, specifying that the successful candidate must be a member of the Church of England, was for a lady's maid wanted 'by a lady and her two daughters residing in Oxford'.

11. Thus an advertiser in the *Hampshire Chronicle* of 23 August 1890 was anxious to secure : 'A small, good-looking, and intelligent Boy, age from 14 to 16. Strong, some knowledge of stable work and gardening, and to make himself generally useful.'

12. Associated Guild of Registries, Leaflet No. 4, London 1901, 3.

13. Dawes, *Not in Front of the Servants*, 103. The Harcourts also used Mrs Hunt's agency according to entries in their account book for Nuneham Courtenay in 1886.

14. 'A Servant's Life, 1866-72', 3.

15. Englefield House Servants' Book.

16. One entry in the book reads, for example : 'Martha E. Foster —30—Ch. Eng.—Father a Clerk in the City—31 Tunstall Road, Brighton. Lady Honyman 18 months—Coton Hall, Whitchurch, Shropshire 1½ years—only left on account of being lowered in health —had abscess in the face. Mrs Townshend 2½ years—Caldecote Hall, Nuneaton, Warwickshire—work too hard—feels quite strong & fit for work—very tall and thin, talks rather fast—well spoken & cheerful, sensible looking—*dark*—no fringe.'

17. *Times*, 18 Aug. 1879. In 1724 Christopher Tancred had advised that testimonials should be 'kept continually on file so that employers and the magistrates could readily investigate their records'. Other writers in the 1750s and 1760s suggested a sort of 'labour passport'. See *Hecht, Domestic Service*, 92.

18. The last attempt was made on 28 March 1904, when the bill was presented by Mr Skewes-Cox, M.P. for Kingston in Surrey.

19. See, for example, *Hansard*, 4th Series, CLXXXV, 1908, 73. A similar bill had been introduced in 1906 and 1907.

20. Thompson, *Lark Rise to Candleford*, 171-2.

CHAPTER 4 (pp. 49-70)

1. Comment by Mrs Anne Ford of Banstead, Surrey, in a letter to the author.

2. 'A Servant's Life, 1866-72', 74-6.

3. 'My First Job', essay submitted in 1961 and preserved at Essex County Record Office.

4. Outside the pages of Mrs Gaskell's novel, the experience of Winifred Foley, as a general maid for a ninety-one-year-old lady in the Cotswolds, bore some resemblance to that of the Cranford maids. Winifred secretly hid her books in the kitchen cupboard; all her kitchen chores were then 'done slapdash quick so that I could poke my head in and have a read'. (Winifred Foley, 'General Maid' in Burnett, ed., *Useful Toil*, 231.)

5. Beeton, *Book of Household Management*, 21.

6. 'Hannah's Places'.

7. *The Lady's Maid*, 2nd ed., London 1877, 82. This pamphlet had first been published in 1838 by Charles Knight & Co. and was apparently reissued without amendment.

8. *Servants' Guide*, 97. I am indebted to Mr H. R. Lover of Kingsbridge, Devon, for a sight of this book.

9. *The Lady's Maid*, 10-11.

10. Turner, *What the Butler Saw*, 126.

11. 'A Practical Mistress of a Household', *Domestic Servants As They Are and As They Ought to Be*, 11-13.

12. Margaret Thomas, 'Behind the Green Baize Door' in Streatfield, ed., *Day Before Yesterday*, 87.

13. *Servant's Practical Guide*, 129.

14. *Longleat Kitchen and Recipe Book* describes the kitchens at Longleat as they were in the nineteenth century; they have been restored by the present Marquis of Bath and can now be visited. (See Plates 5 and 6.)

15. 'My First Job', essay submitted in 1961 and preserved at Essex County Record Office.

16. *The Housemaid*, 35. The anonymous authoress proved to be Harriet Martineau. See Stuart, *English Abigail*, 193. Reminiscences of Mrs Martin of Luton.

17. Walsh, *Manual of Domestic Economy*, 225 states : 'The practice of some masters and mistresses of deducting from servants' wages the value of articles accidentally lost, broken, or injured is illegal, and cannot be defended, unless it was expressly stipulated at the time of hiring that the servants should be liable to make good such damages.'

18. Gathorne-Hardy, *Rise and Fall of the British Nanny*, 276.

19. Gathorne-Hardy, *Rise and Fall of the British Nanny*, 17.

20. Mr V. C. Buckley of Rutland Gate, London, in a letter to the author.

21. Sarah Sedgwick, 'Other People's Children' in Streatfield, ed., *Day Before Yesterday*, 14-15.

22. Beeton, *Book of Household Management*, 1012. Information provided by Mrs E. Bland in a letter to the author.

23. Sheppard, *London, 1808-1870: The Infernal Wen*, 370.

CHAPTER 5 (pp. 71-91)

1. The fluctuations are shown by comparing the 1861 census, which recorded just over 62,000 male indoor servants, with that for 1871, when the total was over 68,000; by 1881 it was around 56,000.

2. Banks, *Prosperity and Parenthood*, 89.

3. Greville, 'Men-servants in England', 813.

4. Hannah Cullwick's Diary, 8 April 1872.

5. *Servant's Practical Guide*, 182. One applicant for such a post, Samuel Trash, wrote in October 1853, that he could 'drive one or two pair [horses] and know well the duties of butler, groom gardener and valet de chambre, and have naturally a good pair of calves and would prefer plain clothes though no objections to livery'. (*Oxford Mail*, 23 Feb. 1973.)

6. Adams, *Complete Servant*, 336-7.

7. Turner, *What the Butler Saw*, 160.

8. Turner, *What the Butler Saw*, 166; *Servant's Practical Guide*, 171.

9. Gorst, *Of Carriages and Kings*, 129.

10. Greville, 'Men-servants in England', 813.

11. *Diary of William Tayler, Footman, 1837*, ed. Wise, 20.

12. Gorst, *Of Carriages and Kings*, 33.

13. Gabriel Tschumi, 'Chef' in Burnett, ed., *Useful Toil*, 197.

14. Greville, 'Men-servants in England', 815-16.

15. *Servant's Practical Guide*, 173. The *Guide* also included among the valet's duties : 'To load for him when out shooting; to stand behind his master's chair at dinner. . . . A valet to an elderly gentleman, besides performing these duties, renders any services that the state of his master's health may require; such as sitting up at night, carrying him up and down stairs . . . or sleeping in his room at night.'

16. Greville, 'Men-servants in England', 816-17.

17. Turner, *What the Butler Saw*, 175; *Servant's Practical Guide*, 185.

18. Mills, *Two Victorian Ladies*, 166.

CHAPTER 6 (pp. 92-108)

1. Gorst, *Of Carriages and Kings*, 132-4.

2. Dawes, *Not in Front of the Servants*, 59.

3. The reminiscences of Mrs Mason are preserved at Leicestershire County Record Office and were written for an essay competition organised by the Leicestershire Local History Council. The second reminiscences are preserved at Essex County Record Office.

4. Dawes, *Not in Front of the Servants*, 73.

5. Statistics produced by Dr D. J. Oddy in a paper on 'Trends in Working-class Food Consumption 1790-1913', given before the Agricultural History Society on 1 December 1973.

6. *Report on the Money Wages of Female Domestic Servants*, 30.

7. *Beeton's Domestic Service Guide*, 4. I am indebted to Mr Wallace H. Denby of Peterborough for a sight of this pamphlet.

8. Lanceley, *From Hall-boy to House-steward*, 161.

9. Hannah Cullwick's Diary, 1870; 'A Servant's Life, 1866-72'. The story of Hannah's relationship with Munby is told in Hudson, *Munby: Man of Two Worlds*.

10. Greville, 'Men-servants in England', 814.

11. Hannah Cullwick's Diary, 1872.

12. Hannah Cullwick's Diary, 1863.

13. *Sunday Express*, 24 Dec. 1972.

14. Jean Rennie, 'Scullery-maid, Kitchen-maid and Cook-housekeeper' in Burnett, ed., *Useful Toil*, 243.

15. 'A Practical Mistress of a Household', *Domestic Servants As They Are and As They Ought to Be*, 6-7. The British Museum catalogue indicates the anonymous author was M. A. Baines.

16. Charlton, ed., *Recollections of a Northumbrian Lady*, 195.

17. Correspondence of Ruth Barrow and John Spendlove. (Northamptonshire County Record Office.)

18. Davies, *Life As We Have Known It*, 28.

19. Countess of Aberdeen, *Mistresses and Maid-Servants*, 9-11.

20. The Annual Reports of the Girls' Friendly Society are preserved at the British Museum. See also Harrison, 'For Church, Queen and Family : The Girls' Friendly Society 1874-1920'.

21. Mrs Lily Gowers of Great Waltham, Essex, for example, recalled that when she was fifteen she went as maid in a large household in Hertfordshire. Eventually she 'had a young man, who brought me a buttonhole of flowers under his bowler hat. When the Housekeeper found out, there was trouble, on the carpet I had to go.' (Reminiscences at Essex County Record Office.) And as late as 1924, Mrs Martin of Luton remembers the warning : 'No boyfriends to come to the house or to be seen standing at the gate,' when she worked for a Sheffield doctor's family.

CHAPTER 7 (pp. 109-132)

1. 'Mrs Motherly', *Servant's Behaviour Book; Rules for the Manners of Servants*. (I am indebted to Miss L. E. A. Liptrott of Ilsington, Devon, for sight of the latter book.)

2. *Address to Young Servants*.

3. Hannah Cullwick's account of 1864.

4. 'Hannah's Places'.

5. 'A Practical Mistress of a Household', *Domestic Servants As They Are and As They Ought to Be*, 4.

6. Accounts of the union are to be found in *The Times*, 23 Apr. and 11 Jun. 1872 and *Dundee Advertiser*, 30 Apr. and 18 May 1872.

7. *Mayhew's Characters*, ed. Peter Quennell, Spring Books, London [1951], 149.

8. Information provided by Miss C. H. Sharpe of Sandown in a letter to the author.

9. Information provided by Mrs R. Cooper of Fearnhead, Warrington, Miss A. Tyler of Torquay and Miss A. Isambard-Owen of Llandudno in letters to the author.

10. Mills, *Two Victorian Ladies*, 162-3.

11. Gorst, *Of Carriages and Kings*, 154.

12. Belley, 'Domestic Service', 180-1.

13. Miss A. Isambard-Owen of Llandudno in a letter to the author.

14. Information provided by Mr C. M. M. Cook of Poole, Dorset

P

and Mr Harold Chorley of Wiltshire in letters to the author. Reminiscences of Mrs A. Jackson of Southsea.

15. 'A Butler', *Hints to Domestic Servants*, 78-9.

16. *Ames Letters, 1837-1847*, 44.

17. At Banbury one of the Guardians put a motion before the Poor Law board requiring that 'all persons taking children from the Union Workhouse for service do allow them 1s. per week wages'. Sadly, nothing came of his initiative, as no one could be found to second the motion. (Entry of 8 Oct. 1891 in the Board of Guardians' Minute Book, Oxfordshire County Record Office.) For the situation in London, see Booth, *Life and Labour in London*, 2nd Series, 4, 216.

18. Information provided by Mr J. H. Fearon of Bodicote.

19. Banks, *Prosperity and Parenthood*, 82, 85.

20. Maidservants' wages book for Taplow Court Buckinghamshire. (Buckinghamshire County Record Office.) Mrs G. Taylor of Pewsey remembers that even in the 1920s beer and tea money were provided for maids at a country house in Roehampton, London.

CHAPTER 8 (pp. 133-148)

1. Mayhew, *London Labour and the London Poor*, IV, 234-5.

2. Munby Diaries, 1862, Vol. 13, 129.

3. Moore, *Esther Waters*, 178-9.

4. Kay, *Social Condition and Education of the People in England and Europe*, 542. Pre-marital sex in a peasant community like Wales may have been due to the need for a woman to prove herself capable of bearing children, who would help on the family holding, before she married.

5. *Third Report of the Royal Commission on the Employment of Children, Young Persons and Women in Agriculture* : Report by G. Culley on the Counties of Pembroke and Carmarthen, 42.

6. *Report of the Select Committee on Metropolitan Hospitals* : Evidence of William Bousfield, Q.1297-1299.

7. A. R. Mills, *The Halls of Ravenwood*, London 1967, 60.

8. Strike poster, Edinburgh, *c.* 1825. (I am indebted to Miss J. Stephen of Bristol for a sight of a copy.)

9. Samuel Adams had been successively groom, footman, valet, butler and house steward, while his wife had risen from maid-of-all-work to housemaid, laundry-maid, under-cook, lady's maid and housekeeper. They therefore had first-hand experience of domestic life before the Victorian era.

10. *Mayhew's London*, ed. Peter Quennell, Spring Books, London [1949], 273.

11. Mayhew, *London Labour and the London Poor*, IV, 289-90.
12. Earl of Denbigh MSS : letter dated 31 Jun. 1803. (Warwickshire County Record Office.)
13. Altick, *Victorian Studies in Scarlet*, 224.
14. Altick, *Victorian Studies in Scarlet*, 229.

CHAPTER 9 (pp. 151-165)
1. Lilian Westall, 'House-maid' in Burnett, ed., *Useful Toil*, 216-18.
2. *The Ladies' Home Paper*, 24 Apr. 1909.
3. Mr Fleming of Surrey in a letter to the author. See also Powell, *Below Stairs*, 45.
4. *Times*, 23 Apr., 18 May and 11 Jun. 1972 and *Royal Leamington Chronicle*, 11 May 1872. See also Chapter 7 for mention of the Dundee union.
5. The records of the union are preserved at the Public Record Office.
6. Membership of the London and Provincial Domestic Servants' Union is to be found in the government report, *Membership of Trade Unions, 1892-99*. See also 'A Servant', *How to Improve the Conditions of Domestic Service*, and Royal Commission on Labour : Minutes of Evidence, Q.31,186-31,190.
7. Information from Miss Jessie Stephen in letters to the author.
8. Terms and Conditions of Employment Bureau, Domestic Workers' Union of Great Britain, pamphlet in the Webb Collection, Vol. XLVII, Item 49, at the London School of Economics. The pamphlet was issued in 1912.
9. The overwhelming majority of members were women; thus in 1912 only 18 of the 245 members were men. Miss J. Stephen briefly served as union vice-president in 1916.
10. *Report of the Select Committee on Metropolitan Hospitals* : Minutes of Evidence, Q.11,955-11,956 and 12,246. Earlier on, one of the commissioners, Earl Cathcart, had noted that among the patients in St George's Hospital in the preceding year had been 7 housekeepers, 16 ladies' maids, 56 cooks, 29 butlers, 37 grooms, 16 footmen, 73 coachmen and 53 general servants—a total of 287. (Q.3,035.)
11. Prospectus of the Servants' Benevolent Institution (in British Museum, 8282.c.74(7)); information provided by the present secretary of the Institution, to whom I am indebted.
12. *Daily Mail*, 20 Nov. 1911.
13. Turner, *What the Butler Saw*, 257. For a report of the Albert Hall meeting, see *Daily Mail*, 30 Nov. 1911.

CHAPTER 10 (pp. 166-184)

1. Burnett, ed., *Useful Toil*, 141.

2. Slater, ed., *My Warrior Sons*, 11-12.

3. Servants' book of Mrs Collier, a clergyman's wife, who lived at Theydon Bois Vicarage, Essex, until 1919 and from then until 1934 at Crowell Rectory, Oxfordshire.

4. Mr F. R. Rainbow of Hemel Hempstead in a letter to the author.

5. Burnett, ed., *Useful Toil*, 141.

6. *Report on Post-War Organisation of Private Domestic Employment*, 4; *Hansard*, 5th Series, XXXI, 1911, 541.

7. *Report on Post-War Organisation of Private Domestic Employment*, 4.

8. Turner, *What the Butler Saw*, 286.

9. Miss A. Isambard-Owen of Llandudno in a letter to the author.

10. Jean Rennie, 'Scullery-maid, Kitchen-maid and Cook-housekeeper' in Burnett, ed., *Useful Toil*, 235.

11. Mrs E. H. Berte of Byfleet in a letter to the author.

12. Mrs D. Duncan of Oxhey, Watford, in a letter to the author.

13. Unpublished reminiscences, kindly lent to the author by Mrs Anne Ford of Banstead, Surrey.

14. Information provided by Mr T. F. Filmer of Shalford, Guildford.

15. Mrs M. Jenner in a letter to the author.

16. Mr Albert Butler of Winchcombe in a letter to the author.

17. Mrs H. Rickard of Marldon and Mrs E. Timms of Chadlington, Oxfordshire, in letters to the author.

18. Marsh, *Changing Social Structure of England and Wales, 1871-1951*, 118, 145.

19. *Annual Abstract of Statistics*, 1970. By 1971, the total British figure was 92,000.

20. Mr George Booth of Elstree in a letter to the author.

21. Tschumi, 'Chef' in Burnett, ed., *Useful Toil*, 202.

22. Mrs Jones of Ramsgate, for example, remembers training in a large house in the 1920s and receiving only 5s. a week : 'They put on you, and you daren't tell your mother, as she would say you were lazy. From there I went to another house for 10/– a week and slept in.' (Letter to the author.) And Ivy Collins of Brighton earned only 10s. a month as a young kitchenmaid. (Letter to the author.)

23. Mrs Peter Black of Buckinghamshire in a letter to the author.

24. Dawes, 'Dying Reign of Pantry', 20; Routh, *Occupation and Pay in Great Britain, 1906-60*, 95.

25. Miss E. C. Howes of Great Wenham in a letter to the author.

Bibliography

MANUSCRIPT COLLECTIONS

Banbury Board of Guardians Minute Books. (Oxfordshire Record Office.)

Barrow-Spendlove Correspondence. (Northamptonshire Record Office.)

Bedford Gaol Records. (Bedfordshire Record Office.)

Brassey MSS. (Northamptonshire Record Office.)

Bulstrode Papers. (Buckinghamshire Record Office.)

Cadland Estate Wages Book. (Hampshire Record Office.)

Census Returns for 1841, 1851, 1861 and 1871. (Public Record Office.)

Mrs Collier's Servants' Book, 1903-32. (In the possession of Mr M. T. U. Collier of Reading, by whose kind permission it is quoted.)

William Cother's Account Book. (Gloucestershire Record Office.)

Dashwood MSS. (Bodleian Library, Oxford.)

Reminiscences of Mrs Florence Davies. (Bodleian Library, Oxford.)

Domestic Workers' Union of Great Britain, Rules, etc. (Public Record Office.)

Elwes MSS. (Northamptonshire Record Office.)

Englefield House Servants' Wages Books, 1885-91. (Berkshire Record Office.)

Ferrers Papers. (Leicestershire Record Office.)

Hackwood House MSS. (Hampshire Record Office.)

Halford Papers. (Leicestershire Record Office. Quoted by kind permission of Mr and Mrs T. G. M. Brooks.)

Harcourt MSS. (Bodleian Library, Oxford.)

Henley Petty Sessions Minute Books. (Bodleian Library, Oxford.)

Huddleston MSS. (Cambridgeshire Record Office.)

Lamport Hall Wages Books. (Northamptonshire Record Office.)

Lloyd-Baker MSS. (Gloucestershire Record Office.)

London and Provincial Domestic Servants' Union, Rule Book, etc. (Public Record Office.)

Milton Manor Wages Books. (Berkshire Record Office.)
Ministry of Reconstruction, Domestic Service Records. (Public Record Office.)
Munby MSS. (Trinity College, Cambridge. Quoted by kind permission of the Master and Fellows.)
    Account of 1864.
    Hannah Cullwick's Diaries.
    'Hannah's Places'. [Autobiographical fragment.]
    'A Servant's Life, 1866-72'. [Autobiographical fragment.]
    Munby Diaries.
Newdigate MSS. (Warwickshire Record Office.)
Oxford Assizes and Quarter Sessions, Calendars of Prisoners. (Oxfordshire Record Office.)
Reminiscences of old people. (Essex Record Office.)
Reminiscences of old people. (Leicestershire Record Office.)
Risley Diaries. (Bodleian Library, Oxford.)
School log-book collections. (Warwickshire, Buckinghamshire, Northamptonshire, Hampshire and Oxfordshire Record Offices.)
Sturges Bourne–Dyson Correspondence. (Hampshire Record Office.)
Taplow Court MSS. (Buckinghamshire Record Office.)
Warwick Quarter Sessions Records. (Warwickshire Record Office.)
Webb Collection. (London School of Economics.)
Wissman family records. (In the possession of Mrs J. Knowles of Chelmsford.)

In addition, the author has received about three hundred letters in answer to an appeal for reminiscences and other material on domestic service which appeared in the *Daily Telegraph*, the *Western Morning News* and the *Oxford Times* in August 1974. This collection contains a wealth of information on the vanished era of domestic service, particularly over the period from 1890. Quotations from the letters or from documents provided by the writers appear in the text and are acknowledged in the notes.

OFFICIAL PUBLICATIONS
General Reports of the Censuses of Population: 1871: PP, 1873, LXXI; 1881: *PP*, 1883, LXXX; 1891: *PP*, 1893-94, CVI; 1901: *PP*, 1904, CVIII; 1911: *PP*, 1913, LXXVIII.
Local Government Board, *Third Annual Report: Report by Mrs Nassau Senior on Education of Girls in Pauper Schools, PP, 1874*, XXV.
Select Committee on Metropolitan Hospitals, *Report, PP*, 1890, XVI.

Royal Commission on the Aged Poor, *Report, PP*, 1893, XV.
Royal Commission on Labour, *Minutes of Evidence, Group C, PP*, 1893-94, XXXIV.
Miss C. E. Collet, *Report on the Statistics of Employment of Women and Girls, PP*, 1894, LXXI, Pt II.
Miss C. E. Collet, *Report on the Money Wages of Indoor Domestic Servants, PP*, 1899, XCII.
Membership of Trade Unions, 1892-99, PP, 1900, LXXXIII.
Royal Commission on the Poor Laws, *Report, PP*, 1910, XLVIII.
Ministry of Reconstruction, *Report of the Women's Advisory Committee on the Domestic Service Problem, PP*, 1919, XXIX.
Ministry of Labour, *Report on the Supply of Female Domestic Servants*, 1923.
Report on Post-War Organisation of Private Domestic Employment, PP, 1944-45, V.
Hansard.
(*PP* = *Parliamentary Papers*)

NEWSPAPERS, ETC.
Daily Mail
Daily Telegraph
Domestic Servants' Advertiser
Dundee Advertiser
Englishwomen's Domestic Magazine
Glasgow Daily Record
Hampshire Chronicle
Jackson's Oxford Journal
Ladies' Home Paper
Leeds Daily News
Morning Chronicle
The Observer
Oxford Mail
Punch
Royal Leamington Chronicle
Servants' Magazine
Sunday Express
The Times

PRINTED BOOKS, PERIODICALS AND PAMPHLETS
Countess of Aberdeen, *Mistresses and Maidservants: Suggestions Towards the Increased Pleasure and Permanence of their Domestic Relations*, Aberdeen 1884.

Countess of Aberdeen, 'Household Clubs', *Nineteenth Century* XXXI (Mar. 1892).

William Acton, *Prostitution*, London 1857; 2nd ed., London 1870.

Samuel and Sarah Adams, *The Complete Servant*, London 1825.

An Address to Young Servants, London 1863.

Richard D. Altick, *Victorian Studies in Scarlet*, New York 1970.

The Ames Letters, 1837-1847 (Norfolk Record Society, Vol. XXI).

Annual Abstract of Statistics, 1970, 1972.

Annual Register for 1829, 1840, 1849, 1851.

J.B., *Servants Defended by One of Their Own Class*, Oxford 1847.

James Bain, *A Bookseller Looks Back*, London 1940.

J. A. Banks, *Prosperity and Parenthood: A Study of Family Planning among the Victorian Middle Classes*, London 1954.

Marchioness of Bath, *Before the Sunset Fades*, Longleat 1951.

Mrs I. Beeton, *Book of Household Management*, London 1861; repr. 1888 and 1906.

S. O. Beeton, *Beeton's Domestic Service Guide*, London [c. 1880].

A. A. Belley, 'Domestic Service: A Social Study', *Westminster Review* (Feb. 1891).

'A Benedict', *Mistresses and Servants, or Servants and Mistresses*, London 1859.

Geoffrey Best, *Mid-Victorian Britain, 1851-73*, London 1971.

Charles Booth, *Life and Labour in London*, 2nd Series, 4, London 1903.

E. W. Bovill, *English Country Life*, Oxford 1962.

W. L. Burn, *The Age of Equipoise*, London 1964.

John Burnett, ed., *Useful Toil*, London 1974.

Elaine Burton, *Domestic Work: Britain's Largest Industry*, London 1944.

'A Butler', *Hints to Domestic Servants*, London 1854.

Jane Welsh Carlyle, *Letters and Memorials*, ed. J. A. Froude, London 1883.

L. E. O. Charlton, ed., *Recollections of a Northumbrian Lady*, London 1949.

Randolph S. Churchill, *Winston S. Churchill: Youth, 1874-1900*, London 1966.

Caroline Clive, *Diaries, 1801-73*, ed. Mary Clive, London 1949.

Charles W. Cooper, *Town and County*, London 1937.

Rose Mary Crawshay, *Domestic Service for Gentlewomen*, London 1877.

Ellen W. Darwin, 'Domestic Service', *Nineteenth Century* XXVIII (Aug. 1890).

Florence Davenport-Hill, *Children of the State*, London 1889.

Margaret Llewelyn Davies, *Life As We Have Known It*, London 1931.

Frank Dawes, 'The Dying Reign of the Pantry', *Daily Telegraph Magazine*, 6 Jul. 1973.

Frank Dawes, *Not in Front of the Servants*, London 1973.

Charles Dickens, *Dictionary of London*, London 1879.

Charles Dickens, 'Old and New Servants', *All the Year Round*, 20 Jul. 1867.

Monica Dickens, *One Pair of Hands*, London 1961.

A. H. Dodd, *Life in Elizabethan England*, London 1961.

Domestic Appliances Gallery, Science Museum pamphlet [*c.* 1973].

Mrs H. Ellis, *Democracy in the Kitchen*, London 1894.

G. R. Elton, *England under the Tudors*, London 1955.

George Ewart Evans, *Ask the Fellow Who Cuts the Hay*, 2nd ed., London 1965.

Violet M. Firth, *The Psychology of the Servant Problem*, London 1925.

Mrs E. C. Gaskell, *Life of Charlotte Brontë*, World's Classics, Oxford 1919.

Jonathan Gathorne-Hardy, *The Rise and Fall of the British Nanny*, London 1972.

Girls' Friendly Society, *Annual Reports* (British Museum Library).

Going to Service, London 1858.

Frederick Gorst, *Of Carriages and Kings*, London 1956.

Lady Violet Greville, 'Men-servants in England', *National Review* (Feb. 1892).

L. and E. Hanson, *Necessary Evil: The Life of Jane Welsh Carlyle*, London 1952.

Brian Harrison, 'For Church, Queen and Family: The Girls' Friendly Society, 1874-1920', *Past and Present* 61 (Nov. 1973).

Molly Harrison, *The Kitchen in History*, Reading 1972.

J. J. Hecht, *Domestic Service in Eighteenth Century England*, London 1956.

Thea Holme, *The Carlyles at Home*, Oxford 1965.

P. L. R. Horn, 'Female Domestic Servants in Victorian Oxfordshire', *Top. Oxon.* 19 (1973-74).

Housekeeping in Northamptonshire 1600-1900, Northamptonshire Record Office, Archive Teaching Unit, Folder 3, 1972.

The Housemaid, London 1839; repr. in Houlston's Industrial Library, No. 20, London 1877.

The Housemaid and the Parlourmaid, London 1877.

'Housing of Domestic Servants', *The Lancet* (19 Aug. 1905).

Derek Hudson, *Munby: Man of Two Worlds*, London 1972.

Ted Humphris, *Garden Glory*, London 1969.

[Leigh Hunt], 'The Maid Servant' in William Hone, *Every-day Book of Popular Amusements*, I, Pt 1, London 1826.

Gervas Huxley, *Victorian Duke*, London 1967.

'Internuncio', *Mistresses and Servants*, London 1865.

Mrs Eliot James, *Our Servants: Their Duties to Us and Ours to Them*, London 1882.

Gareth Stedman Jones, *Outcast London*, Oxford 1971.

'Justice', *Solution of the Domestic Servant Problem*, North Shields 1910.

Joseph Kay, *The Social Condition and Education of the People in England and Europe*, London 1850.

Margaret Wade Labarge, *A Baronial Household of the Thirteenth Century*, London 1965.

'A Lady', *Instructions in Household Matters or The Young Girl's Guide to Domestic Service*, London 1844.

The Lady's Maid, London 1838; repr. in Houlston's Industrial Library, No. 22, London 1877.

'Ladies in Service', *Spectator* 69 (16 Jul. 1892).

William Lanceley, *From Hall-boy to House-steward*, London 1925.

Peter Laslett, ed., *Household and Family in Past Time*, Cambridge 1972.

Peter Laslett, *The World We Have Lost*, London 1965.

Longleat Kitchen and Recipe Book, London 1972.

George S. Layard, 'The Doom of the Domestic Cook', *Nineteenth Century* XXXIII (Feb. 1893).

W. T. Layton, 'Changes in the Wages of Domestic Servants during Fifty Years', *Journal of the Royal Statistical Society* LXXI (1908).

Elizabeth A. Lewis, 'A Reformation of Domestic Service', *Nineteenth Century* XXXIII (Jan. 1893).

Lenore D. Lockwood, 'Domestic Service and the Working-class Life Cycle', *Bulletin for the Study of Labour History* 26 (Spring 1973).

Lily Maher, 'Workhouse Child', *The Countryman* (Summer 1972).

'Maids-of-all-Work', *Cornhill Magazine* XXX (Sep. 1874).

T. G. Mann, *The Duties of an Experienced Servant*, London 1847.

David C. Marsh, *The Changing Social Structure of England and Wales, 1871-1951*, London 1958.

Dorothy Marshall, *The English Domestic Servant in History*, Historical Association pamphlet, G.13, 1949.

Master and Mistress, Religious Tract Society, London 1842.
A. and H. Mayhew, *The Greatest Plague of Life*, London 1847.
Henry Mayhew, *London Labour and the London Poor* (1861), 4 vols, Dover edition, New York 1968.
Metropolitan Association for Befriending Young Servants (est. 1875), *Annual Reports* (British Museum Library).
A. R. Mills, *Two Victorian Ladies*, London 1969.
'Modern Domestic Service', *Edinburgh Review* CXV (1862).
George Moore, *Confessions of a Young Man*, London 1918.
George Moore, *Esther Waters* (1894), Oxford 1964.
'Mrs Motherly', *The Servant's Behaviour Book*, London 1859.
Arthur J. Munby, *Faithful Servants*, London 1891.
Lady Dorothy Nevill, *Reminiscences*, ed. Ralph Nevill, London 1906.
'An Old Servant', *Domestic Service*, London 1917.
Mrs J. E. Panton, *From Kitchen to Garret*, London 1888; 2nd ed., London 1893.
Mrs C. S. Peel, 'Homes and Habits' in *Early Victorian England*, ed. G. M. Young, I, London 1934.
Mrs C. S. Peel, *A Hundred Wonderful Years*, London 1926.
Ivy Pinchbeck and Margaret Hewitt, *Children in English Society*, London 1973.
Margaret Powell, *Below Stairs*, paperback ed., London 1970.
'A Practical Mistress of a Household', *Domestic Servants As They Are and As They Ought to Be*, Brighton 1859.
Mrs Henry Reeve, 'Mistresses and Maids', *Longman's Magazine* 21 (Mar. 1893).
Eric E. Rich, *The Education Act 1870*, London 1970.
John Robinson, 'A Butler's View of Man-service', *Nineteenth Century* XXXI (Jun. 1892).
Guy Routh, *Occupation and Pay in Great Britain, 1906-60*, Cambridge 1965.
B. Seebohm Rowntree, *Poverty: A Study of Town Life*, 2nd ed., London 1903.
Rules for the Manners of Servants, London 1901.
Edward Salmon, 'Domestic Service and Democracy', *Fortnightly Review* (Mar. 1888).
'A Servant', *How to Improve the Conditions of Domestic Service*, London 1894.
Servants' Benevolent Institution, *Prospectus*, etc. [c. 1850] (British Museum Library).
The Servants' Guide, Richmond 1830.
The Servant's Practical Guide, London 1880.

The Servants' Practical Reply, London 1868.

Francis Sheppard, *London, 1808-1870: The Infernal Wen*, London 1971.

Guy Slater, ed., *My Warrior Sons*, London 1973.

Sir H. Llewellyn Smith, ed., *New Survey of London Life and Labour*, II : *London Industries*, I, London 1931.

Noel Streatfield, ed., *The Day Before Yesterday*, London 1956.

Dorothy M. Stuart, *The English Abigail*, London 1946.

'A Suffering Mistress', 'On the Side of the Mistress', *Cornhill Magazine* XXIX (Apr. 1864).

William Tayler, *Diary of William Tayler, Footman, 1837*, ed. Dorothy Wise, St Marylebone Society, Publication No. 7, 1962.

W. M. Thackeray, *Jeames's Diary*, New York 1853.

F. M. L. Thompson, *English Landed Society in the Nineteenth Century*, London 1963.

Flora Thompson, *Lark Rise to Candleford*, World's Classics, Oxford 1963.

Gladys Scott Thomson, *Life in a Noble Household*, paperback ed., London 1965.

Anthony Trollope, *The Last Chronicle of Barset*, World's Classics, 3rd ed., Oxford 1958.

E. S. Turner, *What the Butler Saw*, London 1962.

Richard Greville Verney (Lord Willoughby de Broke), *The Passing Years*, London 1924.

John H. Walsh, *A Manual of Domestic Economy*, London 1857; 2nd ed., London 1873.

Why Do the Servants of the Nineteenth Century Dress as They Do?, London 1859.

Within Living Memory: A Collection of Norfolk Reminiscences, Norfolk Federation of Women's Institutes, 1972.

John C. Wood, *Cooper's Outlines of Industrial Law*, 6th ed., London 1972.

E. A. Wrigley, ed., *Nineteenth-century Society*, Cambridge 1972.

The Young Servant, 2nd ed., London 1837.

The Young Servant's Own Book intended as a Present for Girls on First Going into Service, London 1883.

Index